WHILE
OTHERS
BUILD

WHILE
OTHERS
BUILD / THE
COMMONSENSE
APPROACH TO THE
STRATEGIC
DEFENSE INITIATIVE

Angelo Codevilla

THE FREE PRESS
A Division of Macmillan, Inc.
NEW YORK

Collier Macmillan Publishers
LONDON

The Free Press
A Division of Macmillan, Inc.
866 Third Avenue, New York, N.Y. 10022

Collier Macmillan Canada, Inc.

Printed in the United States of America

printing number
1 2 3 4 5 6 7 8 9 10

Library of Congress Cataloging-in-Publication Data

Codevilla, Angelo M.
   While others build.

   Bibliography: p.
   Includes index.
   1. Strategic Defense Initiative.   I. Title.
UG743.C63   1988   358'.1754   87–35661
ISBN 0–02–905671–3

To Harry V. Jaffa

Contents

Preface

A people without walls is a people without any choice.

—Aristotle, *Politics*

Whether to build walls or any other form of defense has often proved to be more complex a question than common sense might suggest. In Aristotle's time, sophisticated analysts were suggesting that the rapidly advancing technology of siege machinery had made walls obsolete. Hence many argued that cities should rely for their protection only on the ultimate offensive weapon, heavy infantry. Enough walled cities had perished so that anyone could argue, correctly, that walls did not guarantee protection. Indeed, some argued that a people's unwillingness to strike out at their enemies and the option to retire behind walls virtually invited enemies to ravage the surrounding countryside; only a good offense could achieve total protection. By a somewhat different line of reasoning, others argued that building walls behind which one could retreat after raiding one's neighbors would provoke attack.

Aristotle, however, reflected the common sense of mankind when he affirmed the value of the best protective measures available, imperfect though they surely must be. Without walls, citizens would have to keep themselves physically and mentally prepared at all times to kill and be killed. This would engender an unreasonable preoccupation with military affairs and more wars than would otherwise occur. The best that wall-less peoples would expect in the long run was either regime like Sparta's following a string of victories or the foreign domination that would follow a single defeat. Aristotle did not deny that *some* attackers were able to overcome *some* defended walls or that walls might engender in their owners either excessive placidity or an undue taste for adventure. Nor did he deny the possibility that future inventions might make walls obsolete. He simply noted that for most of the situations he knew of, people would be better off living with walls than without them.

Although most peoples at most times have rejected the temptation to do without the best defensive arrangements they could manage, that temptation crops up whenever new offensive weapons are invented. We laugh too easily at the medieval politicians who saw crossbows and then gunpowder as the harbingers of society's end, at the military commanders who thought there could be no defense against them, and at the lawyers who tried to outlaw them. Centuries later, cannon did make walls obsolete—but not fortresses. World War I showed that firepower in combination with trenches and barbed wire had become more impregnable than any stone rampart. This in turn led to millennialist talk about uncrossable defensive lines.

In our time, the perfection of the airplane, the invention of the nuclear bomb, and then of the nuclear-tipped ballistic missile have occasioned talk about the impossibility of defense. But, in ours as in Aristotle's time, the new offensive weapons have been the excuse for, rather than the cause of, the millennialist hope that the long seesaw struggle between military offense and defense has come to an end. In fact, throughout the ages those who have rejected the millennialist urge to neglect either offense or defense, new weapons or old, and have made the most imaginative use of all means at hand are the people who have lived to write about the struggles they have endured.

All of this is to say that the controversy over whether or not to build defenses against ballistic missiles is a political one, thinly clothed in technical terms. There is no dispute among serious, informed people about the technical characteristics of existing ballistic missiles, and little about what current defensive technology can do against them. There *appears* to be a technical dispute, because it is no more possible to know, before the fact, what a defensive system built out of current technology would do against an attack by current missiles than it is to know how well one tank army would do against another. The reason is that both offensive and defensive systems could be used in quantities according to very different strategies and with different levels of skill. In other words, today—as always—technology is only one of the variables in war. More important than the technology is how it is used, and when. Arguments about the adequacy of *future* defensive technology for dealing with *future* offensive threats are especially fatuous. There is no technical ground at all for deciding what is supposed to be the great dispute about President Reagan's Strategic Defense Initiative (SDI): the efficacy of *hypothetical* defensive technology in countering *hypothetical* ballistic missiles in *arbitrary* scenarios according to *arbitrary* standards of performance.

In fact, the current controversy about strategic defense involves a clash of human preferences about the uses to which certain *existing* mechines should and should not be put. The various protagonists in the controversy—including the author—choose to emphasize particular matchups of offensive and defensive technologies. Protagonists find some matchups significant rather than others, because they find the results of these matchups significant. As we will show, all sides to the controversy make their own judgments about whether defense against ballistic missiles would or would not be worthwhile. But calculations of cost-effectiveness depend largely on the value that the calculator places on the results. In short, judgments about the feasibility of antimissile defenses depend most heavily both on how one chooses to define what these defenses are to be and do and on the worth one finds in the results. These judgments, though necessarily expressed in technical terms, are not about technical issues.

Acknowledgments

I thank the Salvatori Center at Claremont McKenna College for giving me two months' head start on this book during the summer of 1985. I am indebted to the Hoover Institution, where I did the bulk of the work, for its impeccable material and intellectual support. Any shortcoming of a book produced at Hoover has to be the author's fault! This book sums up my work in the field of strategic defense since the summer of 1978. Many of the insights herein come from the bright people in industry and government with whom it has been my honor to work: Senator Malcolm Wallop, Maxwell Hunter, Alan Pike, Sven Kraemer, Mark Schneider, Ed Gerry, and many others. While I am solely responsible for the content, I gratefully acknowledge their influence.

Angelo M. Codevilla
Stanford, California
December 1987

1 / *The Myth of an SDI Program: An Overview*

The flesh is willing, but the spirit is weak.

—The Gospel, reversed.

Military commanders had always dreamed of being able to "take out" any enemy position by pressing a button. When the Soviet Union tested the world's first intercontinental ballistic missile (ICBM) in 1957, it was clear that this dream would soon become reality. In short order, ballistic missiles indeed came to fill the preeminent role in warfare once exercised by heavy infantry, mounted knights, artillery, and tanks. Today, on land and on sea, the Soviet Union has at least 2,500 ballistic missiles with ranges over 4,000 miles, and perhaps 2,000 others with ranges between 1,000 miles and 4,000 miles. Altogether, these missiles can deliver some 12,000 explosive nuclear warheads, many to accuracies of 170 yards or better. The U.S. has a total of about 1,500 long-range and 100 short-range ballistic missiles, with about 6,000 warheads of equal or somewhat greater accuracy but much less potency.

So all ballistic warheads are not created equal. The military importance of any warhead depends on its combination of explosive power and accuracy. Almost a half-century ago, the first ballistic missile, the German V-2, carried a ton of TNT some 300 miles but could be relied on to hit only areas as large as London. The 1,190 that were fired sowed much terror, killed 2,724 civilians, but proved to be of no military significance. The first ballistic missiles able to travel across continents were little more accurate than the V-2s and carried payloads only a few times heavier. But by the mid-1950s, a few thousand pounds could mean a nuclear explosive, or enough highly toxic chemicals to do substantial damage to the target areas that these first ICBMs were likely to hit: cities, airbases, and so on. At this point, ballistic missiles were only marginally useful in warfare. To realize their potential, long-range ballistic missiles had to be developed with the capacity to destroy heavily bunkered installations while sparing the surrounding area.

It is important to remember that nuclear explosives release most of their power in the immediate vicinity of where they are detonated. While a 1-megaton nuclear bomb is 1,000 times as powerful as a 1-kiloton nuclear bomb, other things being equal, the big bomb, will devastate an area only *ten* times the size of the smaller bomb. Thus, if one wishes to devastate houses and other "soft" things in as large an area as possible, one will spread relatively low-yield nuclear bombs throughout. These need only be accurate enough to hit the general area. To destroy a single important target, something like a missile silo or a group of tanks, the warhead must yield enough to make up for its inaccuracy. Thus, if one wishes to destroy such things one will make warheads as accurate as possible.

Ever since the early 1960s, builders of ballistic missiles and their warheads have been able to choose between tailoring the devices to destroy large unprotected areas or to destroy smaller ones of military significance. For the most part, the U.S. has chosen the first path; the Soviet Union the second. Very recently, U.S. policy has explicitly stated the need to concentrate on destroying military targets while avoiding civilian damage. But, in fact, the U.S. has not built significant quantities of missiles for this purpose. This is certainly not for lack of technology; throughout the 1970s and 1980s the accuracy of ballistic missiles has improved so much that the newest models can accomplish countermilitary missions with nuclear yields once too weak for the purpose. The very newest guidance systems are so accurate that ballistic missiles can be expected to strike directly on an enemy command bunker, supply depot, or an enemy missile on the ground. This means that, except for very hard targets like missile silos or bunkers, the missile need not be armed with nuclear weapons to do its work of destruction. With such accuracy, a ton of TNT or chemical contaminants on each of the enemy's key weapons systems and command, control, and communication centers can realize the age-old dream of offensive-minded military commanders: to destroy the enemy's key means of resistance at the outset of a war.

Hence, because they are accurate, as well as swift and reliable, modern ballistic missiles are not doomsday machines or scarecrows. They are powerful tools for diminishing an enemy's ability to do damage and therefore to fight and win wars. As they become more accurate, the weapons carried by ballistic missiles are becoming less indiscriminately destructive but more devastatingly effective against important targets. Nuclear-armed ballistic missiles were fearsome in the 1960s because they could rain down senseless destruction on cities. They are far more to be feared in the late 1980s and beyond because, without bringing on Armageddon, they can work more effectively: destroying the electronic nerve centers of armored forces, nuclear weapons storage sites, and most important, other missiles on the ground. Thus, because modern missiles usually carry multiple warheads, one missile fired can prevent many enemy missiles from being launched toward one's own country. Many missiles fired may cripple an opponent's military capacity, and so limit collateral damage as to leave the society largely unharmed—and hostage.

But what is a modern long-range ballistic missile? It is a tube between 30 and 100 feet tall. Those powered by liquid fuels, such as oxygen and kerosene, are made of thin aluminum. Because the skin of the missiles is so thin, some models must be pressurized before being fueled, lest they collapse of their own weight. The missiles powered by solid fuels (typically combinations of powdered metals like zinc or magnesium, an oxidizer and a retardant) are made of synthetic resin. They easily bear their own weight and the heat of the burning fuel, but not much more. Since all long-range ballistic missiles must accelerate to some 15,000 miles per hour while pushing several thousands of pounds of payload, they have to be light.

A missile is called *ball*istic because it begins its flight being boosted up and at an angle by its engines. After its engines are shut down, it floats to the top of its trajectory and then falls to its target, affected only by the force of gravity—much like a thrown ball.

Ballistic missiles are fearsome because they can get to their targets so fast—typically, thirty minutes from Siberia to Wyoming (or vice versa). But they can travel as quickly as they do only *after* going up and out of the atmosphere. Any device that attempted to travel at 20 times the speed of sound against the atmosphere's resistance would have to be heavily armored to withstand the heat of atmospheric friction and would burn up a literally unbelievable amount of fuel. That is why ballistic missiles really begin to accelerate only after they rise into space. Moreover, only in space can the missile be so free from jostling by air molecules as to become truly ballistic, that is, affected only by the impulse of its engines and by gravity. Hence, only in space can its guidance system make the minute adjustments in course that allow the missile to achieve militarily significant accuracy.

A long-range ballistic missile, then—whether launched from sea or from land, from a truck, an underground silo, a ship, a submarine, or an airplane—must have its guidance system programmed for where it is and where it is going. The missile must be pointed more or less upward and given a small amount of electrical power. The engines then burn for up to 300 seconds, propelling the missile until it is about 200 miles up. During this time the missile's exhaust plume, a source of immense energy, is unmistakably visible, even from 20,000 miles away. Within 50 seconds the missile is above almost all of the earth's atmosphere and really begins to accelerate, reaching its top speed of some 15,000 miles per hour. Then the engines stop and drop off, ending what is called the *boost phase* of flight.

After the last stage drops off, the missile begins to dispense its warheads one by one, directing each to a separate target. It also may spread decoys designed to confuse defenses. All of this involves a small maneuvering engine, which is reasonably easy to track through infrared sensors, though not from such great distances. This is known as the *post-boost phase* and may last until the missile reaches the top of its trajectory, usually some 800 miles up. Only after the top of the trajectory is reached are the warheads fused so that they can explode.

The longest stage of the flight, lasting perhaps twenty minutes, begins after the last release maneuver. During this *midcourse phase*, decoys made of tinfoil travel alongside heavy warheads, undisturbed by air. Radars find it difficult to distinguish between decoy and warhead because their shapes reflect radio waves similarly. Moreover, radars have to contend with clouds of thin metallic foil strips called *chaff*. Infrared devices, for their part, have some difficulty distinguishing between warheads and decoys. But while tinfoil decoys quickly become as cold as the surrounding space, warheads retain and radiate some heat.

Roughly speaking, the final five minutes of the flight constitute the *terminal phase*, during which the atmosphere affects the reentering warheads and decoys. The vast majority of decoys—foil balloons—are slowed, destabilized, and heated to various temperatures by the first few molecules of air at altitudes of fifty miles. By measuring variations in speed and movement, sophisticated radars can distinguish the warheads from most decoys. Heat-seeking devices pick up the growing difference in temperatures. Below fifty miles, the atmosphere simply strips away nearly all decoys. The warheads explode either at preset altitudes, when a proximity fuse tells them they have come as close to their target as they are going to, or when a salvage fuse tells them they are being destroyed. If a warhead explodes above roughly twenty miles, for whatever reason, it will do no harm to life or property below. Of course, if the missile is destroyed during boost phase, its warheads will never reach terminal phase. Gravity will cause them to fall back, unexploded, either on the area whence they were launched, or on the North Polar regions. Obviously, if we want to defend ourselves against ballistic missiles the boost phase is the best point at which to do it.

Since 1953, studying the feasibility of defenses against ballistic missiles has been a major industry in this country. Between 1953 and 1958 under the NIKE II program, the U.S. government was making a sincere (if low-budget) effort to defend the country.

But since 1958, the U.S. government has spent money for research and has subsidized a pseudotechnical debate, in part as a substitute for building actual antimissile defenses. In 1983, President Reagan raised the level of rhetoric about antimissile defense and has spent some $6 billion on studies to match hypothetical defense systems against hypothetical attacks. The Reagan administration has also sponsored work on basic technology applicable to antimissile defense. But it has carefully avoided committing itself to preparations for destroying even one attacking missile. Accordingly, the U.S. government, unable to make the political and strategic case for why we should or should not have antimissile defenses, has veiled its vacillation from the American people by "vigorous" funding of research projects. Thus a generation of politicians have claimed to keep their minds perpetually open to changes in technology and pretended to be technology's servants rather than its masters.

This book is about the problems—both technical and political—associated with defending ourselves against ballistic missiles, and about the myths that have grown up around the problems. It lays out the facts by which any educated layman can understand why the U.S. government treats ballistic missile defense as a theoretical rather than a practical task. It shows that the free world's opportunities for protecting itself from the modern world's most destructive weapons are not so different today from what they were twenty years ago, or from what they will be twenty years hence.

Conventional wisdom has it that only as we look forward to the technology of the year 2,000 can we seriously consider protection against ballistic missiles. In fact, in recent years a variety of means have been available to reduce greatly the harm that ballistic missiles can do. But these means are effective against the ballistic missiles that actually exist. It is impossible to ensure their effectiveness for all time. Interestingly enough this is not a new situation. For example, the contemporary debate deals in substantial part with whether devices can be made to discriminate between a missile's warheads and the debris and decoys accompanying them before they reenter the atmosphere. Actually, even as ballistic missiles were being developed in the 1950s, so were devices to make the discrimination. In 1958, the very first flight of a U.S. Thor intermediate-range ballistic missile was watched by radars that discriminated between the warhead and the junk that came with it. Such radars could not possibly deal with today's warheads and decoys, but they could have dealt with anything that might have been thrown against the U.S. from 1958 until the early 1970s. The U.S. government chose not to build a defense incorporating the instruments of discrimination because someday they would have become outdated. In effect, the U.S. government chose to forego the protection it could have had for a period of time, because that period would not last forever.

Today, a variety of instruments and technology on the near horizon can do a competent—though not a guaranteed—job of discriminating between today's warheads and decoys. But we can imagine warheads, decoys, and conditions with which current technology might not be able to deal. By such reasoning, the U.S. government can always reject currently available protection because it cannot totally ensure us against our "instant" images of future threats.

Such decisions, however, have not been technical ones. They have consisted of judgments about whether the extent, the certainty, and the length of time for which the protective devices might remain effective would be worth the cost of those devices. Those making such judgments, of course, are necessarily influenced by how seriously they take the possibility that the Soviet Union might attack the U.S. or its allies with missiles or use the threat of such an attack to coerce us, by how important they think it would be to save as many innocent lives as possible in the event of war, and by how much stock they put in other methods of persuading the Soviets not to attack—methods such as threats of massive retaliation, arms control, or surrender. Obviously, those who accept the moral imperative to save as many innocent lives as possible in case of war, who believe that the Soviet Politburo would not hesitate to threaten or use nuclear armed missiles to blackmail us, and who do not believe arms control or threats of massive retaliation to be serious deterrents are likely to think money well spent if it buys a few years of partially effective protection—especially, if they have some notion of how they would use the intervening time! Those who are differently disposed regarding these fundamental matters are not likely to regard the protection, or the time it buys, as particularly valuable. Though people on both sides of the argument might speak in technical terms to explain that the devices in question are "adequate" or "inadequate," the bases of their decision are not technical at all.

Conventional wisdom has it that America's interest in ballistic missile defense was born on March 23, 1983, because on that date President Reagan spoke of new technology coupled with a dream of a nuclear-free world. Certainly the U.S. government had lost interest in anti-missile defense long before the 1972 ABM treaty. But the American people—had never ceased to be interested in self-protection. The U.S. Senate began to reassert that concern in the late 1970s after the Soviet strategic buildup had discredited the men and policies that had long dominated U.S. government in the field. Those policies rested on the assumption that the Soviets would be content with a relatively small number of city-killing missiles, useful only for threatening Armageddon, and would be unwilling or unable to build an arsenal for actually waging war, including missiles for destroying the enemy's missile launching silos as well as antimissile devices. These policies found their fullest expression in the SALT I agreements of June 1972, which were supposed to keep both the U.S. and the Soviet Union from acquiring such an arsenal. But by the late 1970s, the then-new Soviet SS-18, SS-19, and SS-17 missiles alone represented ten times the silo-killing countermissile capacity that American leaders thought they had arrested by means of SALT I. In other words, by the late 1970s it became undeniable that U.S. policy had given the Soviet Union a free shot at a monopoly in this kind of force, and that the Soviets had taken it. The Soviets had done precisely what we had refrained from doing. They had done precisely the thing that made nonsense of U.S. policy.

It turned out that this rude awakening occurred just as changes in technology were providing unprecedented means for destroying missiles and bombers in the air and on the ground. During this time also, the great debate over ratification of the SALT II treaty convinced most Americans that no one had any plans for making the Soviet Union abide by future arms control agreements more faithfully than it had in the years it used arms control as a screen for a drive to military superiority.

It is important to understand that the people from Congress, industry, and the executive branch of government, who in the late 1970s went to the aerospace companies looking for technology that might be applicable to antimissile protection, were not moved to do so by gadgetry or by millennialist hopes of absolute safety—of stuffing the nuclear genie back into the bottle. Rather, they knew we had no practical way of dealing with Soviet offensive superiority, and they were driven by the desire to save innocent human lives. Their goal was to provide the free world with the best protection possible, and they were delighted to find that the possible was very good indeed. Hence, by 1980 several U.S. Defense Department programs had been established and funded to develop components for space-based and ground-based antimissile systems employing the new technologies of lasers and electro-optics, as well as new developments in radars and data processing.

But there was great reluctance in the U.S. government to acknowledge that the technical elements were useful for antimissile work rather than for antisatellite purposes, or for intelligence. In 1981 and 1982, Senator Malcolm Wallop (R-Wyo.) and his congressional allies, who had nurtured the developments, won overwhelming votes in the Senate for building laser weapons as quickly as possible. At the time, also, the Office of Management and Budget and the General Accounting Office, renowned skinflints, both recommended a radical increase in the funds for space-based lasers.

Hence, when President Reagan spoke to the nation about strategic defense in March 1983, he was not taking a leap into the dark. Rather, he was stepping onto ground that had been well prepared technically and well tested politically. Indeed, by early 1983 President Reagan's own political options about strategic matters had narrowed. He had been elected in part on the promise to undo the effects of what he called a "decade of neglect," during which the Soviet Union had built some 6,000 counterforce warheads to none for the U.S. But by 1982 it was clear to all that his proposed "strategic modernization plan," which justified to the public large increases in the military budget, would do no such thing. By talking about strategic defense, President Reagan successfully shifted the debate onto different ground. Reagan had effectively reneged on one promise. But he covered up this fact politically by making a newer, more interesting one.

President Reagan did not decide, however, to build any antimissile weapons. His science adviser, George A. Keyworth, and others, encouraged his tendency to think of defense against ballistic missiles in terms of a utopian "system" that would make nuclear weapons "obsolete," and that could only be built with technology not then existing. Thus, although conventional wisdom has it that the SDI reoriented U.S. strategy and procurement, in fact it did no such thing. Indeed, the only immediate effect of the SDI on the nation's real military capacity has been that antimissile weapons or components under development in 1983 were either canceled, as happened to everything having to do with nuclear-tipped, antimissile interceptors, or redefined into research programs that were to bear fruit later than originally intended, if at all. Under Reagan, as under his predecessors, antimissile defense would be a welfare program for scientists.

The technical panel that President Reagan empowered to give substance to his vision believed it had a charter to sketch a single multifaceted system that would be effective against all forseeable countermeasures, and that would be built not as the pieces became available but all at once and once and for all. Thus, much like the Keller Commission, appointed by President Truman in 1949 to specify what should be done about ICBMs, President Reagan's Fletcher Panel crafted gold-plated definitions of what is required for ballistic missile defense.[1] Moreover, the Fletcher Panel stated plainly that even these definitions might be made more demanding to take account *not* of what intelligence learns the Soviets are doing but rather of American technicians' own evolving notions. In bureaucratese, such changing of standards is known as the "responsive threat." Thus was the SDI established as a program of research without logical end.

The Fletcher Panel's report, the founding document of the SDI, is a distillation of all the faults of modern American military research and development. Next to it, the Pentagon's twelve pages of specifications for purchasing a drillmaster's whistle and $7,000 coffee makers are marvels of realistic planning. In sum, the panel built an artificial world. By inflating up to a thousandfold the "hardness" of the missile boosters to be destroyed, the panel's report requires antimissile lasers to be much more intense than any now feasible, thus disqualifying currently feasible lasers. By assuming that any battle-management system must identify and track "birth-to-death" every piece of debris, tankage, and so on involved in a missile attack and then centralize all data and all decisions in one computer, the fathers of the SDI have disqualified currently available sensor and data-processing technology. By setting unrealistic requirements for altitude of intercept and discrimination, they have disqualified currently available technology for terminal defense. Indeed, they have disqualified all current technology, and all current decision makers, including the president who commissioned them, from a role in building an antimissile defense. Thus defined, our SDI program can only spend money for many years while bearing no protective fruit.

Nevertheless, conventional wisdom has it that antimissile defense is, as Secretary of Defense Weinberger has said, the "very core" of U.S. strategic policy. The Defense Department's annual report (commonly known as the Posture Statement) for 1986 states plainly that the Soviet Union's superiority in offensive missilery is so great that the U.S. cannot overcome it and should not try. Strategic defense, according to this document, is the *only* avenue available to the U.S. for exiting from a nasty predicament.

But, in fact, if the SDI is the core of U.S. defense policy, that core is soft—or even hollow. This is because it consists not of programs to achieve an antimissile defense but of research programs intended to answer—no sooner than the 1990s—what the Pentagon deems to be a theoretical question: whether ballistic missile defense, as defined by the research program itself, is possible. Hence, in practice, the SDI is a conscious decision to postpone deciding for the forseeable future. It is a conscious decision to mark time, *not to decide until the 1990s* whether or how to reverse the effects of the Soviet strategic buildup of the 1960s and 1970s. A defense policy that recognizes it has but one way of getting out of serious, concrete problems, and as a consequence decides to let the problems worsen for nearly a decade while it looks into *whether* that way is feasible, is not a serious policy.

One does not have to wander far among those responsible for the administration's policy of researching, but not building, strategic defenses to encounter frank avowals that, for many of them, the whole business about "answering a question" is a pretext for quite another policy—one about which they are somewhat more serious, namely, arms control. George A. Keyworth, who as presidential science advisor set the Fletcher Panel's frame of reference, stated publicly in January 1984 that the goal of the SDI is an arms control agreement with the Soviet Union, and that for this purpose only the *ability* to build antimissile weapons need be demonstrated. The weapons themselves need never be built. In 1985,

Gerold Yonas, then the SDI's chief scientist, said at a public forum that the SDI's function is to be "a catalyst for arms control." Accordingly, the notion of exiting from a dangerous predicament through a research program whose researchers seek scientific rather than practical results seems even less serious. This calls to mind President Eisenhower's warning in his farewell address against letting national policy become "the captive of a scientific-technological elite."

One might well ask policy makers responsible for this way of thinking what would happen around 1992 if they were to then conclude that antimissile defense according to their standards was *not* possible, or required yet another number of years of research? What would happen to the vaunted "catalytic effect" on arms control? Would the president of the United States and the U.S. Senate ask the Soviet Union to meet in Geneva to negotiate the terms for permanent U.S. inferiority? No. There would then remain only one honest option. The president could ask the Pentagon's R&D establishment what might be accomplished by building the ballistic missile defenses that current technology would allow. If so, the president of the 1990s might wonder why his predecessor had not done the same thing many years sooner. All of this is to point out that it is disingenuous to say there is only one way out of mortal danger while putting off for ten years whether to take up that way as best one can.

Conventional wisdom has it that current defensive technology is not good enough, but that the stuff in the labs is terrific. In fact, current technology is quite adequate to defend against any attacks that might be attractive to the Soviets. The stuff in the laboratories is indeed terrific—potentially; some of it may never work. But, even as the U.S. government judges current defensive technology against the imaginary standards of the year 2010, the stuff coming out of the labs in 1995 may be judged inadequate according to an even more fanciful image of the year 2020.

In fact, if suitably modified and produced in sufficient numbers, the Navy's Aegis air defense system, the radar at Grand Forks (North Dakota) and the mothballed interceptor missiles associated with it, the large coastal Pave Paws radars, the Army's ERIS/HOE interceptor and its flying optical radar, all would provide the U.S. and its allies with a respectable terminal defense against ballistic reentry vehicles. The space-based laser designed by the Defense Advanced Research Projects Agency, by the admission of a wide variety of experts (including, in curious ways, some from the Soviet Union), would devastate Soviet missile launches during boost phase. Although there is now no sophisticated means of discriminating and attacking warheads in midcourse, nuclear weapons exploded in the vicinity of attacking warheads would kill some and, above all, clear out decoys. Thus, existing technology could not guarantee total protection from an irrational assault against the population. But it would make impossible a militarily meaningful missile attack against the U.S., *while largely protecting the population against the collateral effects of such an attack.* While our growing vulnerability invites attack, the capacity to defend would deter war.

The most concrete illustration of what current technology can do to defend against ballistic missiles is to be found in the Soviet Union. The populated part of Soviet territory is covered by nine huge, modern phased-array radars (three still under construction in 1987) that can "see" incoming warheads thousands of miles away, do some discrimination, and transmit electronic files on the track of each object to antimissile sites in the area of destination. There, other radars use the cues to track the objects more precisely and direct interceptor missiles to destroy them at the edge of the atmosphere. All components of the system are in full production in the Soviet Union. No American knows how many are produced or where they go once they leave the factory.

Also in full production in the Soviet Union is a mobile surface-to-air missile system, each unit of which can defend a relatively small area against a few warheads. When hundreds of units are produced, they will supplement the nationwide system and provide solid protection for lightly attacked targets. This is especially important for all those who live in cities. Ever since President Carter's Decision #59 in 1980, the U.S. has adopted the Soviet practice of not targeting civilian areas per se—indeed, of avoiding them. Thus, few if any warheads would reach such places. Any city where one of these units is located can thus count on surviving a nuclear war. In other words, contrary to conventional wisdom, and given modern, rational, nuclear-targeting policies, cities are relatively easy to protect. The Soviet Union is also scheduled to test a high-energy laser in space in 1988.

Together, the Soviet devices would stand a good chance of intercepting most, if not all, warheads from a U.S. attack if that attack were spread evenly over thousands of targets in the Soviet Union. Hence, as such devices continue to roll off Soviet production lines, the U.S. will have to plan to concentrate any retaliatory attack on fewer and fewer targets to make sure that at least some warheads got through. But as the U.S. could count on destroying fewer and fewer targets, more and more doubts will necessarily arise about whether the U.S. would do itself any good by actually retaliating. This is bad for the U.S. and bad for the cause of peace in the world.

The U.S. could be building similar defensive weapons, only better. As more and more such systems came off American production lines, they would make the prospect of attacking the U.S. less and less rational for the Soviets. Yet, as we've said, one reason why the Reagan administration has rejected all suggestions to build what defenses it can is the prospect that everything we do now could, theoretically, be done much better later.

Indeed, a wholly new terminal intercept radar, several kinds of wholly new interceptor missiles, homing projectiles with guidance systems able to function under 200,000 times the force of gravity, tiny, super-fast pellets guided by laser beams that would direct them by literally shaving them in flight, airborne optical radars able to cover bigger areas—all these techniques are likely to be available to weapons builders in the 1990s and could result in excellent terminal defense weapons by the turn of the century. For defense in the boost phase, the availability of advanced technology is much less certain. Perhaps huge, ground-based free-electron lasers will be available in the 1990s. But whether it will ever be possible to transfer high-power laser beams up through the atmosphere efficiently no one knows; no one knows whether the "pop up" relay mirrors needed for such systems will ever work. Availability of equipment for a discriminating attack against warheads in the midcourse phase is even more uncertain. Space-based radars, space-based infrared and laser systems to provide sharp pictures of decoys and warheads, huge power supplies to run them and their computers must be developed, paid for, and, later, defended. Compared with what would be needed for the support devices, developing and acquiring the weapons for destroying the warheads in midcourse would be child's play. All of this is to say that the promise of future technology is far less certain than the advantages that current technology offers.

Objective observers can only be impressed by how some technologists go out of their way to highlight the difficulties involved in adapting and using relatively well-known tools and then show blind faith in the ability to do other things, the basic scientific principles of which remain undemonstrated. One explanation lies in who holds what government contracts; another, more potent, lies in what the technology managers believe the contracting agency wants them to have faith. The dimension of conventional wisdom that may be farthest from reality is that the nation's technologists, particularly in the aerospace industry, lobby for antimissile defenses. In fact, the reverse is true.

I spent four years fruitlessly asking senior aerospace executives not so much to lobby for antimissile defenses as to answer truthfully questions from Congress about what their companies could do in the field. Of course, on a purely technical level, industry answers questions very well. But, so wary are executives of "getting out in front of the customer" (the military officers who sign their contracts), that the aerospace companies, and the national laboratories do not mind spurning the birds in the hand for the ones in the bush—so long as they are paid to do it.

Conventional wisdom has it that the U.S. is conducting research into strategic defense in part as a hedge against a possible Soviet "breakout" from the ABM Treaty of 1972. The same wisdom also has it that in order to forestall such a breakout, as well as to preserve the option of deploying defenses with the Soviet Union's agreement, the U.S. must make sure that our SDI wholly complies with the treaty. A broad spectrum of what one might call the "foreign policy class" in America feels so strongly about what the ABM Treaty stands for, that it preemptively dismisses the significance of the antimissile devices the Soviet Union has built while supposedly adhering to it. These Americans solicit from like-minded Europeans the implicit threat that unless the U.S. adheres to the spirit of the treaty, it will "lose" Europe. All this wisdom and pressure has led the U.S. government to create an interagency committee (State, Defense, the Arms Control and Disarmament Agency [ACDA]) which, in effect, has written a purely American version of what the ABM Treaty should mean, and which has thereby shaped the SDI research programs to make sure they do not come close to running afoul of that purely American construct.

In fact, however, a close reading of the ABM Treaty shows that it does not restrain either party from producing antimissile defenses—although they may choose not to build them. The U.S. has acknowledged that this "permissive" interpretation is legitimate. Using a loose interpretation of the treaty as well as committing outright violations, the Soviet Union has built, is building, and is developing a wide variety of antimissile devices. When examining intelligence about these devices, U.S. analysts have concerned themselves less with how effective they might be and more with whether they constitute a "breakout" from the ABM Treaty. Concentration on the militarily meaningless legalism of "breakout," as well as on the unrealistic criteria of effectiveness for ABM systems established by the Fletcher Panel, has made it very difficult for U.S. analysts to make sense of the Soviet Union's ominous military preparations.

The controversy about how well the real Soviet and the hypothetical American antimissile defenses would perform is one of history's most pseudosophisticated and unenlightening. Various organizations—including the Soviet Academy of Sciences—have weighed into the *American* debate (the Soviets don't do this sort of thing to themselves) over whether projected antimissile defenses would be 30, 50, 70, or 90 percent effective and over what damage the warheads that got through might do. In fact, though we can learn much from the numbers game, all the figures in it—and the very notion that any offensive or defensive system, from horse cavalry to lasers, can be "X" or "Y" percent effective—are wildly presumptuous. Because it is impossible to know precisely how many missiles with precisely what characteristics would be sent against what targets, and because it is impossible to know precisely how well offensive and defensive systems would perform, any a priori calculations about the results of battles are nothing but the sterile, predetermined interplay of assumptions. By making just the "right" assumptions, one can prove that any percentage of missiles would get through, or none; and that hundreds of millions of people, or none, would be killed.

Life is not a predetermined numbers game; if it were, the number-crunchers would be running the world. At best, the numbers games dramatize the results inherent in the assumptions that frame them. Thus, each scenario and estimate tells more about the mind set of those who developed them than they say about our prospects for safety. Most of the scenarios, true to the dogma of the 1960s, assume an "all-out attack;" that is, that the Soviets would launch everything in their possession regardless of the consequences to themselves, in a militarily senseless attempt to do as much damage as possible to American cities. When the scenarios deal with "limited attacks," as did a General Accounting Office study in 1978, they still assume that a large number of warheads would be directed at large American cities and that people would not take elementary precautions.

However, it is easy to see that if an attacker were intent on doing mindless damage, he would not have to resort to ballistic missiles. For a modest fee, any express freight service would doubtless deliver a few well-disguised bombs to several American cities with no possibility of defense. Yet such damage would be mindless precisely because it would not do an attacker any good to inflict it.

Some of the attacks on the U.S. that would cause the most damage, however, would not only be mindless but also relatively easy to defend against. It should be easy to see that missile attacks designed to do across-the-board damage to society by assigning one or two warheads to thousands of widely separated targets are relatively easy to take care of, because in any given target area they would place little stress even on primitive local surface-to-air defensive systems like the SA-12 system now rolling off Soviet production lines. On the other hand, the kind of attack on the U.S. that would give the attacker the greatest advantage, a "decapitating" attack intended surely to destroy certain missiles and command posts, requires the kind of reliability that even a rudimentary space-based defense can upset. If, for example, an attacker expected roughly one-third of his missiles to be destroyed in boost phase but had no way of knowing *which one-third*, he could not have much confidence that his attack would end up doing him more good than harm.

Looking carefully through the claims and counterclaims of the numbers game, it is possible to see the reality that is being contested: both the U.S. and the Soviet Union possess the technology for taking a large, but uncertain, toll of attacking missiles in the boost phase. Both also possess the technology for self-defense of individual points, whether cities or military sites, so long as only a handful of warheads appear above each. The whole quarrel in the U.S.—there is no parallel in the Soviet Union—is over what use, if any, is to be made of existing technology.

The effective resolution of the intramural U.S. quarrel is that no use at all shall be made of the technology. Why? In part the answer is that no service within the Defense Department has the mission to defend the U.S. against missile—or air—attacks. The Pentagon is divided into "programs" that vie for a share of the defense dollar and are united only in opposing new entrants. For the Navy, each dollar spent on the SDI is a dollar for which it cannot compete. For the Air Force and the Army, each dollar spent on the SDI is a dollar that might be "taken out of hide;" that is, higher authority might order the services to curtail other spending for the sake of SDI. Hence, each service jealously argues against ballistic missile defense because if the U.S. were to pursue it, the inevitable result would be reduced budgets prominence, and general officer billets for U.S. military officers who have made their careers in traditional specialties.

So each service argues that it does not want the "mission." The Army fears that, in the short run, its present programs would be held back to compensate for the additional funds it would receive for antimissile work. Besides, to make use of the new opportunities, many senior Army officers would have to go into fields with which they are now unfamiliar or watch senior ranks to which they aspire filled by eager juniors. The Army has been tempted to ask for the "mission," but has decided against it. The Air Force's view is more categorical: "Our plate is full." It views a major turn toward strategic defense as a demotion for the retaliatory mission that is its principal reason for being. The Air Force sees strategic defense for the U.S. as a disaster for itself—at least in the foreseeable future.

The Strategic Defense Initiative Organization (SDIO), although nominally under the secretary of defense, is theoretically a place where the Air Force, the Army, and the Advanced Research Projects Agency arrive at mutually satisfactory accommodations—much as occurs with the Joint Chiefs of Staff. But the SDIO's officers have neither the power nor the interest to transcend the interests of the organizations on which they depend for their careers. General James Abrahamson, the SDIO's director, sees himself as an officer of the Air Force, which does not want to build antimissile weapons, and as an executor of national policy, which is at best ambiguous. The SDIO's performance thus has illustrated the old axiom that *nothing is more futile than giving charge over new things to people who are not committed to doing them.* The SDIO resembles more the organizations established before the U.S. became serious about ballistic missiles than the ones that actually built them.

Because it is essential that *some* organization have a lively interest in antimissile weapons, there is no good alternative to creating one: a fifth service, the United States Strategic Defense Force. Like the separate military service (the PVO) that is in charge of the matter in the Soviet Union, the new branch of the U.S. Armed Forces would be in charge of conceiving, procuring, and deploying major anti-air, antimissile, and space weapons.

The U.S. government has found it irresistible to make the SDI a bargaining chip in arms control negotiations with the Soviet Union. The foremost obstacle to doing just that is that the Reagan administration's very claim to effectiveness in military matters rests on the SDI. Thus, the administration has gone to great lengths to tell the public that whatever deal it might strike with the Soviet Union must leave the SDI untouched. But the conventional image of a Soviet Union totally committed to killing the SDI and of a Reagan administration committed to antimissile defense could not be further from the truth. The feverish diplomatic activity that has surrounded the SDI stems from the fact that obvious ground for compromise exists. That is, the Soviet Union is supremely interested not so much in getting rid of the line items in the U.S. military budget that are labeled "SDI" as it is in impeding the construction of American antimissile weapons. Meanwhile, the Reagan administration is committed not to the construction of American antimissile devices but to a line item in the U.S. military budget labeled "SDI"—a line item involving everything *but* the construction of antimissile weapons.

No doubt the Soviet Union would be delighted if the United States ceased all research that might possibly be applicable to strategic defense and stopped talking about the subject. But the Soviets know from experience that the U.S. often has technology vastly superior to anything in the Soviet Union, which, for one reason or another, it does not employ in its weaponry. Nor does the U.S. use even the devices it has deployed to the maximum potential. For example, the Joint Chiefs of Staff's military posture statement for fiscal 1987 reports that the U.S. government does not use the full potential of its ballistic missile warning radars for antimissile work.[2] Thus, so long as it is not the SDI's purpose to build antimissile devices, it is possible for the Reagan administration to have its public relations cake and for the Soviet Union to eat out its military substance.

The Soviets know that the SDI was formulated as a research program to culminate in the early 1990s in decisions as to whether or not to *develop* weapons, and that the SDI envisages yet another set of decisions later in the 1990s on deploying antimissile weapons that might come into use by the year 2,000. The Soviets have some experience (the MX comes to mind) in helping to delay new American weapons until they become obsolescent. By their pressure on the SDI, they have helped the Reagan administration to proudly define the present research program as the very limit (and perhaps beyond) of permissible American action in regard to antimissile devices. By so doing, they have helped to gain for themselves a monopoly in the antimissile field until at least the early 1990s. At stake in U.S.-Soviet talks on arms control is how far into the future to stretch that Soviet monopoly. Not surprisingly, given the uninspiring nature of the Reagan administration's commitment to antimissile defense, Congress essentially decided to freeze the SDI's funding. Hence, the program as conceived by the Fletcher Panel—ostensibly intended to progress, in the usual Pentagon way, to fruition circa the year 2000—died. Moreover, as the end of the Reagan administration came into view, many observers who assumed that the SDI had been Ronald Reagan's brainchild assumed that it would pass from the scene along with him.

But this is far from the truth. In fact, interest in strategic defense arose out of the utter failure of the American military policies of the late 1960s and 1970s. Rhetoric aside, those policies continued throughout the Reagan administration and continued to demonstrate their impotence. As a consequence, hardly any responsible person dissents from the proposition that in the 1980s and 1990s, the Western world will have literally no choice other than to accept the Soviet Union's military superiority for the indefinite future or try to undermine it by strategic defense.

Ronald Reagan's presence in office is not necessary to highlight the nation's need for missile defense. On the contrary, his reassuring presence blurs that need.

2 / *The Millennium*

And lo, there was a great earthquake; and the sun became black
as sackcloth of hair, and the moon became as blood; and the stars
of heaven fell upon the earth. . . . And the kings of the earth and
the great men and the rich men and the chief captains, and the
mighty men and every bond man and every free man hid themselves
in the dens and in the rocks of the mountains and said to the
mountains and rocks, Fall on us.

—Revelation

We Will All Go Together When We Go

—Tom Lehrer, song title

In the late 1980s, a consensus seems to be forming that the
Free World must not remain vulnerable to Soviet missiles. Both
Henry Kissinger, always a reliable weathervane, and Zbigniew
Brzezinski have spoken with increasing frequency about the need
to build now what antimissile devices we can. Even more interesting, West Germany's minister of defense, Manfred Woerner, recently wrote that while his country wishes the SDI well for the
far-off future, his country has an extremely serious problem with
Soviet missiles that it must begin solving now. But the growing
consensus about the need for a "partial" or "early" deployment
of antimissile defenses still must overcome the myths that becloud
the straightforward political–military issue of how the U.S. shall
deal with the threat posed by Soviet ballistic missiles. Those myths,
that technical and legal factors, rather than political–military indecision, stand in the way of the United States's self-protection are
the subject of this book.

Whether or not to protect one's self and one's countrymen as
best one can is a moral and political question—not a technical one.

20

From the very beginning of the missile age, men have destroyed missiles and their warheads in flight many times. How many missiles either we or the Soviets might choose to destroy in flight depends more on expertise in strategy, management, and economics than it does on technical wizardry. Moreover, there are two ways of protecting oneself against ballistic missiles that have nothing to do with shooting them down in the air or in space. I am referring, of course, to tailoring one's offensive missiles to destroy enemy missiles on the ground before they are ever launched as well as protecting against the effects of any missiles that reach our soil by building passive shelters. No one contends that these means of antimissile protection are technically problematic. Yet it is easy to see that whether we ought to prepare these protective means has been essentially the same question—strategically and politically—as whether we ought to prepare to destroy missiles in flight. The issue boils down to this: Shall we do the best we can now with the tools at hand, imperfect though that will surely be, or shall we do nothing practical while "looking into" a total solution, either technical or political? So, although the debates on counterforce missiles and civil defense do not shed direct light on whether, say, space-based lasers are technically feasible, the debates show that the whole matter of the technical feasibility of defenses is entirely subordinate to will and strategic judgement. Let us then preface our discussion of more exotic matters with some plain talk about familiar things.

The question of whether missiles should be made and targeted to hit enemy populations, industries, or armed forces is an old one. Indeed, it is an extension of the very same question concerning bomber aircraft.

At the outset of World War II, it quickly became apparent that bombing armies was more difficult than bombing cities. The military benefits to be derived from bombing enemy armies, airfields, and ports were obvious: the enemy's ability to fight and inflict harm would be impaired. Nevertheless, the United States, Britain, and Germany saw fit to devote thousands of aircraft and pilots to bombing cities and industry in the mistaken belief that the effects would impair the enemy's *will* to fight. After the war, American teams poked through the charred remains of baby cribs and neighborhood grocery stores and concluded that the carnage of innocents—some 135,000 died as a result of two nights' conventional bombing of Dresden—had not helped to shorten the war. Rather, bombing had hurt people superfluous to the war effort and had convinced most of the population that they were "in the same boat" as their government against a barbarous enemy. Attacks on industry no doubt helped to hold down production. Nevertheless, Germany's war production peaked in August 1944—at the height of the bombing campaign. Both German and Japanese factories went underground. More important, managers of war production realized that while buildings were easy prey to bombs, machinery and workmen were not, and they organized war production accordingly. Both the Soviet Union and Germany even assembled aircraft in the open!

So, World War II, like most other wars, was won on the battlefield. Had the Allies saved their huge fleets of bombers for the more difficult task of bombing in ways that were significant militarily, they would not only have spared innocents immense pain but also would have ended the war more quickly. But the dearly bought lesson about "strategic bombing" was submerged by the millennialist ideas that surrounded the invention of nuclear weapons. Surely these monster weapons must be able either to paralyze the enemy's will to fight or to wipe his country from the map.

In fact, if only because of their great scarcity, nuclear bombs heightened the criminal stupidity of "strategic bombing." Yet, at first, using them in any other way seemed problematic. It was clear that employing nuclear weapons for countermilitary purposes would require much new technology. After all, hitting any target with a single atomic bomb is much more difficult than doing so with hundreds or thousands of iron bombs. The fact that a single atomic bomb is much more powerful than any conventional bomb helps only to a limited extent. To compensate for the inaccuracy with which gravity bombers could deliver atom bombs and still destroy bunkers, tanks, or ships takes a truly monstrous nuclear yield. Hence, when the first atomic bombs became available, it was by no means obvious where the rare, expensive devices should be dropped.

Had the U.S. chosen to drop its first bomb on a concentration of ships in Tokyo harbor (assuming the U.S. had timely intelligence), an error in delivery of only a half mile—terribly common with high-altitude gravity bombing—might have left every ship afloat. For the same reason, had the U.S. chosen to expend one of its few atom bombs on destroying a particular factory, that factory might have been left unscathed. So the atomic bomb was used pursuant to the same notion of "strategic bombing" that had already devastated Japanese civilians. Nor did the atom bomb destroy more than conventional raids had. The Hiroshima bomb destroyed 4.7 square miles of buildings, the Nagasaki bomb, 1.8. By comparison, the biggest conventional raid on Tokyo had destroyed 15.8 square miles. The ninety largest conventional raids on Japanese cities each destroyed on the average as much as the Nagasaki bomb. So, given its expense, scarcity, and inaccuracy of delivery, the first atom bombs turned out to be simply more efficient city-killers—that is to say, more efficient terror weapons but no more useful than others. Their novelty, however, did provide the excuse that the emperor needed to stop a war that Japan had lost long before.

That is why when, in 1947, President Truman asked the U.S. military for concrete ways in which he could use the nation's twenty-odd atomic bombs to stop a possible Soviet invasion of Western Europe, he found that there were none. Even threatening atomic retaliation on Russia itself made little practical sense. How many of these twenty-odd B-29s would manage to overfly thousands of miles of Soviet territory, through intact fighter screens and anti-aircraft guns? How much less damage would the atom bomb do to brick-and-concrete Russian cities than it had to papier-mâché Hiroshima? Surely the damage would be far smaller than what Soviet cities had suffered while the Red Army defeated the Wehrmacht! So, if the U.S. were ever to make nuclear weapons useful substitutes for the millions of Americans who would otherwise have to brave privations and shed blood to guard America's freedom, we would have to make these weapons more numerous. Above all, we would have to make the means of delivering them far more accurate and reliable. The U.S. military, especially the Army, set about that task.

However, because another set of pressures has been at work, the U.S. government has never fully committed itself to using nuclear weapons to minimize damage to ourselves and our allies by striking the Soviet military. That is because the dropping of the first atomic bombs, followed so swiftly by the end of the war, had an intoxicating effect on public opinion and, above all, on intellectuals—ever ready to catch the bug of millennialism. While the newspapers were awash with things "atomic," and with talk that the newly harnessed power might spell perpetual peace or universal doom, Bernard Brodie and other eminent military analysts (who should have known better) were writing a little book along those lines, *The Absolute Weapon*,[1] which is worth examining because it became—and remains—the intellectual currency of the dominant tendency among U.S. policymakers.

The book purports to explain the consequences of a scientific discovery. Instead, it purveys an attitude, justified by the supposed total and everlasting ability of the U.S. and the USSR to destroy one another. It proceeds less by argument than by "Gee Whiz" remarks about the power of nuclear weapons. Although the writers never deny that nuclear weapons have finite effects and that prudent preparations for dealing with nuclear attack necessarily affect its results significantly, they give the impression that nuclear weapons would be targeted primarily on cities and, therefore, that their use preordains total destruction.

The book's logical contradictions are resolved by the exaggerated hopes and fears the authors attach to "the bomb." The book's thrust is that before we can speak of a defense against atomic bombs being effective, the frustration of the attack "for any given target area" must be complete.[2] The reader agrees instinctively that one atom bomb is surely enough to destroy *any* target. But few stop to think that Brodie's axiom—one's enough—is true of bullets aimed at human beings and of artillery shells aimed at buildings, that it omits any consideration of the vast differences in the yield of nuclear weapons or in the accuracy of delivery, and that it is quite false as regards nuclear weapons aimed at targets hardened to withstand a given combination of yield and accuracy. More important, the reader easily loses sight of Brodie's qualifier, "for any given target area," and is led to assume that unless a nuclear attack is *totally* frustrated at *every* point, it succeeds totally. In fact, Brodie helps the reader forget his qualifier by arguing that the attacker has the incentive to apply vast resources to getting each and every weapon on all targets.[3] One might ask how this could be? Surely in the nuclear age, as ever before, attackers have the option of concentrating their efforts on overwhelming one objective. But, in the nuclear age, perhaps more than before, such concentration invites disastrous military consequences. After all, if one wastes one's own nuclear assets while the enemy keeps his, the future belongs to an outraged enemy.

Brodie's second main thrust is that "superiority in the number of bombs is not in itself a guarantee of strategic superiority" because "if 2000 bombs in the hands of either party is enough to destroy entirely the economy of the other, the fact that one side has 6000 and the other 2000 will be of relatively low significance."[4] Again Brodie invites the reader's knowing smile. True, numbers have never, *by themselves*, guaranteed superiority. Moreover, if one could *totally* destroy one's adversary by pushing a button, one would need no more. But what *is* total destruction, and would the possession of "X" number of bombs give one the ability to carry it out? Would the outcome not depend on how they were targeted? What *about* one's adversary would one wish to destroy by rationing one's stock of 'X' bombs among enemy targets? Why would one want to destroy the adversary's economy? If one could, through one's own bombs, cut down the proportion of the adversary's stock delivered upon one's self would that not take priority? Such questions do not arise for Brodie's readers. Awe of "the bomb" forecloses them.

The final thrust of Brodie and the other authors is that since "the bomb" is too powerful to be used, henceforth the threat of it will wring peace, even from the heart of dictators, because "in no case is the fear of the consequences of atomic bomb attack likely to be low."[5] Again, a kind of understated humor subverts sober thought. Of course the fear won't be "low," just as the fear of a knife at the throat or at the groin is never low. But how high will it be, given a dictatorship well prepared for nuclear war and a democracy whose military leaders content themselves with Brodie's witticisms?

For the first fifteen years of the nuclear era, American military supremacy was so great, and American military leaders faced so few momentous choices, that their increasing verbal adherence to the tenets of *The Absolute Weapon* seemed irrelevant. General Maxwell Taylor, perhaps the premier military intellectual of the time, expressed the thoughts of many when he wrote:

> The avoidance of deliberate general atomic war should not be too difficult, since its unrenumerative character must be clear to potential adversaries. . . . a nation need only feel reasonably sure that an opponent has some high yield weapons, no matter how indefinite their exact number, to be impressed with the possible consequences of attacking him.[6]

It was not necessary to go to a military expert to find out that anyone would be "impressed" by the prospect of nuclear retaliation. But one might have expected such an expert to dwell on how one might make an enemy's arsenal less impressive to ourselves while making ours more impressive to him. Taylor, however, like many, was merely "impressed."

Yet what American military leaders thought did not matter. America could deliver many bombs on the Soviet Union but did not want to, while the Soviet Union's intentions were irrelevant because it could hardly deliver any weapons on the United States. So for the U.S., the discussion was theoretical because the danger was theoretical. Thus, although American leaders spoke freely about destroying the Soviet Union by massive retaliation for any Soviet aggression anywhere, they did not have to define what they meant. The theoretical plan was, in case of war, to disgorge the U.S. arsenal on an "optimum mix" of Soviet civilian and military targets.

All of this changed *circa* 1960 when the prospect arose that the Soviet Union could bypass our air defenses by lobbing ballistic missiles at us. When the possibility of damage to the U.S. became real, the Kennedy administration rightly charged its predecessor with not having an explicit strategy for limiting damage to the U.S. in case of war. Relying on the new Atlas, Titan, and Minuteman missiles, as well as on the new reconnaisance satellites that pinpointed Soviet missile bases, Kennedy's secretary of defense, Robert McNamara, was able to declare:

> The United States has come to the conclusion that to the extent feasible, basic military strategy in a possible general war should be approached in much the same way that more conventional military operations are. That is to say, principal military objectives in the event of a nuclear war should be the destruction of the enemy's military forces, not his civilian population.[7]

Later in 1962, before the American Bar Association, McNamara elaborated: "In any case, our large reserve of protected firepower would give our enemy an incentive to avoid our cities and stop a war." At this time, McNamara took no action to diminish U.S. air defenses or to interfere with the effort to develop defenses against missiles. The purpose, after all, was to limit damage to the United States.

Yet, beginning in 1963, Robert McNamara changed his mind and the shape of the U.S. military. Whether he was impressed by his aides' commitment to the tenets of *The Absolute Weapon*, or frightened by the Cuban missile crisis, or desirous of cutting the strategic forces' share of the budget in order to fight the Vietnam War, or simply shrinking from the prospect of endless innovation in offensive and defensive weapons is irrelevant. In fact, his purpose ceased to be the limitation of damage in case of war, and became the absolute avoidance of war through the policy of "mutual assured destruction" (MAD) in case war occurred.

When, in late 1963, it became clear that the Soviet Union was going to emplace its new ballistic missiles in blast-resistant silos, the U.S. faced a decision: Shall we target the silos and continue to improve our missiles in order to do so effectively? The answer from McNamara's Pentagon was "No." He later explained that our safety comes from a willingness to "destroy the attacker as a viable 20th-century nation," regardless of what happens to ourselves, and not from any "ability to partially limit damage to ourselves."[8]

Defining the appropriate level of destruction was a problem. Pentagon analysts sought the "flat of the curve," that is, the number of Soviet cities hit, after which hitting another would cost more than the damage inflicted. Give or take a little, McNamara's Pentagon settled on a figure:

> I would judge that a capability on our part to destroy, say, one-fifth to one-fourth of her population and one-half of her industrial capacity, would serve as an effective deterrent. Such a level of destruction would certainly represent intolerable punishment for a twentieth-century industrial nation.[9]

McNamara's calculations about the Soviet Union did not take into account a very different value system from his own, and his calculations about what damage our weapons would cause were proved wrong in tests by the Boeing Corporation.[10] Moreover the very notion that it is possible to compare the value of a number of human lives destroyed with the cost of destroying them is a lunacy of which only modern social science is capable. But right or wrong, McNamara not only explicitly took up the "absolute weapon" rhetoric of the Eisenhower officials that he had criticized,[11] he acted wholly consistently with that rhetoric. Against the will of the Joint Chiefs of Staff at the time, he made new U.S. missiles incapable of striking Soviet missiles. He oriented American targeting toward populations and later went out of his way to assure the Soviet Union that the U.S. would do nothing to protect the American people against Soviet nuclear weapons, whether dropped by bombers or delivered by missiles. He also selected for promotion to the highest military rank people who agreed with him. Hence he created a new establishment; the Pentagon possessed a new ideology and a new way of doing things. What McNamara did has never been substantially undone. He was the last Secretary of Defense who mastered the Pentagon. His successors, especially those appointed by Republican presidents, have acted largely as cheerleaders for an establishment that they did not have the mind or the heart to shape.

Decades later, when the MAD policy came into disrepute, eminent men who had been associated with the Pentagon during that policy's heyday tried to explain it as a mere "declaratory policy,"[12] and not as a wholesale abandonment of the intention to limit the amount of damage that the Soviet Union could do to the American people. Yet these very explanations concede that *because of this "declaratory" policy, the U.S. did not develop the missiles with the combination of power and accuracy needed to destroy Soviet missile silos.*[13]

It is essential for us to note that the issue of whether or not to develop such missiles has not been at all technical. Since 1967, the U.S. has watched the Soviet Union deploy so-called counterforce missiles. Thus there has been no question as to whether or not it could be done. The question has been whether it should be U.S. policy to have a large stock of such missiles. The U.S. policy community's answer has been, consistently, "No." The whole purpose of the U.S. delegation at SALT I between 1969 and 1972 was first to inculcate in Soviet minds and then to cement in solemn treaties the doctrine that John Newhouse, the sympathetic official chronicler of those negotiations, summarizes as "offense is defense, defense is offense . . . killing weapons is bad, killing people is good." Nowadays it is easy to say that this was never "really" U.S. policy. But it is utterly impossible to understand the United States' central demand in SALT I, and the U.S. negotiators's central boast after the treaty was concluded except in the light of this formulation.

Our negotiators above all wanted to stop the building of Soviet counterforce warheads at 300 (atop an equal number of SS-9 missiles), and they thought they had done so. Alas, when the Soviets completed the conversion of their 308 SS-9 missiles to the SS-18 missile model 4—each of which carries 10 warheads—and the installation of their SS-19 and SS-17 missiles, the Soviets possessed approximately 6,000 counterforce warheads.

But the U.S. defense and foreign policy establishment's intention not to build counterforce missiles has persisted even after the Soviet Union deployed *20 times* the 300 counterforce warheads it had at the time of SALT I in 1972. Since that time, a coalition of defense experts, liberals in Congress, and editorial writers have argued successfully that the U.S. should not do the same because to do so would be to give ourselves the false impression that we could significantly limit damage to ourselves by striking first. In addition, if the U.S. had missiles that put Soviet silos at risk, argues this coalition, the Soviet Union would likely be tempted to launch its missiles in a crisis rather than risk losing them. To the question, why, given that the Soviet Union already has offensive missiles able to limit damage to itself should the U.S. be the only one to bear this risk, the coalition answers that the Soviet Union's possession of counterforce missiles, though regrettable, does not change the "facts of life" of the nuclear age, namely, that nuclear weapons cannot be used rationally to anyone's advantage, ever, under any circumstances.

These "experts" have granted that yes, of course whoever has counterforce missiles can prevent some of the other side's weapons from landing on his soil. Responsible liberals admit that the Soviet counterforce missiles are not targeted on U.S. cities, that they could destroy 90 percent of our land-based missiles on the ground and nearly all of our bombers, and that half of our missile-carrying submarines are in port at any given time. They admit further that such losses would drastically reduce what the United States could do to the Soviet Union. Indeed, that they would eliminate all U.S. options other than "busting" a limited number of Soviet cities. But, the argument continues, because Soviet counterforce strikes cannot wholly eliminate this U.S. option—no matter how irrational or how unlikely to be exercised—such an assault by the Soviets could not prevent "nuclear devastation." Sooner or later the Soviets will learn as much. Indeed, they probably already have.

But, one might ask the U.S. Defense establishment, if the Soviets learned this lesson, why did they waste a generation's efforts to build their counterforce missiles? Out of the Pentagon, the CIA, and the universities comes the chorus: This Soviet decision had to be the result of simple, mindless, bureaucratic inertia, or perhaps a temporary weakness in face of the temptation to gain a meaningless advantage. At any rate, continues the chorus, were the U.S. to possess counterforce missiles, America's leaders would tend to think they had limited options for fighting a nuclear war that in reality they do not have. The chorus concludes that nuclear weapons have wholly and forever removed the freedom of action of U.S. and Soviet leaders. Aristotle is irrelevant.

Though a succession of defense secretaries and presidents have spoken in opposition to axioms of the 1960s, none has acted decisively against them. Secretary of Defense James Schlesinger formally modified Robert McNamara's declaratory MAD policy by announcing that henceforth the U.S. would seek to exercise "limited nuclear options." In 1980, President Carter's Decision #59 formally made Soviet missile silos the number one priority target for U.S. missiles. Nevertheless, the U.S. government's ability to protect the American people, or to frustrate Soviet strategy by destroying Soviet reserve missile forces, remains near zero. Beginning in 1980, the U.S. did in fact assign its most potent warheads to Soviet missile silos. But since these warheads were never designed for that purpose, the new policy remained largely empty, and the American people remain unprotected.

Albert Wohlstetter may be correct that MAD was only a "declaratory policy" in that its authors never had the intention of actually destroying Soviet civilians, and that the effect of MAD was primarily to help its authors limit the U.S. to a MAD capability (MADCAP) and no more! But surely Wohlsletter understates the case when he writes, "MADCAP did not lead to any persistent thought about how to improve the force to make it increasingly discriminating."[14] In fact, the very reasons why certain people thought up the policy of MAD (or MADCAP) in the first place are the same that, as of 1985, led such prominent members of the U.S. defense establishment as Senator Sam Nunn (D-Ga) and National Security Adviser Robert MacFarlane to agree to drastically limit the deployment of the MX—the only American missile designed from the ground up for the purpose of striking Soviet missiles on the ground.

The defense establishment's deliberations over various basing modes for the MX have eclipsed the question: Do we want the ability to destroy as many Soviet missiles as possible before they are launched, or do we not?[15] The opposition, in order to shield themselves from the charge of not wanting to protect their country, confined themselves to pseudotechnical questions about the missile's ability—in any given way it was based—to survive attacks. But the reams of comparative studies, the technical-sounding speeches by Senator Sam Nunn and others on the feasibility of possible basing modes, are a smokescreen. If anyone were really looking for a way to base a 200,000-pound missile like the MX so that the other side could not shoot at it, one need look no farther than the Soviet Union, where the local version of the MX, the SS-24, is riding the country's rail network. When they were not talking about fantastic basing modes, the opponents of the MX were talking about problems with management.

Thus in the 1980s, if the concerned public failed to look at the Soviet Union, it was left with the impression that somehow the state of the art of missilery had not been pushed far enough to permit the U.S. to deploy counterforce missiles. The likes of MacFarlane and Sam Nunn, not really believing in damage-limitation and eager to shield themselves from the charge of wanting to fight a nuclear war, confined themselves to the pseudotechnical, pseudostrategic question of whether the U.S. was going to "modernize its weapons" to "keep up" with the Soviet Union in some ill-defined contest.

But why modernize? Why agonize over basing modes? If threats to "bust" a few cities are enough of a deterrent, what practical good does it do to keep up with the Ivans? The question of whether to try to use offensive forces in a rational protective way or as irrational threats is the only real question—and it is not even remotely a technical one. If we wished to pose the same kind of threat to Soviet missile forces that these pose to us, we would only have to build relatively low-tech counterforce missiles like those of the Soviets. But the U.S. government is not trying to do that. Despite the declaratory policies issued since 1974, we are living largely with the tools of the declaratory policies of the mid-1960s that the government has no intention of carrying out—and, indeed, has consciously rejected. The U.S. government is in no hurry to acquire any other tools fit to carry out any other policy.

For the same reasons, over the past generation, the U.S. government's fundamental attitude on these matters has pushed an even lower-tech means of self-protection, civil defense, into the realm of pseudotechnical contention. But there is no shadow of doubt that the neglect of civil defense, otherwise known as passive defense (digging shelters; reinforcing buildings or machinery; storing food, medicine, and tools; training personnel) is the result of adherence to the ideology of the absolute weapon, or MAD. The Secretary of Defense's annual report for 1978 said:

> U.S. policy for some time has been to avoid the development of large first-strike forces and major damage-limiting capabilities through active and passive defenses. Restraint in both cases, it was hoped, would demonstrate to the Soviets that the United States did not intend to threaten their capability for assured destruction.[16]

In fact, authoritative commentaries on the SALT I and ABM treaties[17] stress that in order for strategic stability to exist, both U.S. and Soviet societies must be equally (and totally) vulnerable to retaliatory attack. *Thus, the many objections to mounting a serious defense for the American people that allege such a defense would be ineffective hide the fact that they measure effectiveness not in terms of lives saved but rather in terms of shoring up a preferred policy.*

By the mid-1970s, the U.S. intelligence community had amassed solid evidence of a massive Soviet civil defense program, including single-purpose blast shelters for workers at key factories, for all the country's leadership at all levels, as well as for 10 to 20 percent of the general urban population. In addition, subway systems and literally uncountable buildings have been modified to give various degrees of blast and fallout protection. These multi-purpose structures are not normally counted in CIA estimates of Soviet civil defense. Food storage areas, and indeed all workplaces, are built with an eye to protection against blast and fallout. Some 100,000 full-time personnel under military control train to, in the words of Maj. Gen. Altunin, "liquidate the consequences of an enemy attack."[18]

Of course, there is no agreement about what these facts mean. How well would these preparations serve the Soviet Union in case of U.S. retaliation? That depends on how many and what kind of warheads remained to the U.S. after a counterforce strike, and on how many of these the U.S. chose to launch against what. The CIA, assuming that the full weight of an undiminished U.S. strategic arsenal would be disgorged on Soviet centers of population, has claimed that the Soviet government would have to evacuate its cities to hold casualties down to 5 percent of the Soviet population.[19] But of course if the U.S., as is likely after a Soviet first strike, would have but a fraction of its arsenal remaining, and, as is certain, would use only a fraction of that remainder (and that probably not against cities), then even without evacuation and in the absence of any antimissile defense, Soviet casualties would be well below this figure. No one can be certain, and the CIA did not factor rationality into the hypothesis of U.S. retaliatory strikes. Nevertheless, the CIA concluded: "[The Soviets] cannot have confidence, however, in the degree of protection that their civil defenses would afford them. . . . The intelligence community does not believe that the Soviets' pursuit of civil defense would embolden them deliberately to expose the USSR to a higher risk of nuclear attack."[20]

The CIA's basis for this conclusion was not secret knowledge of conversations among Soviets on this topic. CIA had no such knowledge. Instead, CIA analysts made the judgments about Soviet civil defense that *they* and other members of the U.S. foreign policy establishment *have made about American civil defense.* Here, too, the facts are not in dispute, since building shelters and measuring their resistance to blast or radiation is easy. The cost of backhoes, concrete, and labor is easily calculated. Thus, the Defense Department's study of what various kinds of civil defense systems could do for the U.S. and what they would cost was straightforward.[21] Even though the study assumed, against all evidence, that the

Soviets would target the U.S. population, it concluded that whereas with no civil defense perhaps only 20 percent of the U.S. population would survive, a five-year, $60 billion (FY 1979) program for building blast shelters in urban areas would ensure that about 90 percent of Americans survived. When the study takes into account that the Soviets might not target the population per se (i.e., reality), survival rates approach 100 percent. As for the effective hardening of industrial equipment, the conclusion of the Department of Defense's Nuclear Agency was that the Soviet procedures (whose validity the Boeing Company's tests had proved) would largely protect U.S. industry for a price tag ranging between $300 million and $3 billion.[22] But the facts cannot possibly speak for themselves. While some deem satisfactory the insurance of 170 million lives for $3 billion,—18 dollars for each American—others do not.

In December 1978, the Arms Control and Disarmament Agency (ACDA), using assumptions about the Soviet civil defense system very different from the CIA's, and assuming that the U.S. would target cities and then, alternatively, industry, came up with a figure of twenty-five–thirty-five million Soviet fatalities, i.e., about 9 to 13 percent of the population, and 65 to 75 percent of "key Soviet production capacity," an index known to ACDA alone. Presenting that study to Congress, and arguing against a U.S. civil defense program to match the Soviet Union's, ACDA's deputy director concluded that nothing "could render a large-scale nuclear war anything but an unparalleled disaster for the Soviet Union. We see nothing that indicates the Soviets have a different view."[23] Nevertheless, any reasonable person might well ask what someone who does not wish to reverse the prospect of 80 percent of the American people dying and 87 percent of the Soviet people surviving would have to "see" in order to be impressed? ACDA Director Paul Warnke's statement in the same controversy was an answer of sorts to the question. It cited no facts; indeed, it judged irrelevant any fact other than the unspecified "vast destruction" of nuclear war. He said:

> *There can*, in my opinion, *be no question* of the fact that the Soviet leadership *must recognize* the futility of the Soviet civil defense effort. . . . The Soviets *cannot be judged* so blind and reckless as to assume that *any* present or prospective shelter program . . . may make it possible for them to utilize strategic nuclear war as a means of achieving political objectives. . . . I believe it is *completely unrealistic and totally destabilizing to consider* that civil defense can play any genuine part in the strategic balance. Any conclusion that we should seek to match whatever it is that the Soviet Union may be doing

in the civil defense field *could lead only* to a mindless race in this area, with the result being a diminution of stability in time of crisis.[24] [Emphasis added.]

The voice of the establishment could not be clearer: We should not even think about the difference between 80 percent of us dead and nearly all of us alive, even as we acknowledge that our enemies have already completed preparations that by themselves, without counting air defenses or antimissile defenses, would keep some 90 percent of them alive. The voice of the establishment says that what we could do to subtract hundreds of millions of lives from the vagaries of international strife is only a threat to a notion of "stability" that requires that they be hostage. Thinking about what the Soviets have done heightens that threat by breaking the solipsistic reasoning that this notion of "stability" demands. This voice of the establishment is so authoritative that it has made dead letters, literally non-sense, of repeated statements by presidents as well as chairmen of the Joint Chiefs of Staff to the effect that U.S. policy is to come out of any conflict in better shape than our enemies, that only if we can expect to do this can we deter war, and that to this end, in the words of a spokesman for the Pentagon, ". . . we can't tolerate marked asymmetries in relative population vulnerability."[25]

In fact, the U.S. government has more than tolerated this disparity. The Carter administration, despite its declaratory commitment to limiting the damage to the U.S., embodied in P.D. 59, did not revive civil defense. Even more significantly, the very Reagan administration that has talked so much about protecting the American people in the next millenium by ultra high-tech means not only has failed to provide for, or even encouraged the use of, picks and shovels to provide elementary protection now. Indeed, the Reagan administration thoroughly silenced and disavowed T. K. Jones, one of its deputy undersecretaries of defense for research and engineering, who dared to encourage civil defense. Ronald Reagan's major activity in civil defense was to place it in charge of one Louis Giuffrida, who had been in charge of his bodyguards, and who was later forced to resign by revelations of extravagance in remodeling his office. Like its predecessors, the Reagan administration has defined civil defense as a low-profile activity that produces an endless succession of paper studies on the feasibility of this and that—studies whose time to be translated into concrete and steel somehow never comes.

Thus, as we begin considering claims and counterclaims about

what can be done with tools somewhat more difficult to comprehend than picks and shovels, it is important to remember that
during the last generation the U.S. government has passed up
chances to protect against ballistic missiles or bombers by methods
well on *this* side of the technological horizon. The choice before
us at any given time is always whether or not to use the tools on
hand at that time. During the past generation, almost as much
as ever, American politicians have declared themselves four-square
in favor of protecting the American people's lives and property.
Given that the U.S. Constitution specifies this as the primary purpose of government, and that politicians must get elected, this is
not surprising. But words and deeds can differ. In daily life we
come across professions of devotion to many worthy goals, and
judge them according to what those who profess them actually
do. Claims of devotion to the purpose of people protection should
be judged by the same practical standard.

Why then are so many American policy makers so unwilling to
try to meet their constitutional responsibility? Two answers ring
true, but beg the question. The first is inertia. In the 1960s, Robert
McNamara made a revolution in the Pentagon. He ended hundreds
of careers and made hundreds of others for people who thought
as he did. These people now *are* the U.S. Defense Establishment.
Defense Secretaries Laird, Schlesinger, Richardson, Brown, and
Weinberger, and Presidents Nixon, Carter, and Reagan, each for
their own reasons, have reigned over McNamara's establishment
but not changed it substantially. The second answer is the doctrine
of MAD—embodied in men, weapons, and procedures in the Pentagon, as well as in the ideology of American liberalism. Granted
that most people in Washington are moved less by ideas than by
concrete pressures. Yet insofar as they do not take refuge in procrastination based on technical "agnosticism," and explain to
themselves their unwillingness to try to limit damage as best they
can, they can only refer to MAD—a doctrine part of whose seductive
power comes from its easy prescription: Do nothing.

But the fundamental reason why anyone can find inertia and
MAD acceptable can only be that he or she attaches relatively
little importance to the things to be defended and does not think
it likely that the occasion for defending them will arise. The typical
member of the defense establishment does *not* believe that each
of us has a duty to preserve each innocent human life. Whether
he is in government, industry, or journalism, he also does not
believe that the U.S. government and society stand on a qualita-
tively different moral plane from those in the Soviet Union and,

therefore, that it is his duty to move earth—if not heaven—to preserve the American way of life. Why these attitudes reign supreme is a matter of some dispute. The U.S. government's increasing official neutrality about whether people are or are not made in the image and likeness of God cannot help but contribute the Pentagon's increasing ethical vacuum. But on the other hand those in government who follow the U.S. Catholic Bishops' 1983 pastoral letter on war also cannot explain why the moral difference between the U.S. and the Soviet Union might sanction war to preserve American society, or why it might be wrong to threaten to slaughter innocents rather than to defend the country. In other words, for certain people, the passing of our civilization and of most of us in it would not be a great evil because they do not believe there are objective standards by which to distinguish evil from good.

Because such people find little meaning in the issues that divide the U.S. and the USSR, they value most highly any chance, however remote, to establish a kind of sleepy, perpetual accommodation with the Soviet Union that would gloss them over. To gain that chance, they are willing to risk much. Besides, they genuinely cannot understand why the Soviet leaders would feel strongly enough about anything to make war. After all, they themselves would not make war for any reason in the world. In other words, they feel no pressing need for a shield because they do not wish to do things in the world that would require a shield, and cannot imagine that anyone else would do them. In fact, one cannot read American liberals' testimony against civil defense, counterforce missiles, or any form of ballistic missile defense without being struck by *their preference for the absence of a shield precisely because this absence helps keep what they believe to be the American people's worst qualities from asserting themselves in the world*. Thus the argument over antimissile defense, at bottom, is about how much labor and risk the preservation and advancement of this civilization are worth.

Our story, then, is one of technical bounty out of proportion to the moral insight and strategic competence of those who have been in charge of using it.

3 / The More Things Change . . .

The tests by themselves will have little effect on the decision as to whether we will or will not proceed into production.

—Robert McNamara, on the Nike Zeus ABM, 1962

The technology of anti-aircraft defense and of ground-based defense against ballistic missiles has grown apace with that of ballistic missilery. Air-defense missiles and antimissile missiles involve many of the same technical elements as do ballistic missiles: rocket propulsion, radar, infrared sensors, and miniaturized data processors for terminal guidance, as well as long-range, computer-driven radars for tracking and battle management.[1] Since 1945 the technological progress of these three kinds of missiles, ballistic, air defense, and ABM—has been rather even. But it has not been applied evenly. In the Soviet Union, as each technology has matured, it has been applied in an evolutionary manner to ever more sophisticated offensive and defensive operating forces. In addition, the number of all three kinds of missiles in Soviet forces has expanded steadily. This determination to apply new technology to all the military uses where it is applicable as soon as it becomes available results from a steady commitment to increase Soviet military power across the board. U.S. authorities, by contrast, have not had such a commitment since World War II. Instead, they have shifted emphasis from bombers to special forces, to missiles, to the navy, etc., in search of the magic "fix" *du jour* for the country's military problems, or as a result of purely bureaucratic struggles. This has meant that the "star" of air defense, ballistic missiles, and missile defense has fluctuated, which in turn has meant stops, starts, and sharp changes in the development and application of new technology.

Air defense was a booming business in the U.S., beginning in the late 1940s, absorbing both the latest technologies and much production money. But until *circa* 1955, U.S. officials were not interested enough in ballistic missiles to apply present technology to them. For a decade thereafter, while ballistic missiles were all the rage in Washington, the U.S. government deemed the technology available for them to be quite good enough. Meanwhile, in the 1960s, as air defense lost favor, U.S. officials decided that the job which the technology of the day was doing was not worth doing. Thus, air defense became something to be researched for the future, not done in the present.

After *circa* 1966, the same fate befell American ballistic missiles. Somehow, U.S. officials decided that before new models were built, or the ICBM fleet were expanded, much more research and development should be done. Consequently, the pace of innovation slowed dramatically. Whereas the Minuteman ICBM had gone from "go ahead" to first deployment in a bit more than three years, twenty years passed between the initiation of a program for a successor to Minuteman and the MX's first tentative deployment in 1986. Defenses against ballistic missiles, for their part, became interesting to U.S. officials about two years before ballistic missiles did, that is, *circa* 1953–54. That was due to the fact that antimissile defense was growing out of air defense. But interservice rivalries kept the antimissile mission from being assigned to any service. Since that time, ballistic missile defense in the United States has not been a job to be done—in the hands of people who want to do it—but a question to be studied—in the hands of people who spend a substantial proportion of their effort figuring out "technical" reasons for studying the field *ad infinitum*. Thus we will see that the waves of enthusiasm and reticence that have made ballistic missiles, air defense, and ballistic missile defenses "technically" feasible and "cost effective," or the opposite, have had very little to do with the state of the art and much to do with the basic choices of American policymakers.

In 1945, both the Army and what was to become the Air Force had a substantial stake in defense against hostile aircraft. The Army was eager to improve its antiaircraft guns and to supplement them with surface-to-air missiles (Project Nike had begun in 1944). The Air Force, while pursuing its very lively interest in better fighter-interceptor aircraft (at its peak, the Air Force had 2,612 of them), also entered the field of surface-to-air missiles—which it called ground-to-air pilotless aircraft. The Air Force, jealous that the Army had flying things to shoot down airplanes, successfully lobbied to restrict the operating altitude of the Nike missiles and the size of their aerodynamic control surfaces. To pacify the Air Force these were no longer to be called "wings" but rather "fins." At any rate, the Army eventually deployed 274 Nike batteries to protect individual cities and military bases; the Air Force deployed 439 long-range BOMARC nuclear-armed cruise missiles intended to blow big holes in attacking bombers should they use the large-formation tactics of World War II. The Air Force also largely built and staffed the vast battle management network: 81 distant early warning (DEW) radars stretched across some of the world's most inhospitable terrain, from Alaska to Greenland; 286 other long-range radars stretched across Canada. Eleven large radar picket ships and 137 other gap-filler ships covered the seaward approaches to North America. Sixty-eight ground control centers and seventy-seven large EC-121 aircraft provided the brains for the whole system. Military personnel totaling 207,000 were employed directly in running it, and almost that number again of civilians built and tested the equipment. The total air-defense bill for the decade 1950–1960 came to about $200 billion (1980 dollars). In other words, this was a huge enterprise by any standards.

Those involved in that enterprise were very much aware of its technical shortcomings. Just about all the electronic equipment employed vacuum tubes instead of the semiconductors that became widely available in the 1960s. Maintaining radars, rudimentary computers, and communications based on vacuum tubes in the high Arctic was a nightmare. The interceptor aircraft had radars on board good enough to work in foul weather—so long as they were looking *up* or *out*, not *down*, at their targets. But then again, the long-range bombers of the day could only fly high. Radars capable of seeing targets clearly against ground clutter had not yet been invented, but moving target indicators were common. Anyhow, U.S. interceptor aircraft carried some 16,000 air-to-air rockets (named Genie) loaded with 2-kiloton nuclear warheads. The new Nike Hercules and anti-aircraft missiles also assuaged doubts about their accuracy by carrying nuclear warheads. The computers that managed the system filled whole rooms, experienced frequent breakdowns, and could not be connected to each other. Each part of the system had to stand or fall on its own, with the sole hope that human judgment somewhere along the line would channel more resources into hard-pressed sectors.

Anyone familiar with the standards used in the U.S. military's research and development process since the mid-1950s cannot help but marvel at how such imperfection was tolerated. The U.S. air defense system of the 1950s, like most of the weaponry that won World War II, could certainly not have passed muster in the modern Pentagon. Yet, it passed muster literally without serious question: there was a job to be done, and it was done with the best tools at hand.

Incidentally, the job succeeded totally. This is not to say that it was possible, around 1962, to guarantee absolutely that no Soviet bomber could have dropped a single bomb on an American city. But the U.S. air defense system effectively guaranteed that the Soviet Union's 210 turboprop Bears and jet-powered Bisons could not possibly have carried out any sort of meaningful military mission against the U.S. Had the Soviet Union sent its whole force into the teeth of our defense, no one knows what would have happened. Perhaps a few would have got through; perhaps all would have been shot down over the unpopulated parts of Canada. But very surely, regardless of how much harm it might have done to the U.S., the Soviet Union could have done itself no good by such an irrational attack. In fact, the Soviet Union not only did not challenge the U.S. system with an attack, it did not challenge it by quantitative or qualitative improvements in its bomber force. Not until the late 1960s, when the U.S. had largely dismantled its air defense system, did the Soviet Union decide to build the Backfire, and later the Blackjack, bombers. These new Soviet bombers are a response to an American invitation.

By 1981, however, state-of-the-art bombers were not really needed to bomb the U.S. The DEW radars are down to thirty-one, leaving huge gaps. The backup radars in Canada, the picket ships, all of the surface-to-air missile batteries, and all but some 200 interceptors are gone. Intruding aircraft have a free ride into the U.S. Every day during the 1980s, in the absence of serious air defenses, countless aircraft violate U.S. borders to carry tons of illegal drugs to places as widespread as Oregon and Florida, California and Pennsylvania. Deep inside Cheyenne Mountain, Colorado officers of the North American Aerospace Defense Command watch helpless as the little dots representing the drug-runners move across their screens. In the 1980s, in the era of look-down/shoot-down radars, of tracking radars so fine that they can produce a picture of each airplane, of computers so small, cheap, accurate, and reliable as to bear no comparison at all to the ones that daunted the Soviet Union's best equipment a generation ago, the U.S. could be bombed by cargo planes!

Interestingly enough, the Soviet Union built its post-World War II air defense system on top of the anti-aircraft guns and prop-driven fighters that had held off the Luftwaffe. By 1950 it had rudimentary jet interceptors and by 1955 its first surface-to-air missile, the SA-1. But not until 1960, with the SA-2, had the Soviet Union begun to close its territory to high-altitude penetration whether by bombers or intelligence aircraft. In sum, Soviet air defense was about seven years behind U.S. air defense until, in the 1960s, the U.S. system stopped reflecting the state-of-the-art in sensors and data processing and all but disappeared. The Soviet air defense system, however, kept on growing and by 1980 incorporated up to 4,000 interceptor aircraft, the newest with look-down radar, some 10,000 air defense radars, and some 10,000 launchers for surface-to-air missiles—most embodying the latest technology. As a result, the U.S. no longer even thinks about sending high-altitude bombers to the Soviet Union. In the 1980s, U.S. B-52 bombers (designed during the Truman administration) have been reduced to carrying weight-inefficient cruise missiles to be launched from great distances. In 1983, the U.S. stopped production of these air-launched offensive cruise missiles because it judged that the Soviet air defense system could intercept them with its state-of-the-art SA-10 tower-mounted radar and defensive surface-to-air missiles. The U.S. hoped that the next generation of cruise missiles and the new B-1 bomber might be able to get through Soviet air defenses. But because the U.S. is not counting on this, it has limited production of the B-1.[2] Thus, the Soviet air defense system in the 1980s and 1990s has succeeded in precisely the way that the U.S. air defense system succeeded in the 1950s and 1960s.

The reason why the Johnson, Nixon, and Carter administrations dismantled the U.S. air defense system seemed simple enough: the Soviets had built long-range ballistic missiles. Since we could not (or did not choose to) defend ourselves against ballistic missiles but relied wholly on the threat of retaliation with our own ballistic missiles to deter any and all major wars, why spend money to defend ourselves against airplanes? By this line of reasoning, Soviet aircraft are a lesser threat than Soviet ballistic missiles with which we have dealt cost-free by threatening retaliation with our own ballistic missiles. Thus, even as the technology available for air defense improved, and its costs were dropping, air defense ceased to be cost-effective according to a peculiarly latter-day American standard.

But one need not look far to see that the cost-effectiveness of threats of mutual destruction can rest only on a single premise:

that all major powers choose to remain wholly vulnerable to ballistic missiles indefinitely. After all, to the extent that either side provided itself with any kind of protection against ballistic missiles, or credibly threatened to do more harm unto the other than the other could do unto it, threats of missile reprisals would no longer be equally effective. So, whether one side were attracted to war by the perception of unequal vulnerability, or for any other reason, that side would find bomber aircraft useful to roam the enemy's country, striking down attempts to regroup—especially if the opponent had no air defenses. In other words, if there were a war between the U.S. and the Soviet Union, and we were somehow not consumed by it in the first moments, Americans would soon regret the techno-managerial logic by which their leaders have dispensed with anti-aircraft protection.

By contrast, the constantly growing Soviet air defense system continues to reduce the value of the bomber aircraft and cruise missiles of the United States. The Soviets obviously have understood the air threat on its own terms, and as one of many threats. Thus, they have sought to cover themselves against it as well as they could. This point is most relevant to the Reagan administration's claims that it waits only for technology to end the strategic vulnerability of the United States. No. The decision to do without air defense, like the decision to build it in the first place, has scarce relationship to technology. The talk of cost-effectiveness, however, illuminates the *value* that these officials place on the military things they choose to do and not do.

The development of long-range ballistic missiles also shows that technology is subordinate to political choice, which can hold it back or call it forth in very different ways. In a perceptive history of the space age, Professor Walter McDougall writes: "The rocket teams of both superpowers protested that they could have launched a satellite years earlier if left to do so without political or military interference. But the genius of the engineers was only a necessary, not a sufficient, condition."[3]

The U.S., although it got nearly all of Nazi Germany's rocket team, plus all of its records and almost all of its equipment, nevertheless lost the race for the first intercontinental ballistic missile as well as for the first earth satellite because its leaders were not especially interested in winning those races. Meanwhile, without help from the Germans, American rocketeers on project Nike far outstripped the Soviets in the development of surface-to-air rockets. The explanation? Good engineers with a goal! Later, the United States exploited its technical superiority to go to the moon, because

American politicians chose to respond in this particular way to popular pressure for achievements in space.

Soviet leaders, by contrast, knew what they wanted from their long-range rocketeers and why they wanted it long before the rocketeers could deliver. The few members of Werner von Braun's rocket team who had fallen into Stalin's hands were interested in space travel, as were, indeed, their colleagues who wound up in the United States. But the Soviet leadership wanted missiles, not space travel. The Politburo had decided to build intercontinental rockets long before it possessed the atomic bomb, and long before it knew the bomb could be made small enough and powerful enough to be used as a warhead on a missile. Research was fine, Stalin said, but the Soviet Union needed intercontinental strike systems as quickly as possible.

Stalin realized that the Red Army's heart was not in the high-level development of the new weapons, so he established a separate organization to do the job and endowed it with high-level "pull." The first political commissar of what would become the Soviet Strategic Rocket Forces was none other than Leonid Brezhnev.

As for the complex leadership of the United States, it was cool not just to space travel but to missiles as well. Among the many technical advantages then enjoyed by the United States was a superior ability to fabricate rocket nozzles resistant to high heat. This allowed von Braun's team in Huntsville, Alabama, to use the NAVAHO engines—bigger and more efficient than could be built in the Soviet Union. But many years would pass before von Braun received the authorization and the money to build missiles around those engines. Meanwhile, Soviet engineers, who did not have the metals and propellant for big, efficient engines, did have a mandate to deliver a product. So they got around their technical problem by clustering twenty relatively inefficient engines. The result was the world's first intercontinental rocket, the rocket that launched Sputnik and that is still in use today as the world's most prolific space-launch vehicle.

In the U.S., no military service or unit—indeed, no one—was assigned responsibility for building long-range rockets. Rocketry was divided into many technology programs, none with a mission or a deadline. The services, however, were jealous enough to fight for the *option* to build such rockets. They did not intend to exercise those options, because to do so would have taken money out of current programs, but each wanted to protect itself against the possibility that some time in the future, any of the other services would have a monopoly on a new mission and new budgets.

Absence of purpose engendered bad technical judgments. Vannevar Bush, then the foremost expert on military research and development, had declared in 1945 that no one knew how to build an ICBM and that one would not be built for a long time to come. By 1949, he could no longer rule out the possibility that some might be built, but he thought the cost would be "astronomical." Bush and a host of others were satisfied that anything reentering the atmosphere after an intercontinental ballistic flight would be heated by friction to temperatures higher than any material known to man could withstand. He was right, and, in a way, he is still right. But engineers who started rather than stopped with that fact have been able to get around it in two interesting ways: with materials whose surfaces ablate (or peel off) as they burn, cooling the rest, and with materials that dissipate heat almost as fast as they absorb it (as in the tiles of the space shuttle).

The truth is that the research and development establishment was not interested in building ICBMs, and ridiculed those who wanted to. Thus, Vannevar Bush spoke for thousands of bright, but smug, people:

> Some eminent military men, exhilarated perhaps by a short immersion in matters scientific, have publicly asserted that we are interested in high-trajectory guided missiles spanning thousands of miles. We have been regaled by scary articles . . . we even have the exposition of missiles fired so fast that they leave the earth and proceed around it indefinitely as satellites, like the moon, for some vaguely specified military purposes.[4]

This, in 1949, when the U.S. aircraft industry and the Army's rocket team were sitting on reasonably concrete plans and on basic technology nearly identical to those used for U.S. ICBMs and satellites almost a decade later. This was also three years after the Douglas Corporation's satellite report of 1946, which proved to be a road map for what happened a decade later, when the U.S. government chose to act.

At about the same time, however, Americans began to learn that what our "best and brightest" were saying could not—or at least should not—be done was in fact being done on the Russian steppes. Prominent outsiders, notably then-Senator Lyndon B. Johnson and Hanson Baldwin, the military correspondent of the *New York Times*, charged the government with ignorance, confusion, and a lack of policy. In 1950, as a response to these pressures, as well as to those of the Korean war, President Truman appointed K. T. Keller, president of the Chrysler Corporation, as his special adviser in this field. Mistaking this move as a decision rather than as a move to defuse the pressure for making a decision, the press touted the birth of a new era of push-button warfare with the President's new adviser as its czar.

Of course, he was no such thing. Keller appointed a blue-ribbon technical panel that recommended a long-term research and development program. The panel also defined the program's goals: a rocket able to carry a 10,000-pound payload 5,000 miles with an accuracy of 0.01 degrees. Until we could build that, the government would not think about building long-range ballistic missiles. Therefore, for the foreseeable future, we would build nothing.

This filibuster-by-technical-definition lasted almost four years, until news of the Soviet H-bomb—and of Soviet missile tests— caused a new panel to be appointed. The new panel found that a rocket carrying one-third the payload with one-half the accuracy that had been previously specified—something we had known how to build for some years—would be worthy of being called an ICBM after all. Armed with this new report, Trevor Gardner, a junior civilian at the Pentagon, made a fuss about unrealistic technical requirements, and finally, in 1954, a special organization was created within the Air Force specifically to produce an ICBM. The Soviets were far ahead.

Beginning in 1955, however, the U.S. was gripped by something of a mania for rocketry. The industrial teams commissioned by the Army, the Navy, and the Air Force simultaneously built excellent ballistic missiles quickly. The Army's Jupiter and the Air Force's Thor went from initiation of the program to the first operational squadrons in twenty-eight months. Thor's main booster is still in production. The Navy's Polaris program managed to develop, test, and field highly complex systems for expelling newly designed solid-fueled missiles from submarines underwater, to light them off at precisely the right time, to stabilize guidance systems mightily upset by having come through the water, and to guide the missiles to distant targets—all in four years. The Air Force developed the Atlas in four years, during which it was also developing superior follow-on missiles, the Titan and the Minuteman. By the early 1960s, the U.S. had far outstripped the Soviet Union and had ordered the 1,000 Minuteman land-based missiles and the 600-odd Poseidon sea-based missiles that would be the bulk of America's strategic forces for over a generation.

But although the early 1960s made long-range ballistic missiles part of the U.S. armed forces, these years also saw the rise within the Pentagon of a new elite that assigned to these weapons the essentially nonmilitary role of ultimate scarecrow. That elite's father, Secretary of Defense Robert McNamara, in 1967 vetoed the Navy's plan to arm its sea-based ballistic missiles with the combination of nuclear yield and accuracy that would have made them countermilitary weapons rather than city-killers. Finally, as we have already seen, although the *declaratory* commitment of the U.S. to countermilitary ballistic missiles began in 1974 and became unequivocal in 1980, the Pentagon's elite has passed this commitment through a technical-managerial filter somewhat like that which had slowed down ballistic missiles in the first place. Instead of building large numbers of counterforce missiles with the technology on hand, the Pentagon defined its problems in terms of decades-long development programs for the sophisticated MX and for the very sophisticated Trident D-5 submarine-launched missiles. As of January 1987, ten MX missiles were deployed and the first Trident D-5 was over two years away. Meanwhile, by 1987 the Soviet Union had long since used the materials at hand to build an offensive missile force that, if fired, would drastically reduce the ability of the United States to fight back.

On November 26, 1956, Secretary of Defense Charles Wilson refused to resolve the struggle among the military services over which of them should be assigned primary responsibility for developing and, above all, for operating U.S. defenses against ballistic missiles. He thus unintentionally set up a situation that has persisted ever since: none of the services would have a strong interest in performing the antimissile mission, while some would have a strong interest in making sure that the mission was not performed. Wilson's memorandum assigned to the Army the development of antimissile missiles with ranges up to 100 miles, and to the Air Force the development of a nationwide radar network, along with more comprehensive defenses. In January 1958, Wilson's successor, Neil MacElroy, confronted the fact that the Army had a product, the Nike Zeus, ready to be built and deployed, while the Air Force had none. He decided to reduce the Air Force's role in the antimissile field to providing long-range radar warning and tracking data to encourage the Army to develop the Nike Zeus. Just as in the case of ballistic missiles prior to 1954, responsibility was parceled out according to arbitrary criteria; no one agency had the tools or the mandate to build and operate weapons to perform a mission. In fact, this was a decision not to decide about deployment, about the roles and missions of the services, and about strategic doctrine. As part of this decision, Secretary MacElroy commissioned the Advanced Research Projects Agency (ARPA) to look for better ways of defending against ballistic missiles. Both the Air Force and ARPA thenceforth have been potent interest groups, promoting the thinking underlying that decision and all subsequent ones in this field, to wit: The nation's money is best spent not on self-protection and the ability to fight wars but on the threat of senseless retaliation and on research into ever better antimissile technologies without logical end.

To understand the controversies over Nike Zeus and its successors, let us glance briefly at their technical basis. Ground-based defenses against ballistic reentry vehicles are akin to defenses against aircraft. Radar "sees" the object, and provides initial guidance to a surface-to-air interceptor missile. That is then guided to a near-collision with the target, either based on the radar waves bounced off the target, by homing in on the heat it radiates, or by a combination of both. The differences between air defense and missile defense lie in the nature of the target. While a heavy bomber may have 20 square meters of surface that reflect radar energy, reentry vehicles (RVs) may expose only one-half a square meter. Hence, to see RVs accurately, the radar waves must be relatively short and must be transmitted in short, frequent pulses. While aircraft move at hundreds of miles per hour on unpredictable courses, RVs move at over ten thousand miles per hour on totally predictable ballistic trajectories.

Aircraft are relatively difficult to decoy physically (as with clouds of tinsel strips called chaff) and easy to decoy electronically, while RVs are nearly impossible to decoy electronically and easy to decoy physically, before they reenter the atmosphere. However, once a ballistic RV has begun to reenter the atmosphere, it is very difficult to decoy. But by then, the defense has only a few minutes to act. Of course, RVs come from an apogee in space and are thus in line-of-sight with a defensive radar while still many hundreds of miles away, whereas even a high-flying aircraft may not come over the horizon until it is less than 200 miles away. Thus, in order to "see" an RV, a radar must emit pulses that are powerful (able to travel far), of short duration, and of short wavelength (or else they would not return a coherent image of something small). Long wavelengths are fine for acquisition alone. But to establish very precise tracks and to tell the difference between RVs and decoys, short wavelengths and short pulses are better. The radar must also be able to follow an RV's fast angular motion without losing sight of other RVs.

The ballistic warheads of the late 1950s and 1960s had radar cross sections of about 2 square meters. The radars of the earliest

Nike Zeus—mechanically-steered "dish" type radars—could manage to discern them at distances of 600 miles (later, 1,000 miles). As the warheads got closer to the defended city or military installation, the warhead's location, course, and speed—i.e., its track—would be transferred to ever more precise radars, would become clearer, until the Zeus missile itself would be launched. The nuclear warhead of the Zeus would explode perhaps 100 feet from the reentering warhead and destroy it perhaps 75 miles away from the area to be defended. On July 20, 1962, after many administrative delays, the first of three Zeus missiles on Kwajalein atoll in the Pacific intercepted dummy warheads launched from Vandenberg Air Force Base in California, one of which was accompanied by decoys not yet deployed on operational U.S. offensive missiles. The hardware worked.

But Zeus had many shortcomings. Because dish-type radars relied on a single mechanically-steered beam to scan areas, they could not "stare." Despite the ingenious track-while-scan Lunberg lens, the ability of any dish-type radar to follow the track of many warheads simultaneously was limited. Also, the Zeus radar could barely distinguish decoys. Also, because of the administratively imposed limitation of its range, Zeus was strictly a point-defense weapon, meaning that any Zeus site could defend its own area and the area in the "downstream shadow" of its coverage but no more. Hence, almost as many Zeus sites would have to be built as there were areas to be defended. Moreover, as is the case with all fixed point defenses, any given site could be overwhelmed by attacking it with one more warhead than it had interceptors, or with more warheads than its radar and computers could handle at any given time. Still, by the time the decisions were made not to produce Zeus, the Soviet ICBM force had ever greater shortcomings. The Soviet's first-generation ICBM, the SS-6, was proving more dangerous to those who fueled it than it was to the U.S. By the time of the all-too-famous Cuban missile crisis, during which myth has it that Khrushchev was fingering "the button" of Armageddon, the Soviets had perhaps fourteen SS-6s. They did not have over 200 SS-7s and SS-8s until 1967. The first decoys came later. Thus during most of the 1960s, perhaps fifty Zeus sites would have made nonsense of any Soviet missile attack.

As others have noted,[5] the string of decisions between 1958 and 1962 not to build Zeus but rather to use it as a technical stepping-stone was a strategic, and above all, a managerial, one. But it was presented to the country as a choice dictated by technology. In Congressional testimony, the Air Force argued that because the decoys and penetration aids it was studying could theoretically defeat Zeus hardware, ballistic missiles would always get through and therefore Zeus was unworkable. ARPA argued that the many new technologies that were being investigated by its project Defender—including lasers, particle beams, space-based rockets, and even antimatter beams, as well as new radars—would soon offer more comprehensive solutions to the ballistic missile problem. ARPA agreed that Zeus should not be allowed to meet the Army's projected operational date of mid-1962. Congress, however, was sympathetic to the Army's plea, expressed by General Maxwell Taylor:

> My reservation is this area arises from the unopposed ICBM threat and my conviction that the importance of obtaining this unique anti-missile weapon at the earliest possible date outweighs the possible financial risks inherent in initiating selective production.[6]

Zeus was the only ABM available. Why not use it? The administration's answer to Congress dodged the question by redefining it. The administration said it was all in favor of an ABM "if *it* can be successfully developed"[7] (emphasis supplied). By definition, the "it" that existed was not "it."

By the administration's definition, an ABM was something that could intercept warheads farther out than Zeus, that could handle far greater numbers of warheads simultaneously, and that could reliably discriminate warheads outside the atmosphere. Could Zeus, the ABM that existed, be modified to become the "real" ABM that did not yet exist?

The question boiled down to this: Can we make wholly new kinds of radar, as well as two new kinds of missiles, one with a range longer than Zeus and one much faster? The answer was clearly "yes."

Of course the Nike Zeus missile was constantly being improved in range and performance. The main missile for the new system, Spartan, was to be virtually a re-named Zeus. According to one wag, the name was really an acronym for *S*uperior *P*erformance *A*nd *R*ange *T*hrough *A*nother *N*ame. The real change, however, would come in the radar. Improvements in miniaturization and data processing would allow more radar power to be put out of small, individual transmitters and would allow many transmitters to work together as if they were one. All of this would take some time, but the path of development was clear. The new instruments would be ready for testing in 1963 and would be called Nike X.

At the heart of Nike X was the phased-array radar. This kind of radar, was first developed during World War II and has become commonplace as computers have grown in their ability to make it function. The phased array features fixed arrays of small, powerful transmitters that radiate one after the other. By doing so, the waves from each transmitter interfere with one another so as to steer a broad beam in the desired direction. Thus, the set of sensors receiving the signals that a phased-array radar had bounced off an object then build an image of that object somewhat in the way that a television set's picture tube builds a picture. The picture's quality will vary with the number of transmitters and receivers per unit area, with the wavelength, and with the power of the radar. But, because their beams are broad and composed of smaller ones, phased-array radars, like the human eye, have the theoretical ability to see everything in front of them; in short, to "stare." Moreover, the computers that sort out the returns from phased array radars can artificially "compress" the returning pulses so as to produce finer images. Although modern phased-array radars (PARS) intended to see RVs a thousand or more miles away are still the size of large buildings, ones with ranges of hundreds of miles can fit on the back of a truck. Small phased-array radars fit on aircraft. The author has seen one that is ten centimeters in diameter.

The density (number per unit area) and quality of a phased array's transmitters and receivers, as well as its power, set the outer limits of its performance. But the actual *use* to which a phased array is put depends chiefly on the computer software that generates the transmitter's wave, sorts the reception into images, analyzes them for size, shape, mass, movement, and tracks them. Depending on the software for processing it, the raw information coming into a phased array's receiver becomes either intelligence about the nature of the RVs, warning that RVs are coming, or precise track files on each RV transfered to other PARS, whose job is to guide surface-to-air missiles to intercept them.

The area that a radar's waves can usefully cover is commonly called its "footprint." The idea of Nike X was to cover the northern approaches to the United States by large PARs with large footprints. These would have sorted the attacking RVs according to destination and passed the appropriate bundles of track files to an undetermined number of smaller missile site radars, which would have directed Spartan missiles (maximum range, 400 miles) to intercept RVs far out in space (hence, due to imperfect discrimination, some of the Spartan interceptors might have been wasted on decoys). Those RVs which escaped the Spartans and entered the edges of the atmosphere would have been totally separated from their much lighter decoys and would have been engaged very quickly by high-acceleration missiles called Sprints, guided by the same missile site radars.

No one seriously contended that the systems would not work as advertised. The deficiencies of Nike X were not technical. As Secretary McNamara explained to Congress, much more was involved than Nike X's ability to intercept warheads. First, it would have to prove itself able to stop the sophisticated offensive countermeasures that the Soviets might develop in the "out years" at a cost inferior to the cost to the Soviets of buying these countermeasures. But, no one could know what these countermeasures would be or what they would cost, or the cost of modifying Nike X to meet them. More important, to see how "cost-effective" Nike X was, its contribution to the security of the U.S. also would have to have been measured against that of other things the U.S. could do for itself—more missiles or civil defense.[8] Of course, it was easy for anyone to see that, dollar for dollar, civil defense is by far the most effective way of protecting people against the effects of war. But McNamara and the Kennedy-Johnson administration used this standard of "cost-effectiveness" at the margin not as a reason to build civil defense, but as a reason *not* to build Nike X. This conceptual tool is quite useless for understanding international affairs and war. It is of dubious applicability to economic matters as well. After all, the worth of things is often unrelated to their cost. Nevertheless this artificial construct has been quite useful as a bureaucratic device for curtailing U.S. strategic forces.

As Secretary McNamara first explained to Congress in 1965, given the assumption that the Soviets are interested in causing civilian casualties, there is no quantifiable chance of holding U.S. casualties below 80 million, which is totally unacceptable. Hence a dollar spent on enhancing the security of our ability to harm the Soviet Union—which contributes to the *total* avoidance of nuclear war and which in turn is the *only* chance of avoiding totally unacceptable casualties—is surely better spent than a dollar whose contribution at the margin is within a spectrum of casualties that is itself beyond the pale. By this standard, it makes sense for the U.S. to spend huge sums to protect U.S. ballistic missile submarines and to make sure that American land-based missiles could be fired under any circumstances.

But by this standard of cost-effectiveness, the Nike X was impossible to justify. As the secretary of defense later explained,[9] even if every urban area were effectively protected by Spartans and

Sprints, the Soviets could still explode their RVs on empty, undefended areas, like the Mojave Desert or the Pacific Ocean, *upwind*
of the defended ones in a manner calculated to raise contaminated
particles and douse the cities with fallout, which would cause
many casualties unless expensive shelters were built. In the mid-
1960s, the response of the steadily dwindling group of Army officers
willing to swim against the tide was to propose to add Spartan
missiles to the system, thus making more likely the interception
of RVs not directed at cities or at American missile bases. But
this attempt to meet impossible criteria did not last long. Given
these criteria, protecting the U.S. population against a Soviet "all-
out" attack could not possibly be cost-effective at the margin—
by definition.

What, then, could advocates of ABMs do to sell their program
within the McNamara framework? The answer was to transform
Nike X into a device to defend American offensive missiles—not
people. This was a bureaucratic-strategic judgment, not a technical
one. For President Johnson, who again was presented with this
option, there was also a political consideration: Congress had been
pushing the Eisenhower, Kennedy, and now his administration
to deploy an ABM system because congressmen believe their constituents want to be protected. It was generally considered politically futile—even suicidal—to propose an ABM system that openly
eschewed doing the best possible way of doing that job.

Hence, in 1965–67 a consensus grew in the Pentagon that a few
features should be added to this latest version of Nike X that
could be sold as in fact giving the American people the only kind
of antimissile protection that was undeniably feasible: that against
a "light" attack aimed at cities. Some objected that the Soviets
would attack such a light defense heavily, and that therefore the
administration's program could be justified only as a step toward
a "heavy" defense, or not at all. The Johnson administration handled this commonsense objection by publicly leaving open the
option of a "heavy" defense, even though it had foreclosed that
option in private. Meanwhile it made political hay by claiming
that the new ABM system would protect the U.S. from the one
country most likely to attack: China.

This fit well with the Johnson administration's effort to depict
China rather than the Soviet Union as the liveliest danger to the
U.S. Whether the administration did this in a sincere misreading
of the Sino–Soviet quarrel or as a conscious deception, it gave
American public opinion the impression that the Soviet Union
was a worthy negotiating partner and that China rather than the

Soviet Union was the reason American draftees were dying in Vietnam. Regardless of the reason, an administration that considered the Soviet threat too big to deal with gave the convenient impression that it was hardly worth worrying about, while at the same time pouring money into fighting a China that would not do us harm. For good measure, it justified its actions by appeals to technology!

Hence, the Johnson administration came up with a plan, called Sentinel, for concentrating most of our Spartans and Sprints near missile sites and submarine ports and placing a few Spartans where they could give light cover to broad areas. Nonetheless, Robert McNamara strongly opposed President Johnson's 1967 decision, made in preparation for the 1968 election, to actually deploy Sentinel. His speech announcing that decision was a masterpiece of damning by faint praise. McNamara reiterated that the system would not be effective against the only kind of strike he thought the Soviets could or would mount. He assured the Soviets that Sentinel was not the sign of a major commitment to antimissile defense, but the exact opposite—that it was chosen precisely because the U.S. government did not believe in defense.

After the 1968 election, the Nixon administration, led by Henry Kissinger, acted essentially to embody the substance of McNamara's speech in the U.S. ABM program. The result was the third and last major version of Nike X, Safeguard, which concentrated entirely on protecting U.S. missile sites and submarine ports. Defense was made exclusively the handmaiden of offense. By this logic, the American people would spend heavily to defend their people-killing weapons but would leave themselves and their families defenseless. Seven large PARS—at Seattle (Washington), Malmstrom (Montana), Grand Forks (North Dakota), Detroit (Michigan), Boston (Massachusetts), Los Angeles (California), and Albany (Georgia) would have ringed the continental United States. The PARS would have identified incoming warheads and decoys, provided some discrimination, divided the attack into "bundles" of tracks according to destinations, and "handed off" the information to the missile site radars (MSRs) located at the same sites and also at five other sites—San Francisco (California), Cheyenne (Wyoming), Whiteman (Missouri), Dallas (Texas), and Washington, D.C. These radars in turn would have guided Spartans and Sprints to intercepts. Safeguard, as conceived in 1971, would have protected U.S. strategic weapons against perhaps 2,400 RVs—many more than Soviet ICBMs had at that time, but half as many as they were projected to have by 1980.

Once formulated as a prop for the policy of mutual assured destruction, the ABM program lost the political support it had always enjoyed. Even the Army, seeing that the program had no future, began to skim funds from the program to benefit the "real" Army of tanks and trucks and cannon. Whereas the Johnson administration had felt constrained by public opinion to maintain an ABM program for the defense of the population that it really did not want, the Nixon administration was quickly under pressure from Congress to abandon a missile-protection ABM that it wanted only half-heartedly. The administration's ambivalence toward Safeguard stemmed from the knowledge that, to take account of the possibility that by 1980 the Soviets would have 5,000 RVs able to destroy U.S. missile silos, it would have to plan for a possible doubling of the system and for a significant upgrading of the computer technology then in hand. The bottom line is that the Nixon administration was unwilling to do this.

Interestingly, during these years the national intelligence estimates agreed strongly (but wrongly) that the Soviets were not trying for a capability to kill silos, only people. The administration could have followed the logic of the estimates and focused the Nike X on defending the U.S. population. But it did not, in part because unlike McNamara and the CIA, Nixon and Kissinger did not believe that the Soviets had accepted permanent nuclear inferiority, or even parity.[10] Instead, they believed that the Soviets really were trying to build a counterforce missile force. But they also believed that the Soviets could be taught, or forced out of that goal, by a "hard-line" U.S. administration that would conduct "hard-nosed" negotiations, complete with concrete threats. Hence, the Nixon administration logically favored having an ABM even less than did the Johnson administration. But Kissinger and Nixon valued Safeguard more because they looked upon it as something that could be used to "bring the Soviets around" to its view of the world. For Kissinger and Nixon, the American ABM was to be at once a bargaining chip and a pedagogic tool in the service of MAD.

The arms control process was even more of a pedagogic tool for the Nixon administration than for its predecessor. In the end, Kissinger and the Nixon administration staked their reputations on the belief that they had successfully taught the Soviet Union to behave as McNamara had thought it would of its own accord. They believed that their success was embodied in the ABM Treaty. This limited both the U.S. and the Soviet Union to two (later reduced to one) antimissile sites, each with only 100 launchers for antimissile interceptors. More important, it represented a commitment, which the U.S. has thenceforth taken seriously, not to build the basis for an antimissile defense.

The U.S. defense bureaucracy believed that the SALT I agreements of May 26, 1972, consisting of the ABM Treaty and the Interim Agreement on Offensive Weapons, had solved their strategic problems. Gerard Smith, chief negotiator of the accords, stated to the Senate Armed Services Committee that the ABM Treaty had removed the near certainty that U.S. offensive weapons would have had to contend with *8,000* (!) effective Soviet ABMs by 1980, while the Interim Agreement had removed the near certainty that Soviet offensive weapons would threaten American missile silos. The expenditure of many billions of dollars, now unnecessary, would not so surely have achieved the twin objectives of American strategic policy—safety for our own weapons, and capability of our weapons to strike the Soviet people. The Soviets, said Smith, did us this big favor in exchange for the same favor in their regard. This mutual act assured strategic stability indefinitely. Henry Kissinger, Smith's superior, argued that the Soviets had finally learned that "an attempt (by either side) to gain a unilateral advantage in the strategic field must be self-defeating."[11] Kissinger, like the authors of *The Absolute Weapon* evidently believed that in the age of nuclear weapons, any increase in capability by either side could ultimately result only in a reestablishment of the balance of terror at a more terrible level. For him and for the American foreign policy establishment he headed, the age of major strategic reversals had ended.

The SALT I-ABM Treaty also solved a political problem that McNamara and his close associates in the 1960s had never been able to confront directly: the American people's demand for security through military superiority. MacGeorge Bundy later wrote that the Kennedy-Johnson administration's commitment to military superiority had been intentionally "misleading." According to Bundy, "What we did not say so loud was that the principal use of this [American] numerical superiority was as a reassurance to the American public and as a means of warding off demands for still larger forces."[12] Through SALT I, Nixon and Kissinger had taught the American Congress, if not the people, that antimissile defense was impossible, or at least a less reliable path to security than agreements with the Soviet Union. Since SALT I, there has been no congressional constituency for strategic weapons comparable to what existed up to that time.

The SALT I-ABM Treaties also made into official dogma all the arguments that had been made against antimissile defense—that it was neither technically nor economically up to competing with the offense. This had to be so. After all, if this were not so, why was antimissile defense abandoned by both sides? The dogma also led the Kissinger–Nixon administration to deny strenuously the very facts that had convinced them the treaties were needed, i.e., the facts that had earlier convinced them that the Soviets really were building a rational fighting force and that an effective ABM was part of that force. After all, if ABMs really work, why would any rational nation get rid of them? And if U.S. intelligence shows that the Soviets are continuing to build such forces after the treaties, what good were the treaties? Hence during the rest of the Nixon administration, as well as during the Carter administration, senior intelligence officers committed to this point of view suppressed this sort of intelligence. Meanwhile senior U.S. military leaders, no less committed to this point of view, looked at all ABM technology through the prism of the dogma. But the dogma was an illusion.

In reality, the SALT-ABM Treaties proved the shortsightedness of those in that now much-diminished group in the U.S. Army and the U.S. defense community who had bet the fortunes of antimissile defense in the U.S. on going along at first with limiting the role of ABMs to protecting irrational retaliatory forces, and then with using ABMs for bait to lure the Soviets into promising to eliminate the threat they had worked so hard to pose. When the sole U.S. ABM site allowed by the ABM treaty was completed in 1975, it epitomized the arguments that had been made against ABMs: It was by definition inadequate and incomplete. It was indeed insignificant in relation to the threat, and it was surely anachronistic in a world officially characterized by U.S.–Soviet cooperation to make nuclear war irrational. When Senator Ted Kennedy made these very arguments in support of his amendment (to the Fiscal 1976 Defense Appropriations Bill) to dismantle the site, the only possible counter would have been that this operationally insignificant site could have been a stepping-stone to something more useful. But if that had been so, why was not the administration proposing to build a more extensive, strategically significant defense? And why had the U.S. made a commitment to the proposition that no antimissile defenses could be useful? The Kennedy amendment of 1975 succeeded because it followed the grain of over a decade of U.S. policy.

In the aftermath of the ABM Treaty, the Army and ARPA both continued to work on technologies related to ABMs. But both worked without a mandate to turn out a product—indeed, with the understanding that they should *not* do so, and that any device they might come up with would be inadequate by definition. Nevertheless, within a few years of the signing of SALT I, harsh reality began to dispel the dogma.

4 / A Leap in the Dark?

In the beginning, the disease is easy to cure and difficult to recognize, but, as time passes and the disease is neither recognized nor treated, it becomes easy to recognize and difficult to treat.

—Machiavelli, *The Prince*

In the 1980s, defending the U.S. against ballistic missile attack has become one of the foremost issues in American politics. Conventional wisdom has it that this happened because Ronald Reagan, speaking on national television on March 23, 1983, leapt into the unknown after a private dream and took the U.S. government with him. But this is not so. Instead, rather than leaping in the dark, President Reagan let himself be dragged by the well-lighted logic of events during the previous decade. Even so, he let this logic drag him into rhetoric only, while the opposite logic of the American foreign policy establishment kept a firm grip on his actions.

During the 1970s, the Soviet Union built precisely the kinds of war-winning missile forces that we had sought to forestall by entering into SALT I. Hence, arms control lost credibility as a means of protecting the United States against such Soviet forces. Moreover, by the late 1970s no responsible American could figure out a way of exiting the predicament caused by the Soviet build-up of offensive missile forces by building great numbers of American offensive missiles. Thus, by the end of the decade, logic argued for shifting the U.S. effort toward antimissile weapons. During the 1970s, advances in technologies applicable to antimissile defense also pointed in the same direction.

But in human affairs, individuals decide for themselves whether or not to be open to logic. This, then, is a story about how individual human beings acted and explained their actions with regard to ballistic missile defense. Granted that given the logic of events, the rebirth of interest in ballistic missile defense in the United States might well have come about even if none of the individuals involved had existed. Major events always result from the confluence of various people who, without reference to one another, come to similar conclusions and further the logic of those conclusions in circumstances in which they find themselves. Nevertheless, it is worthwhile recounting who did what, when, and why to revive interest in antimissile defense, if only because the rebirth of this interest began a quarrel that is a long way from being settled. Thus this account of the origins is essential to understand why the quarrel has developed as it has and to understand literally where everyone involved in the quarrel is "coming from."

The reader should know that I am myself part of the story. Between 1977 and 1985, I served as a staff assistant to Senator Malcolm Wallop (R-Wyo.) on the U.S. Senate Select Committee on Intelligence. Accordingly, I contributed heavily to what he said and did as he developed the concepts and fostered programs to reverse the U.S.–Soviet military imbalance through strategic defense. Even though I often attended meetings and acted alone on these matters, I always acted in Senator Wallop's name and with his approval. Hence, unless otherwise indicated, I fully identify here with Senator Wallop's views and initiatives.

This discussion explains to some extent why a senator and a staffer serving on the U.S. Senate Select Committee on Intelligence, rather than people in other positions, should have played a role in advocating the use of modern technology to defend the country against ballistic missiles.

It makes sense to begin by explaining something about the technology by which American satellites collect intelligence about Soviet strategic weapons, because these satellites were part of the rebirth of strategic defense in two important ways. First, they provided much of the data that showed the Soviet ICBM force to be a serious war-winning weapon. Second, it so happened that the technology developed largely for these intelligence satellites also turned out to be quite useful for countering ballistic missiles.

Divisions of responsibility and bureaucratic jealousies have produced deep ignorance of intelligence technology among Pentagon officials in charge of U.S. strategic forces. There is also a division of labor in U.S. intelligence between those who deal with the technology of collection and those who analyze the facts collected. This means that intelligence officers in charge of coming up with estimates of Soviet missile forces have only the remotest notion of the technology that produces the data they work with. Hence, by default, it happens that the offices of the intelligence committees of Congress are in fact among the very few places in the world where hard data on Soviet strategic forces and knowledge of U.S. intelligence technology routinely come together. Although exposure to this combination of facts does not mandate our conclusions, it does explain how Senator Wallop and his staffer on the committee were among the few to become interested in using the technology of intelligence collection to counter the Soviet missile force, the details of which collection had revealed.

We mean to make clear that Senator Wallop and I were not driven to embrace modern means of antimissile defense by any love of gadgetry or by any sort of technological imperative. Rather, we were moved by a long-standing, deep personal commitment to securing the safety of the American people, by a visceral disgust with the doctrine MAD, and by the judgment that antimissile defense is the most effective way of dealing with Soviet missile superiority. Our exposure to the fine points of the Soviet missile threat provided the goad, and our exposure to intelligence technology and to the aerospace industry lighted a path we were disposed to follow anyhow. All this said, we nonetheless believed that the technology we came to know was exciting itself.

Consider, for example, the United States' KH-11 imaging satellite.[1] Although in the late 1980s commercial camera companies advertise instruments to the public that are based on the principle that this satellite pioneered,[2] the KH-11 was perhaps the greatest technical wonder of the mid-1970s. Orbiting the earth at altitudes of 150 to 300 miles, this huge tube would aim at points perhaps 500 miles away on the earth below—a missile site, for example, that it was programmed to provide an image of. As it moved through the sky, the KH-11 would "track," or continually change orientation, to keep the desired object in its sights before being ordered to shift to another target to repeat the exercise. The satellite's accuracy and steadiness were so great that as it sped over the earth, it could follow even small objects, certainly smaller than a missile. How could the KH-11 see things so far away? Like the finest astronomical telescopes, it had a very large, exceptionally fine, concave mirror to focus light onto its focal plane. But, instead of carrying film on its focal plane, the satellite carried arrays of photoelectric sensors. Each of these registered the light that reached them, performing a function analogous to that of the granules on photographic film (indeed, analogous to that of the nerve endings in the retina of the human eye). The impressions from each of the sensors were relayed to the ground in digitized form, and a computer put them back together, forming a snapshot image of what the satellite had seen.

Another satellite wonder of the age was set in a much higher orbit. Its smaller, less accurate telescope was equipped with a focal plane filled with tiny heat-sensing devices (infrared detectors). Even from very great distances, these little sensors could notice the flashes of Soviet missile tests well enough to tell from whence they were coming, to register roughly where they were going, and to distinguish one missile from another. One may well imagine that the computers for controlling the satellite (plus the KH-11, plus many others)—to coordinate what they should be looking at, for maintaining each satellite in the right orbit—were tiny, powerful, and quite sophisticated.

So, as we gathered knowledge learning about Soviet missiles, we developed ways to recognize distinctive rocket exhausts from afar, to focus on small faraway objects, and to follow them as a hunter does ducks. We could also automatically control the satellites doing the work. In other words, by the late 1970s *if one looked at intelligence technology with the eyes of someone interested in antimissile defense*, one realized that our technical intelligence programs had invented and deployed all of the technology elements necessary for shooting at missiles during the boost phase, except for the "gun" itself.

Meanwhile, during the time we monitored Soviet warheads as they reentered the atmosphere heading for test targets on the Kamchatka peninsula, the United States had vastly improved the state-of-the-art of the radars and fine infrared optical instruments needed for precisely locating and identifying the warheads. The United States' large, phased-array radar in Alaska's Aleutian Islands, code-named Cobra Dane—as well as a smaller one called Cobra Judy that was mounted on a ship and driven by rapidly improving computers—became able to produce rather precise images of these warheads and their accompanying decoys, as well as to measure their movements. Optical heat-sensing instruments, either lofted within a few hundred miles of the paths of these reentering warheads or flown near the warheads' path by high-flying aircraft, produced surprisingly good infrared signatures of both warheads and decoys. Thus, by gathering intelligence about Soviet reentry vehicles, we had much improved the tasks of decoy discrimination and computer target management that had vexed previous plans for a U.S. ground-based ABM system.

So, by the late 1970s, any American who examined the *technology used by U.S. intelligence* to determine what the Soviets were doing would also learn (whether he realized it or not) much about technology applicable to both ground-based and space-based anti-missile defense. Of course, the *substance* of what the U.S. learned about the Soviet missile force in the late 1970s led reasonable people to conclude that antimissile defense is essential for the U.S.

The essence of what the U.S. learned about the Soviet missile force in the 1970s is that the Soviets had fielded a new generation of intercontinental missiles. They had replaced their 308 SS-9s with 308 SS-18s. Thus it became clear that instead of threatening us with 300 counterforce warheads (as the U.S. government had supposed they would under SALT I), those silos would threaten us with over 3,000. The Soviets had replaced 500 of their SS-11s with 360 SS-19s and 150 SS-17s. Thus, instead of 510 warheads of dubious effectiveness for counterforce purposes, these silos would present us with a threat of 2,760 true counterforce warheads.[3] By 1979 U.S. intelligence had noticed that the Soviets had built five of the kinds of large phased-array radars that had been the backbone of America's planned ABM System (this number became six in 1983 and nine in 1986). The U.S. had also noticed that the Soviets had tested, and were beginning production, of the missile interceptors and local radars to fill out a nationwide ABM defense system. The Soviets were also giving their air defense equipment the capacity to intercept reentering warheads.

These and other facts about both Soviet forces, and about U.S. intelligence technology, were the grist of the national debate over the SALT II Treaty that began in 1978—a year before President Carter signed the treaty. That debate took place in the shadow of the fact that under SALT I, the Soviets had brought about precisely the situation that the United States had sought to avoid— and indeed believed it had avoided—by entering into arms control negotiations in the first place. We had tried to avoid "Minuteman vulnerability" (a shorthand term for the Soviet capacity to deliver a near-disarming first strike), and that very vulnerability was now upon us. We had tried to prevent the Soviet Union from laying a base for nationwide, ABM defense, and that base was growing before our eyes. It seemed that every week Paul Nitze, then a private citizen, would issue a paper showing that under the terms of the proposed SALT II Treaty, the Soviet Union's superiority in offensive forces would continue to grow. The proponents of SALT

II did not deny what had happened under SALT I, and that America's strategic predicament would continue to worsen under SALT II. Their main argument in favor of ratifying SALT II was that without it, America's predicament would get even worse. Nobody, but nobody, argued that SALT II would produce a good situation for the U.S. In other words, the SALT II debate was the logical (if not the effective) end of the arms control movement.

Wallop realized both the importance of the Soviet ICBM force and the opportunity that intelligence technology offered for dealing with it. He approached the SALT debate as an opportunity to focus the country's attention on what it could do for its own safety. But before he could teach, he had to learn a mass of detail. Thus in 1978 he set about reading up on Soviet strategic offensive and defensive forces.

From his seat on the Senate Intelligence Committee (and as ranking member of its key subcommittee on the intelligence budget) Wallop studied the United States' intelligence technology. Beyond committee responsibilities, he sought out specialists in various parts of the U.S. government and industry who might have information about what new technology was being developed in the U.S. for possible antimissile use. Here he first sought out the U.S. Army's Ballistic Missile Defense Advanced Technology Center (BMDATC) in Huntsville, Alabama, and a group of aerospace engineers in industry under contract to the U.S. Defense Advanced Research Projects Center (DARPA), the most prominent of whom was Maxwell Hunter of the Lockheed Missiles and Space Company. In November 1978 Wallop visited Huntsville. The Army's BMDATC is colocated at Huntsville with another Army installation, the Missile Intelligence Agency (MIA). By looking at what both agencies were doing, one could see that there was literally more technology applicable to ballistic missile defense (BMD) than U.S. officials knew what to do with. The MIA explained the Soviet Union's development of the SA-12, a mobile surface-to-air missile system comparable to the U.S. Army's projected SAM-D that would be able to destroy incoming ballistic RVs as well as aircraft. But the BMDATC told the senator that the Army had intentionally downgraded the radar technology in the SAM-D project so that as the system matured and was renamed Patriot, it would only be able to defend against aircraft, not RVs.

The MIA laid out the intelligence from Soviet tests of two surface-to-high-altitude interceptor missiles. One, the SH-8, is cone-shaped, very fast, and a somewhat larger copy of the Sprint ABM interceptor that the U.S. had abandoned upon signing the ABM Treaty. The

Sprint was quite workable as a last-ditch means of catching RVs that had penetrated the atmosphere. But the SH-8 was a better device, because its guidance system would use the faster microprocessors of the late 1970s rather than those of a decade earlier. The other, the SH-4, is very much like the United States' Spartan, an interceptor which was designed to reach hundreds of miles into space, but which the U.S. had abandoned along with the rest of its ABM system. How much better a Spartan-type interceptor might be could be learned at BMDATC, which had commissioned Lockheed to develop a heat-seeking instrument package called the homing overlay experiment that could be shot into space in the path of incoming warheads and decoys, and guide a rocket to a direct collision with the warhead. They also showed early plans for a version of an optical probe, to be carried on high-flying aircraft.

The MIA also showed Senator Wallop how recent increases in the power of its computers greatly enhanced its ability to process radar information about thousands of warheads and decoys in flight so as to simultaneously keep track of each and sort out the tracks according to their destinations. But because of the ABM Treaty, the U.S. had intentionally not built radars capable of supplying such information. But the computer simulation showed that if the data were made available, more than enough computer power existed to turn it into a constantly updated, accurate picture of an incoming attack that would be very useful to a defensive network—if that were to be created.

The Army's presentations had about them an aura of make-believe. Anyone listening to them would logically be moved to ask: At what point do you actually turn any of this stuff into working weapons or sensors? The Army's answer was that it was literally not allowed to think about that question. The commanding officer, General Meyer, said: "Our mission is to keep up a certain level of effort and to come up with ideas about what is feasible, primarily to serve as a reference point for our own intelligence people as they evaluate Soviet ABM developments. National policy is that antimissile protection is bad. That is why if our ideas are judged a threat to national policy, we are asked to modify them." He explained that "Washington" had forced the redesign of the Army's newest surface-to-air missile system, the SAM "D," so that it would have no ability to intercept ballistic reentry vehicles, because "somebody" was worried about possible charges that it would violate the ABM Treaty.

Similarly, and for the same reason, "Washington" was now pressuring Meyer's command to design the homing overlay experiment so that each interceptor rocket would carry only a single vehicle to collide with an incoming warhead, rather than about a dozen vehicles. Doing this would require a lot of redesigning, and thus would slow down the program. Moreover, dedicating one whole rocket to kill one warhead would make the whole concept less efficient. But such were the signals from on high, and the Army obeyed them. We shared with Meyer our belief that the American public, on whose behalf the work was being done, would hear only about how much money was being spent (about a fourth of a billion dollars a year), and that despite the expenditure of money and time, we just could not come up with antimissile weapons!

Sometimes, however, a tiny amount of money coupled to a neat idea can help to push major changes along. So it was with a set of simple experiments on the vulnerability of missiles to lasers ordered by the Army. It was managed by, among others, John Hagferstration, an Army civilian engineer. Up until 1978, the conventional assumption was that for a laser to kill a missile, the laser would have to heat the missile's surface until it burned through. So, early experiments on laser effects had been carried out by attaching heat-measuring devices to sheets of aluminum or other materials, pointing a laser at them and counting the seconds until the laser burned a hole in the material. Hagferstration's team, however, tried something different. The skin of a missile during boost phase, they reasoned, is not a sheet of material peacefully sitting on a stand. Rather, it is a cylinder already heated by atmospheric friction, by proximity to a very hot exhaust, and, above all, bearing up to ten times the weight of the missile because of rapid acceleration. What would happen, then, if a laser were to hit the skin of a missile during boost phase? Given its tiny budget, the team could only deal in approximations. It built a series of aluminum cylinders, placed them under physical and thermal pressures approximating those of a missile under boost phase, attached the calorimeters, and hit the cylinders with an old, very-long-wavelength, carbon-dioxide laser.

The results were eye-opening. The cylinders did not last long enough for the laser to burn a hole in the material. Instead, after the laser had placed a small amount of energy onto the cylinders— about 80 watts per second per square centimeter—the cylinders self-destructed. In other words, the little laser simply pushed the missile mockups beyond their ability to endure the stresses that were already on them. The ratio between the energy required to cause this to happen to a missile mockup made of a given material and the energy required to burn through that material turned out to be roughly one-to-six. This little experiment naturally led those who were looking for ways of defeating ballistic missiles to ask how easy or difficult it would be to place in orbit a means of delivering that small amount of energy on a Soviet missile in boost phase a few thousand kilometers away.

Senator Wallop found that several sets of people had been at work on this problem for some time. The most important of these were working on contracts let by the Directed Energy Office of DARPA. Lockheed's first contract in this field, for all of 15,000 dollars, had come in 1971. By fiscal 1979 the directors of that office, Douglas Tanimoto and Alan Pike, were working with only $24 million. Nevertheless, they had made it possible for groups at the Lockheed Missiles and Space Division (Sunnyvale, Calif.) and TRW (Redondo Beach, Calif.) to develop useful technology and plans for carrying that technology to fruition in a space-based laser weapon. The man in this group who most fully grasped how the disparate technologies being developed by the U.S. government might be integrated into an antimissile laser was Maxwell Hunter, an engineer at Lockheed.

Max Hunter, an aeronautical engineer who began his career designing airplanes at the end of World War II, had made his name in the aerospace industry in the 1950s as chief design engineer for the Douglas Aircraft Company on such programs as Nike Zeus, the Thor intermediate-range ballistic missile, and the Saturn 5. In 1962 he had gone to Washington to serve on the staff of the National Space Council and had played a role in the moon program. Later, NASA awarded him a medal in recognition of his pioneering work on the "stage-and-a-half" concept of the space shuttle. But in the aerospace industry of the 1970s, Hunter was an anachronism, a throwback to the days when engineering teams existed to make things rather than to satisfy government requirements unrelated to putting weapons in the field. So although Hunter had unusual latitude within his company to influence programs and to talk about them with policymakers in Washington, he was not himself in charge of any program.

Wallop soon developed good personal rapport with Hunter and Pike, as he learned about angles of diffraction and absorbed fluences. Thus, Hunter and Alan Pike introduced Senator Wallop, who had majored in English at Yale, to a field of technology that closely paralleled the one that Wallop was already learning about from the perspective of the Intelligence Committee.[4]

By mid-1979, Wallop had learned enough to publish an article in the respected military journal *Strategic Review*, entitled "Opportunities and Imperatives of Ballistic Missile Defense."[5] The article explained why the U.S. had no choice but to regard the Soviet ICBM fleet as the primary military threat, why ballistic missile defense was the best option for dealing with that threat, and what new technologies were making antimissile defenses especially attractive. Although Wallop had previously talked this way with his colleagues in the U.S. Senate, this was the first time that he went public. Because many have charged Wallop with advocating only one antimissile device, the chemical space-based laser, it is worthwhile noting that in this article, at the very outset of his campaign, Wallop advocated a variety of ground-based defenses as well as space-based lasers. Indeed, he advocated these protective weapons (rather than others) simply on the grounds that they could be built. The article was noteworthy enough to warrant coverage by the *New York Times'* military analyst, Drew Middleton.[6] But the article had been written less for the public than as a briefing paper for other senators and for a presidential candidate—Ronald Reagan. Reagan read it in typescript in the summer of 1979.

That summer, Reagan's interest was being piqued by a visit to the North American Air Defense Command's headquarters inside Cheyenne Mountain, Colorado, where he had been shocked by the United States' ability to watch as nuclear warheads traversed space on their way to this country, coupled with the United States' unpreparedness to intercept any of them. Following this experience, his campaign aide, Martin Anderson, proposed in a memorandum (Campaign Memorandum #3) that Reagan make advocacy of antimissile weapons into a main theme of the presidential campaign. Later that summer, Malcolm Wallop urged the same thing while he, Reagan, and their mutual friend Senator Paul Laxalt (R-Nev.) were grilling steaks at a barbecue near Lake Tahoe. Reagan was enthusiastic but designated Michael Deaver as the man on his campaign staff who would do the work. Deaver, however, agreed with then-campaign manager John Sears that it was a bad political idea and made sure that candidate Reagan did not make antimissile defense a feature of the subsequent campaign.

Nevertheless, as Wallop discussed antimissile defense with the people whom Reagan had designated to be his principal advisers on national security affairs, Richard Allen and William Van Cleave, he found them enthusiastically receptive. Unfortunately, however, during his presidency, even more than in the campaign, Reagan was drawn more to the Michael Deavers of the world than to the William Van Cleaves.

Throughout the fall of 1979 Wallop worked to brief as many

senators as possible to lay the groundwork for formally placing the question of modern antimissile defenses before the Senate and the country. He found no lack of eager listeners. Among them were Howell Heflin (D-Ala.), who held a small hearing on the subject in his subcommittee of the Commerce Committee in December 1979, and Ernest Hollings (D-S.C.), then chairman of the Budget Committee. Nevertheless, Wallop felt that it would be better if his colleagues got the facts about what currently available technology could do against ballistic missiles directly from those in industry who were doing the work. But Senator Wallop did not have any position on any committee that would have allowed him to schedule a hearing and call witnesses. So he decided to do the only thing available to him: to ask such experts from industry as he could cajole into coming, to brief such senatorial colleagues as he could persuade to listen. Top executives of aerospace companies, who had allowed Wallop free access to their staff and laboratories, refused to let any of their employees take part in such meetings with senators as representatives of the company, citing fear of retribution from the executive branch. But these executives proved willing to allow Max Hunter to recruit like-minded rank-and-file engineers to talk with senators as interested private citizens.

Thus on December 11, 1979, Max Hunter of Lockheed, Joseph Miller of TRW, Gerald Oulette of Draper Laboratories, and Norbert Schnog of Perkin Elmer met in the Russell Senate Office Building with Angelo Codevilla and Sven Kraemer of the Republican Policy Committee to refine the presentation they would make to the senators on the following day. Since the presentation would be for "senators only" in the Capitol's National Security Room (S-407), staffers of the senators who had put the meeting on their schedules stopped by to get a preview of what their bosses would be seeing. One ensuing incident is worth recalling. Rhett Dawson, who worked for Senator John Tower (R-Tex.) as minority staff director of the Armed Services Committee, made quiet, derogatory remarks as he listened. Then Senator Tower came in, along with four other senators, and asked the four engineers if he could hear them then because he could not attend on the following day. After Senator Tower had made glowing remarks about the presentation Dawson also praised it loudly—as he scampered after Tower.

It is difficult enough in the U.S. Senate to gather more than a few senators for a hearing of a committee to which they belong unless a "hot" national issue is up and the meeting will give the senators a chance to be on television with a celebrity. Meetings of groups to which the senators do not belong, with people who represent nobody, held in a closed setting, without even the attraction of sumptuous food, normally do not even draw aides. Nevertheless, at noon on December 12, fifteen senators assembled in S-407, then used primarily for the Intelligence Committee's classified hearings, for a lunch of bad sandwiches, and for talk on weapons that the military had not asked for.

Dr. Joseph Miller, the most prominent figure in the field of chemical lasers, explained how the device he was building at TRW could become a 3-foot by 15-foot cylinder that would put out 10 megawatts of continuous laser power by consuming about 50 kilograms per second of liquid hydrogen and fluorine. Dr. Norbert Schnog showed that as far as the technicians at Perkin Elmer and Kodak were concerned, the technique of building very large, good quality mirrors out of smaller segments had been mastered. The technology could be improved, of course, but if the nation decided it needed large mirrors for laser weapons, Perkin Elmer and Kodak could tool up now and produce them. Dr. Gerald Oulette, who had worked on pointing-tracking technology at Draper (but was not aware of even more advanced work with intelligence satellites) showed how modern micro computers can precisely move an array of electrooptical receivers so as to keep a small laser beam that has been bounced off a target very precisely near the center of the array. He showed that although much engineering work remained to be done to turn the basic technology into a pointer-tracker able to function with a laser weapon, the technology for making such a pointer-tracker was there.

Max Hunter reviewed the engineering tasks that would have to be accomplished in order to turn a 5- or 10-megawatt laser, a big mirror, and a pointer-tracker into a laser weapon able to strike down missiles. The list of tasks included isolating the mirror and pointer-tracker from the violent vibrations that the laser would surely cause, building the fuel pumps and the rest of the satellites' "housekeeping" system, as well as protecting the satellites' body with basic armor and its optical sensors with "optical fuses." Hunter then explained that the difference in time and cost between such a program being run according to the Defense Department's normal regulations and on a commonsense basis was at least a factor of three. Finally, he explained that even as few as four first-generation, crude, space-based lasers would be able to make it impossible for long-range bombers to travel between the U.S. and the USSR, and would likely destroy most submarine-launched ballistic missiles. As few as twenty-four of these weapons would likely annihilate the number of missiles that the Soviets would reasonably be expected to use in a counterforce attack against the United States.

The senators reacted favorably. Henry Jackson (D-Wash.) asked how quickly a missile-killing laser could be assembled. Hunter answered that the schedule depended more on government regulations than it did on engineering. Under the current research and development (R&D) system, he said, a "normal," untroubled program would take twelve years, a normal accelerated program could bear fruit in eight, while we might expect that the occurrence of controversies such as had surrounded the MX might well push initial operational capability out well beyond twenty years. "I know," said Jackson. "But how fast could we do this if we Americans really become impatient with regulations and work under wartime conditions?" Each of the engineers thought that their teams could deliver something workable within about two years, and Hunter thought that under pressure, he could not imagine that as much as another two years would be required to cobble it all together.

How much would the first copy cost? asked Hollings. Something between $2 and $3 billion was the answer. "That's less than the cost of an aircraft carrier," Hollings replied. "I'd love to slip that into the budget." Daniel Moynihan (D-N.Y.), Harrison Schmitt (R-N.M.), and Jake Garn (R-Utah) expressed eagerness to hurry the day when the U.S. would have such defensive weapons in orbit. Wallop concluded the meeting by reminding his colleagues that even the technologies they had just heard about were just a few among many that could be, and should be, put into use. If we built all of the antimissile weapons that we have the ability to build, we would be able to defeat any attempt at a reasonable countermilitary strike against the U.S. We would also be able to largely protect the American people against the consequences of such an attack. Wallop said that he would be introducing an amendment to the Armed Services Authorization Act for fiscal 1981, and he asked for his colleagues' support.

Within hours, the meeting became known in the Pentagon as the "gang of four" presentation, and a variety of officials moved quickly to try to undo its effects. The then-chief of the Air Force's R&D, General Kelly Burke, began a campaign of private contacts that later surfaced in the press to discredit the notion of space-based ballistic missile defense.[7] The Army's chief civilian in the field of ballistic missile defense, William Davis, wrongly but passionately regarded the presentation as a threat to the Army's homing overlay experiment and called on Robert Fuhrman, then president of Lockheed Missiles and Space Company, to muzzle Max Hunter on pain of cancellation of contracts. Only letters and telephone calls from senators to Fuhrman kept Davis's threat from having its intended effect. A similar threat from elsewhere in the Pentagon, however, caused Gerald Oulette to leave Draper Laboratories. But the main campaign against the "gang of four" was waged by Seymour Zeiberg, deputy undersecretary of defense for research and engineering, who had previously expressed scorn for the Wallop article in a way reminiscent of Vannevar Bush's scorn for ICBMs.[8] In addition to making calls to key senators and staff dismissing the entire concern with space-based anti-missile defense, Zeiberg commissioned a "study" by one Victor Ries to discredit Wallop's entire effort.

In February 1980, Zeiberg and his deputy, Larry Lynn, came to see Angelo Codevilla in the Senate Intelligence Committee's old office on the ground floor of the Dirksen Building armed with his study. They contended the study showed that the article Senator Wallop had published in *Strategic Review*, as well as his line of argument with his colleagues, and of course the "gang of four" briefing, were so technically wrong-headed as to bring ridicule upon Wallop. But if Codevilla could manage to cause Wallop to cease and desist, he (Zeiberg) would not distribute the study widely, and Wallop need never know what an inexcusably bad job I had done as Wallop's aide on these matters.

The "study" argued that in the unlikely event that laser battle stations could be built as the senator had described, some 1,444 (instead of 24) would be required to do the job the senator had defined. The cost, according to the "study," would be about $1.5 trillion. After all that, the Soviets could negate the effect of the entire system by coating their missiles with 3 millimeters of cork. The evidence presented in this "study" described the results of an experiment which, it argued, showed that as cork chars, it becomes a near-perfect reflector of radiant heat. The evidence for this was a curve that quickly become asymptotic to the axis representing reflectivity. But the curve itself was based on only 3 data points, 2 of which were on the gently sloping end of the curve and the last of which was entirely off the curve in the opposite direction. Hence the evidence actually showed that charring cork had a slight reflective effect at first, which effect vanished as the charring increased. Moreover, the "study's" analysis had also ignored the fact of heat transfer.

Other parts of the analysis were of similar quality. The hardness of Soviet missiles was off by a factor of 6, having been figured on the basis of energy required for burn-through of sheet aluminum rather than for collapse of a working booster. The beam quality and jitter had been factored in unrealistically. All of this produced an estimate of range that was off by a factor of 10. This, in turn, produced a calculation of the proportion of total stations available at any given time that was off by a factor of 6. All of the stations' effects on targets were figured as if all stations would shoot only at maximum range and therefore with minimum effect, which threw in another factor of over 2. Multiplied together, these factors account for the difference between Wallop's and Zeiberg's estimates of numbers of stations. Zeiberg also figured the cost of the stations by extrapolating, pound-per-pound in orbit, from the cost of electronic intelligence satellites, whose weight consists disproportionately of expensive electronics rather than primarily of relatively cheap fuel, structures, and reflectors. The study, in other words, was an unsophisticated hatchet job.

I eagerly took a copy, showed it to Senator Wallop, and reproduced it for the widest distribution I could manage, as an example of how political commitment can overcome elementary professional standards. The ensuing controversy over the study's competence caused Zeiberg some embarrassment. William Perry, President Carter's undersecretary for research and engineering, was no friend of strategic defense. But he is said to have reprimanded Zeiberg.

As a result of this controversy, Senate staffers who, in the spring of 1980, went to the Pentagon looking for ammunition against the course of action that Wallop was urging on the members of the Armed Services Committee came back empty-handed. Sure, the staffers found plenty of snickers from officials who opposed building space lasers, but none of these officials felt willing or able to deny that a space-laser weapon like the one Wallop was talking about could be built. Wallop was surely crazy, but the Armed Services Committee staff could find no one in the Pentagon willing to follow in Zeiberg's footsteps. Without a hard reason for saying "no" to something that was obviously appealing, senators on the Armed Services Committee increased the money that would be available for work related to space-based lasers from $48 to $68 million—an increase of 40 percent!

Still, Senator John Culver (D-Iowa), chairman of the subcommittee in charge of this field, sought an official statement from DARPA against Wallop's well-advertised proposal. Instead, DARPA's classified reply to Culver, signed by its director, Robert Fossum, laid out a business-as-usual schedule that would have placed a 5- (or possibly 10-) megawatt laser in orbit by 1991, and an accelerated option that would place such a device in orbit by late 1986. The cost for this prototype was to be $2.7 billion on the business-as-usual schedule, and $2.1 billion on the accelerated schedule.[9] Fossum, of course, made it clear that the administration was opposed to the accelerated option. But this mattered not at all! Wallop's opponents wanted to be able to laugh his amendment off the floor with a single authoritative statement that what he proposed doing could not be done. Instead, Fossum's letter meant that if Wallop's opponents joined in a detailed discussion of his proposal they would be reduced to quibbling over a few years in Wallop's proposed schedule. Few elected officials, then as now, feel comfortable saying in public that the U.S. ought to remain undefended.

Meanwhile, the fact that the building of antimissile laser weapons was a live issue began to get serious play in the daily press.[10] The coverage by major magazines had been and continued to be even more extensive. *Aviation Week and Space Technology* had four articles on the subject in 1978, two in 1979, and two in the first half of 1980. *Business Week* and *Commentary* had run favorable pieces, too.[11] Finally, a June 18, 1980 report in the *New York Times* told of a U.S. national intelligence estimate predicting that the Soviet Union would place a high-energy laser weapon in orbit during the mid-to-late 1980s—1984 to 1988. Nevertheless, Wallop was under no illusions that he would succeed in turning around U.S. policy on the first try. He was surprised at how close he got.

The Wallop Amendment of 1980 called for the addition of $160 million to the $68 million already budgeted for work relating to space lasers. More important, it called for a redirection of this work so that the individual pieces of technology that it would develop would produce not mere experiments but rather components that could be bolted together into a weapon suitable for mass production. As the amendment came up for consideration, opponents were spreading condescending remarks in both Democratic and Republican cloakrooms. But on the floor, the replies to Senator Wallop's presentation did not attempt to contradict any of the facts he presented, nor to denigrate the objective he sought. The opposition's public thrust was that great (but unspecified) questions of feasibility were involved which the Senate was not equipped to discuss, that the administration and above all the military services strongly and unanimously opposed the amendment, that Senator Wallop had come upon something of potentially great value—for which he deserved to be commended —but that this was not the time to rush into a huge project.

The opposition's main argument rested on management rather

than on technology or strategy. The Senate should follow the managerial preferences of the Department of Defense about the rate at which money should be spent. This argument was used both by leftists, like Senator Culver, who opposed U.S. anti-missile defenses outright, and by those who, like Senator John Warner (R-Va.), oppose it because it would discomfit the U.S. military's present priorities. Senator Culver summed up the opposition's position by quoting a comment by one Richard Airey (whom Culver referred to as "manager of all DOD high-energy laser programs"): "as an alternative to immediate acceleration, it is recommended that the Defense Department be allowed to accomplish the planning and evaluation necessary to identify development options and report back to Congress in time for a decision to be made affecting the 1982 defense budget."[12] The vote was 39 in favor of the Wallop Amendment, 51 opposed[13]—an excellent result for Wallop considering the novelty of the proposal, the huge forces against it, and the total absence of lobbying—much less arm-twisting—on its behalf.

The amendment got as far as it did simply because no elected official feels comfortable voting against any proposal that can be described, fairly or not, as protecting his constituents' lives. And Senator Culver, himself, provided proof of the amendment's success. He felt obliged, in order to round up the votes to defeat it, to promise to write into the report accompanying the bill a requirement that the Pentagon produce by January 1981 a study of when space-based laser weapons might become available and the effect they might have. The report language asked the Pentagon specifically to solicit the advice of industry. Preparing that report became the responsibility of a somewhat chastened deputy undersecretary, Seymour Zeiberg.

In fact, by the summer of 1980 the highest-ranking people of Jimmy Carter's Pentagon had already completed several months of internal struggle over how to handle the Congress's evident eagerness to fund high-energy laser weapons. In 1979, as Wallop was rounding up allies, the Defense Science Board established a task force under John S. Foster to recommend what to do about the issue. With two exceptions, the group's eleven members were heavily committed against the very notion of antimissile defense, by any means.[14] Not surprisingly, the group strongly recommended that the secretary of defense steer funds away from laser-related technologies applicable to space and toward such tactical applications as defending ships against low-flying cruise missiles. However, in the summer of 1980 Secretary of Defense Harold Brown wrote a letter to the three service secretaries ordering them to make space-based laser weapons a priority. This happened because Brown's principal adviser on high technology matters, Dr. Eugenio Fubini, thought that the peculiar potential of laser weapons could best be realized in space, and because, as Brown, Fubini, and William Perry discussed the question, Perry somehow did not find it within himself to advocate the views of a supposedly expert panel that included Victor Reis, whose attempted hatchet job on the Wallop plan had made his deputy look bad.

Hence, during the summer of 1980 no one in the Defense Department—never mind the Congress—objected as DARPA increasingly shaped its three principal programs in the high-energy laser field (which quickly became known as the DARPA triad) with a view to accomplishing the goals for which Wallop was gathering public support. That the effort was not intended to be mere research into technologies judged immature for weapons work may be seen by DARPA's award to Boeing of a contract for "systems integration of triad technology" (SITT)—i.e., to begin the engineering of a functioning space laser weapon.

This did not mean that Perry and Brown had relented in their unfriendliness to ballistic missile defense. It did mean, however, that as men possessed of intellectual self-respect, they could not justify denying the existence of the technical elements of space-based laser weapons. This serious attitude, reported in *Aviation Week and Space Technology*,[15] spread through the media and added to the effect of Wallop's initiatives. The events on the Senate floor in July 1980 and the following month the adoption of a plank favoring strategic defense in the Republican National Platform of 1980 heightened the interest of the press.

When Ronald Reagan was elected in November 1980, many believed that the development of laser antimissile weaponry was a foregone conclusion. The major aerospace companies adjusted their organization to be ready to enter the new era. Martin Marietta, for example, concentrated all of its work relevant to space lasers in a new products division, while Lockheed significantly shifted its laser weapon work out of the research labs and into the same group that produces intelligence satellites. In other words, they expected orders for production. Investment houses, too, noticed that something was stirring, and on November 22, 1980 the First Albany Corporation held a well-attended seminar for venture capitalists and financial advisers on the future of space-based lasers. One of the speakers, the Pentagon's Walter LaBerge, reflected the view of many in the Department of Defense that the technology and the need had ripened together, and that the Pentagon would go along with the new administration on this point. Almost anyone who looked at the *Washington Post's* five-column headline on December 26, 1980 reporting that President-elect Reagan had pronounced himself in favor of building space-based laser weapons to defend the U.S. against ballistic missiles would have concluded that the new administration would make it happen. In fact, however, while the Congress and the public were to hear much more about antimissile defense, the Reagan administration itself was already raising obstacles to such defense that the public—and, indeed, Reagan himself—would never fully understand.

No sooner had President-elect Reagan chosen Caspar Weinberger to be his Secretary of Defense in December 1980 than he effectively banished from the Pentagon virtually all those who had advised Reagan on military policy during his five-year drive to the presidency. Weinberger, who has never been accused of having any ideas of his own on military policy, was determined to turn over control of such policy to the uniformed military and to the Pentagon establishment in general. But, of course, with the change of administration, the very top of that establishment left—for our purposes, these were Harold Brown, William Perry, and Robert Fossum, director of DARPA. Since Weinberger's connection to the world of defense technology was not intellectual, he chose people regardless of their views of the job they should do. He did this first of all by choosing as his deputy his personal friend Frank Carlucci, who was serving as Carter's deputy director of central intelligence. For his chief of research and engineering, Weinberger chose one Richard de Lauer, who readily admitted in casual conversation that his company (TRW) had been about to fire him. De Lauer's opposition to antimissile defense was not ideologically rooted, as Perry's had been, but, he lacked the restraint and intellectual self-respect of his predecessor. For DARPA, Weinberger chose Robert S. Cooper, who had been one of the more adamant foes of missile defense on the Defense Science Board. Presumably that is not why Weinberger chose him, but choose him he did. Meanwhile, at the White House, again for reasons wholly unrelated to policy, one George A. Keyworth was chosen as the president's science adviser. Keyworth, in turn, assigned the White House portfolio on space and defense science to Victor Reis, who had demonstrated his zeal against missile defense both as Zeiberg's ghost writer and on the Laser Panel of the Defense Science Board.

Hence, by early 1981 any insiders who examined the new roster of players on the question of missile defense in general and of laser weapons in particular should have concluded that those members of the bureaucracy who opposed these endeavors need no longer fear an intellectual challenge at the top, while those in the bureaucracy who favored defense would face nothing but hostility all the way to the top. And if they ever got to the top, a hearing from the secretary of defense would do them no good because the secretary (and the president) would not (or could not) engage the issue intellectually.

The first sign that, rhetoric aside, the Reagan administration was to be less friendly to antimissile defense than its predecessor came when, on February 22, 1981, the National Security Division of the Office of Management and Budget (OMB), under its new chief, William Schneider, formally suggested to the Pentagon that it be allocated $502.9 million for fiscal years 1981–1983—over and above what the Pentagon had applied for—to accelerate DARPA's work on space laser weapons. Now OMB, the U.S. government's official Scrooge, does not normally go around *adding* to agencies' budgets. Agencies, for their part, do not normally look half-billion-dollar budgetary gift horses from OMB in the mouth. But in this case, the Pentagon's James P. Wade, who had been Seymour Zeiberg's deputy, took the most unusual step of turning down the money, confident that he would not be contradicted within the new administration. He was correct.

By March 1981, however, the Pentagon had completed the study mandated by Congress, which concluded that without radical acceleration, it could, by 1990, place into orbit a 10-megawatt chemical laser with a 10-meter mirror, able to project about 1,200 joules per square centimeter at a range of 3,000 kilometers. By 1994, said the report, the department could have in orbit "a fleet" of 10-megawatt, 10-meter battle stations. But, the report concluded, the department should not do this because the Soviets could respond by "hardening" their missiles beyond the ability of chemical lasers to penetrate them, and because the safety of the laser stations themselves could not be assured.

On April 7, 1981 Larry Lynn, who had been Zeiberg's deputy in the preparation of the study, asked to brief me. He said that it was the position of his team and of the Defense Science Board that "decisions on space lasers should be taken without regard to the capability such lasers would have against the fourth and fifth generation of Soviet ICBMs. Rather, the criterion for judging the adequacy of any laser should be its ability to destroy the toughest missile we could possibly think of building." This was an important step. In the polemics surrounding the questions, Lynn and many others would continue to tell the uninformed that current technology is inadequate. Gone for good from the formal debate, however, was talk of the infeasibility of such weapons or of their alleged ineffectiveness against known missiles.[16]

Although the study was classified, its broad conclusion, that laser weapons are for real, was well reflected in the media.[17] For example, on April 12, 1981, Senator John Glenn (D-Ohio) appeared on "Meet the Press" and said he favored "Lasers in space . . . They could be defensive weapons from above the atmosphere—as ICBMs come up you could hit any weapon that would be coming over to attack the United States." Wallop sought to parlay this generally favorable climate into decisive action by the U.S. government. It is interesting to see how he succeeded and how he failed.

Senator Wallop tried to enlist the president and the secretary of Defense in support of a pro-BMD amendment he would offer to the fiscal 1982 Pentagon authorization bill. But his letter to Weinberger of May 7, 1981 was answered (a month later) with a Pentagon party line much more hostile than Harold Brown's. James P. Wade and Larry Lynn even persuaded Weinberger to formally withhold from Congress the report on the feasibility of laser weapons, judging it too favorable, and to submit it to John Foster's Defense Science Board panel so that this panel could then submit to the Congress its own less sanguine recommendations. Weinberger, of course, had no idea that he was being manipulated into endorsing an antidefense position that his predecessor had spurned.

At any rate, Weinberger advised his Republican friends on the Armed Services Committee, John Tower and John Warner, to fight Wallop. This tactic would prove effective against Wallop because he found it difficult to understand why these conservative colleagues, and a conservative secretary of defense would engage in it. After all, he knew that these men lacked both the acumen and the facts to decide on their own that this was a bad idea, and that they most certainly lacked any ideological incentive to oppose him. He realized that they were voicing the views of a bureaucracy opposed to antimissile defense. But he could not conceive how strongly nor for how long they would do this. Only bitter experience would convince Wallop otherwise.

During the weeks before the fiscal 1982 authorization bill came to the floor, Tower and his staff gave Wallop and his staff the impression that they, too, wanted to make sure that space laser weapons and other anti-missile devices were built as quickly as possible, and that only fear of embarrassing "our" administration held them back from fully supporting his amendment. They professed to want a compromise amendment that would convince the administration to do the right thing. Wallop agreed in principle.

But from the very first he had reason to doubt what Warner and Tower meant by compromise. One afternoon Warner brought John Foster to Wallop's office. Foster, apparently assuming that Wallop understood these matters only on Warner's level, argued that Wallop's notion of antimissile lasers was praiseworthy, but that the Defense Science Board had determined that to achieve this dream, "current technology" would have to be improved by a factor of one million, and that any more than $50 million per year added to long-range research would be counterproductive.

Wallop instantly pointed out that by "current technology," Foster must have meant the Air Force's flying laser laboratory. That, Wallop said, employs a 400-kilowatt laser operating at a wavelength of 10.6 microns. This is worse by a factor of over 100 than the 10-megawatt laser operating at a wavelength of 2.7 microns that would result from the laser portion of the DARPA triad. The Air Force laser was also operating with a mirror one-tenth the size of the one that the triad would produce. This would imply an increase of a factor of 100 in power delivered on the target, while the accuracy of the triad's pointer-tracker is about 100 times greater than that of the Air Force's pointer-tracker. Thus, said Wallop, the DARPA triad represented the improvement by a factor of one million that Foster was talking about. "I presume," concluded Wallop to Foster, "that you know this and therefore that you mean to advance the DARPA triad as quickly as possible." Then he went on to show that to do this well, an additional $250 million a year would be needed.

Foster, taken aback, began to agree with Wallop. Warner said he saw what seemed like a budding consensus and that he was pleased. Then the bell rang summoning the senators to the Senate floor for a roll-call vote. Warner said "Looks like we're on our way to a meeting of the minds here. John [to Foster], why don't you and Malcolm's guy finish this conversation for us. Malcolm, you'll agree to whatever John and Angelo come up with, won't you?" Wallop said "yes," and the two senators left the room. No sooner had they done this, and I had begun to ask Foster which of the Wallop amendment's specific directives and funding levels he would want to change and why, than Foster cut off the discussion with a smile, saying "Look, let's not waste our breath. We recommended a maximum of $50 million more for long-range research, and I'm not about to agree to anything else." With that, he left.

The Wallop amendment would have given an extra $15.2 million to DARPA and $41 million extra to the Air Force, along with rather detailed instructions to go beyond its The SITT contract it had just issued, and produce a prototype chemical laser weapon. The money would also have accelerated work on other laser technologies (free electron lasers, excimers, and X-ray laser). On May 13, however, a few moments before the amendment was to come to the floor, Tower and Warner met Wallop by the corner couch of the Republican cloakroom and confronted him with a stark choice: Cut the amendment to a $50 million add-on without detailed instructions, or Tower would lead the Armed Services Committee against it. If Wallop agreed to do so, however, Tower and Warner promised not only to lead the Armed Services Committee in Wallop's support but also to uphold the amendment in the House-Senate conference committee and to use their influence as chairmen to make sure that the administration "took the hint."

Wallop knew that neither Tower, nor especially the man who would have to fight him on the floor, John Warner, the chairman of the Nuclear and Strategic Forces Subcommittee, had the wherewithal to argue against him on this subject, that he would have easily embarrassed them had they tried, and, most important, that they would have had a difficult time explaining a vote against his amendment. He had a nice bipartisan list of cosponsors—Fritz Hollings (D-S.C.) and Robert Dole (R-Kan.), among others—and he stood a fighting chance even against Tower and Warner. But he thought it important to purchase their goodwill. So he revised his amendment to add only $50 million and wrung a compromise from Tower and Warner to establish a space laser program office within the Air Force. Thus, instead of giving detailed legislative instructions on how to build the weaponry, the amendment established an office with the mandate to do the job and some extra money to get started. Not bad.

Although the amendment then passed without significant opposition (91 to 3)—even such liberals as Ted Kennedy (D-Mass.) and Donald Riegle (D-Mich.) voted for it—one could see in the floor debate a hint that Wallop had made a mistake in trusting Tower and Warner. Warner placed into the record a statement by John Foster, of the Defense Science Board, to the effect that the space application of laser weaponry should not be emphasized—which Warner characterized as being the position that he, Wallop, and Foster had agreed upon.[18] In fact, however, this was the very position that Harold Brown had rejected in 1980 and that Wallop and DARPA had successfully overcome. Warner, therefore, argued that the amendment would do neither more nor less than affirm

Foster's position. Warner took a note from Armed Services staffer Frank Gaffney and, minutes later, to leave no doubt, broke into a pro-Wallop speech by Senator Hayakawa (R-Calif.) to voice for the first time a theme that would later become a staple of the opposition—especially of the Soviet Union's opposition—to American antimissile defense: "This is a weapons system which can be used offensively and defensively, and human life can be lost as they use it."[19]

By August 1981, all doubt about Tower and Warner's intentions had vanished. Tower, Warner and their staff—Ronald Lehman and Frank Gaffney—dropped the entire Wallop amendment during the House–Senate conference on the authorization bill. So, as far as the final version of the joint bill was concerned, the amendment never happened. For a congressional committee's leadership to abandon a part of its chamber's bill that had passed so overwhelmingly was virtually unprecedented. For them to do it after having promised their personal support in order to avoid an embarrassing floor fight was the very definition of a breach of the Senate's folkways. In other words, their actions were anything but casual.

The little saga of the 1981 Wallop Amendment would drag on yet another year. In September 1981, Wallop attached his amendment to the fiscal 1982 *appropriations* bill for the Defense Department. It passed overwhelmingly. This time the chairman of the Defense Appropriations Subcommittee, Ted Stevens (R-Alaska), played by the rules and, without opposition in the House–Senate conference, kept the Wallop amendment in the final version of the bill. However, John Tower then called the Pentagon's comptroller and threatened that if the Pentagon spent even a penny of the money appropriated under the Wallop amendment, he would retaliate by cutting the Pentagon's fiscal 1983 budget. Tower's argument was that this money, although lawfully *appropriated*, had not been *authorized*. Of course since the Constitution requires only appropriation, and since authorization is merely a procedure internal to Congress, his argument had no legal standing whatever. But because a committee chairman's threats are always weighty, the 1981 Wallop amendment's funds were not released for spending until yet a second Wallop amendment had passed in 1982.

Why did Tower and Warner act as they did? Few have ever heard these men discourse on the substantive merits of *any* question—much less on the merits of rival technical claims. No one has ever claimed that they had either the desire or the capacity to learn enough about antimissile weapons to have an intelligent opinion about them. Their animus, then, was the reflection of that of their friends in the Pentagon, a large majority of senior generals and admirals. There is nothing new, of course, in the fact that senior military officers oppose new weapons—and especially the establishment of new missions—on the ground that these would jeopardize funding for current programs. By definition, only current programs have constituencies that will stand up for them. It is very significant, then, that throughout Wallop's efforts, his support came from members of Congress, such as Fritz Hollings (D-S.C.), Jake Garn (R-Utah), David Boren (D-Okla.), and Howell Heflin (D-Ala.), people who are pro-defense but who do not have strong personal ties to the military, while the main opposition to Wallop came not from left-wing senators but from the military and their conservative friends. These preferred not to attack in the open with arguments but to foreclose debate by saying "all is well—trust us."

The arguments against Wallop in 1981 were that he, indeed, had pointed out the future, that the Defense Department was grateful for the hint, had the situation well in hand, and was proceeding as fast as possible. Any more money or direction would just throw sand into the gears. However, the very fact that it had taken a law of Congress to make the Air Force establish a mere program office in this field—program offices are normally established by the stroke of a colonel's pen—spoke loudly otherwise, as did the fact that the Air Force staffed that office with passed-over lieutenant colonels and kept it on a short leash.

In 1981, however, the media and much of the Congress saw only that the Wallop amendment had passed. It concluded that the nation was going to have space lasers and that the only question left to resolve was precisely how to proceed. During 1981 and 1982, the Wallop office received over 300 calls from the media on laser weapons and innumerable approaches from industry lobbyists. As one of them remarked: "The cat of population protection is out of the bag, and it's not about to be stuffed back in."

In the summer of 1981, the General Accounting Office audited the space laser program and, in a classified report completed in 1982,[20] concluded that doubling the program's funding was the most reasonable of several options. Most important, the report concluded that the program should be given the clear goal of producing a weapon. Also in the summer of 1981, retired General Daniel Graham formed an organization, "High Frontier," to rally public opinion in favor of building ballistic missile defenses. Although High Frontier pushed only the "kinetic kill" approach earlier developed by Boeing and L.T.V. under Project Defender and opened itself to much criticism by using some faulty numbers, few observers understood this. High Frontier's effect has been to massively raise consciousness about ballistic missile defense at the grass roots. Interest on the part of the press, domestic and foreign, rose again.

But behind the scenes, valiant efforts were being made to stuff the cat back into the bag. In October 1981, George A. Keyworth, the president's science adviser, had told a breakfast gathering of 200 aerospace executives that he had spent three-fourths of his time since coming to Washington trying to "turn off" congressional pressure for space-based defenses. Keyworth and his deputy, Victor Reis, had been reasonably successful in dampening the industry's expectations and in strengthening the resolve of bureaucrats in the Pentagon who feared that the president might weigh in on the side of antimissile defense. He had also come to an agreement with Anthony Battista, the Democratic staffer in charge of R&D for the House Armed Services Committee, to divert the Congressional thrust for space-based lasers to long-range research.

In March 1982, however, stung by Wallop's complaints about him to friends in the White House, Keyworth asked to meet with Wallop. He told a bemused senator how much he admired his efforts, and how much Wallop had contributed to national security. But then, with trembling voice and shaking finger, he pointed to me and exclaimed that I had done incalculable harm by perverting the Senator's healthy support for long-range research into a campaign for immediate utilization. Calming down, he explained that in the past the National Labs had suffered heavily because of public disillusionment with nuclear fusion, whose proximity had been oversold, and that he was out to keep such harm from recurring. When I objected that the state of fusion technology was not comparable to that of space lasers, Keyworth snapped, "You don't know what you are talking about." At this point Wallop said that he himself was less interested in the labs than in preventing possible harm to the country from Soviet missiles. However, he added that differences of opinion about relative expertise should be quickly settled. Would Keyworth and I, he smilingly asked, be willing to take an exam in the field and promise that the one who scored lower would never touch the subject again? At that, Keyworth left.

Despite the comic relief, by 1982 Wallop and I realized that while we might win all the intellectual and public relations battles, our opponents had a monopoly of the executive branch and were making inroads into the Congress. In the House of Representatives,

Anthony Battista the powerful and knowledgeable staffer who has virtually run the R&D subcommittee for a decade had made a bold move. He wholly eliminated funds, in the jargon, "zeroed," the space laser budget for fiscal 1983. This ensured that whatever funds or directives the Senate added would have to be bargained against his "zero" bottom line.

The money that House Armed Services took out of space lasers, it put into long-range research on advanced shortwave-length lasers that were indisputably not ready for use. *Indeed, the novelty of the fight for the fiscal 1983 budget was that all of the previous two years' doubters about the feasibility of existing lasers had instantly become faithful believers in, and ardent proponents of, laser devices that did not (and still do not) exist.*

In late March 1982, George Keyworth and Robert Cooper—officials of the Reagan administration—visited John Warner to persuade him to ditch that part of the president's budget dealing with space lasers and adopt the contrary plan drafted by the Battista Democrats in the House. Warner was eager to go along, and later explained to Wallop that he intended to lead his subcommittee in that direction. When Wallop protested strongly and asked Warner questions that Warner did not understand and would not have enjoyed dealing with in public, Warner called a meeting of all concerned to "hash this thing out." This "thing" was the proposition that Keyworth, Cooper, and Battista had used to justify the zeroing of current lasers: They could not protect themselves and destroy missile boosters. The participants were to be Keyworth, Cooper and his staff, Battista and Congressman Dickinson (one of the Congressmen under whose authority he works), Warner and his staff, and Wallop and myself. The place was the secure room under the Capitol dome, S-407.

Keyworth and Cooper were embarrassed. They could be sure that Wallop would make a fuss at the White House if they appeared to undermine the president's budget request, which still formally endorsed the DARPA triad. Nor could they count on sidestepping the merits of the case with a show of their credentials. Of course, they knew that the facts were against them, and that Wallop would force them to acknowledge that. Keyworth did not show up and sent Victor Reis instead. Cooper came but let Alan Pike do the talking. Pike, of course, was of a different persuasion than Cooper. He pointed out that even if shortwave-length lasers could be developed, they would not be superior to the existing chemical infrared lasers for purposes of defending themselves against attack by anti-satellite missiles. That is because laser stations would typically be trying to destroy such interceptors at ranges between 1,000 and 100 kilometers, and at such short ranges the power of the laser is far more significant than the wavelength.

As they travel from the source, laser beams diffuse themselves in proportion to the square of the distance. Hence, as a target moves closer to the source of the laser, the amount of flux deposited on it increases exponentially. Thus, if a 10-megawatt laser with a 10-meter mirror is able to project about 1,200 joules/cm^2 on a target 3,000 kilometers away and that distance is cut by a factor of 3 to 1,000 kilometers, the amount of flux on the target will increase by a factor of 9, to 11,000 joules/cm^2. That amount of power is not trivial; it is roughly equal to the level of radiant energy on the surface of the sun. If the range were reduced by a further factor of 10, to 100 kilometers, the flux on target would increase by a factor of 100 to 1,100,000 joules/cm^2. At such fluxes, wavelength is simply not a factor. As for the laser's potency against offensive missiles, Pike argued, 1,200 joules/cm^2 is quite enough to destroy any missile ever built or designed. There are vitreous materials that resist such fluxes, but there is no reason to believe that missiles can be made of them.[21]

Warner asked if anyone disagreed with these statements and seemed somewhat surprised when no one did. He had understood the discussion enough to realize that as a consequence of it, it would be out of the question for him to try to kill the space laser program. Congressman Dickinson had understood enough to turn sharply to Battista and ask why he was hearing it for the first time. Cooper, Reis, and Battista, who fully understood the discussion, seemed delighted that it had not taken place in front of a larger audience. Wallop, for his part, was terribly disappointed that the entire Congress and the Secretary of Defense had not been able to look in.

Wallop had two objectives: to enact legislation causing antimissile weapons to be built, and to publicize arguments such as the one that had taken place in Room S-407. But the two purposes could not easily be pursued simultaneously. To make the substantive argument most fully on the floor of the Senate would be to insult Warner and Tower by asking them questions they could not answer and then answering them himself, thus pointing out their duplicity; in short, making an absolute pest of himself. In the Senate, pests always get much publicity and are often paid off. But sometimes they are ostracized. On the other hand, he could use subtle threats of making trouble together with sweet reason, working with Tower and Warner to get his amendment passed while getting publicity the hard way, by cerebral talks with elite reporters. The danger in this route is polite attention from the press, growing respect from senators not involved in the fray, and betrayal from those who are. He chose the second route and paid the price. He thought too well of Tower and Warner.

Wallop rightly believed that, lacking any position of power in the Senate with regard to such matters, his only asset was his ability to pose the choice: Do you or do you not want to build these protective weapons? The best example of his ability to marshal the evidence to convey the starkness of this choice was an editorial that William Gregory, editor of *Aviation Week and Space Technology*, published on April 26, 1982 after an interview with Wallop. Gregory, along with the General Accounting Office, noted that the bureaucracy was simply not trying to produce a prototype laser weapon and assess its usefulness. Why not, he asked?

The 1982 version of the Wallop amendment was intended to pose that very question as clearly and starkly as possible. Hence, Wallop decided not even to propose any increases in funding but rather to mandate that the Secretary of Defense build a laser ABM weapon as quickly as possible and present the Congress with the bill. The amendment directed the Secretary of Defense to give the program the kind of streamlined management practiced in super-secret intelligence programs, to proceed to systems integration, and to report how he was going to do the job. Wallop stated that no one any longer argued that it was infeasible to build the weapon, that the General Accounting Office had pointed out that the technology was being wasted by purposeless management, and that the North American Defense Command had generated a Statement of Operational Need for such a weapon. We need the weapon, Wallop said. Technology would let us have it, but management will not. Shall we have it or not? he asked.[22] The amendment passed by voice vote.

Warner supported the amendment the way a rope supports a hanged man. He urged its passage but stated that he understood it as nothing more than a reaffirmation of the current program and as a chip for bargaining with the House of Representatives, which had zeroed the program. That is precisely how he used the amendment. In the House–Senate conference, he and Tower dropped it in exchange for Battista's agreeing to restore the status quo. Despite personal commitments to Wallop to the contrary, Tower and Warner again negated the support that Wallop had marshaled in the Senate. Of course the administration did not object. This effectively ended any hopes of using legislation to "help" the Armed Services Committee push the administration, or to show the administration that there was a congressional majority that wanted antimissile defense. In effect the administration saw congressional sentiment for antimissile defense as something to be fought and rejected antimissile defense in ways impervious to argument. Those in the Senate who were in charge of military matters were also opposed and beyond the reach of argument.

Just how far beyond argument the administration's position was may be seen not just from the fact that it never explained why it preferred not to have these weapons but also from incidents showing that at the highest level, the Reagan administration is *unable* to make responsible decisions on such matters. In September 1982, frustrated by not knowing why the Secretary of Defense was effectively opposing him, and believing that Weinberger, like Harold Brown, was someone who could be led by his mind, Wallop arranged a luncheon meeting with him to "hash it out."

Weinberger brought along Fred Ikle, the undersecretary for policy, and Richard DeLauer, undersecretary for research and engineering. Wallop brought Alan Pike, who was in the process of leaving DARPA, and me. After almost an hour of spirited conversation between Pike, de Lauer and me, during which de Lauer agreed with every one of our technical points but still maintained that "enormous technical difficulties" stood in the way of dealing with hypothetical future missiles, Wallop asked Weinberger to render judgment. "Who's right, who's wrong, and why?" he asked. Weinberger replied that he was not qualified to make such judgments. He really did not know enough, because he had far more important things to do. Did he not agree, asked Wallop, that the Soviet ICBM force is the number one military threat to the U.S. and that the revolution in antimissile technology is the most important strategic development since the atom bomb? Yes, answered Weinberger. What other matters were more worthy of the secretary's judgment? continued Wallop. These matters are indeed essential, said Weinberger, but other people, not he, would make judgments about them. Then Wallop suggested as gently as he could that perhaps those other people were exercising the reality of the secretary's function.

To attack this stone wall of unarticulated opposition, Wallop would have had to attack the competence and sincerity of important people of his own party in a publicly compelling way. He also would have had to attack the veracity of several key members of the administration, e.g., Robert Cooper, in a similar way. This would have been tough enough had he been a chairman of a key subcommittee in the field, which would have allowed him to hold hearings, call witnesses, and embarrass individuals, much as Lyndon Johnson had done in the field of space policy in the 1950s. (But note that Democrat Johnson had the luxury of pushing against an administration of the opposite party, somewhat as Wallop had done before the 1980 election.) But now without even membership on either the Armed Services or Defense Appropriations Panels, Wallop could only warn his friends about, say, Robert Cooper's dissimulations and suggest sharp questions. But he, for one example, could not be at the meeting of the Defense Appropriations Subcommittee that Senator Stevens held at his suggestion in September 1982, where Cooper, answering questions that Wallop had written, falsely asserted that the triad technology was being brought along as fast as technology would allow, whereas in fact Cooper had already ordered significant reductions in the scope of the programs.

With appropriate orchestration, Cooper's radical reduction, (in Pentagonese, de-scoping) of the laser program could have been made national news. In fact, Cooper had ordered the design of the main laser scaled back from a likely 10 million watts—sufficient for antimissile defense—to 2 megawatts, useless as anything but a test bed. He had also ordered the removal of the infrared search telescope from the pointer-tracker, making sure that that project would not yield an instrument that could simply be bolted onto a laser weapon. He had also removed from the project that was building the main mirror the instruments that would have allowed the main mirror to respond to the pointer-tracker. In the hands of a subcommittee chairman interested in following in Lyndon Johnson's footsteps, Cooper would have been placed under oath, surely embarrassed, and possibly prosecuted for perjury. But without a committee position, and unwilling to attack his own party's administration head on, Wallop simply had no leverage.

Wallop's strategy had been to publicize the fact that the technology existed to make effective antimissile devices. His primary sources of information had always been industry and DARPA. But on most occasions, Cooper was able to monopolize testimony after he took over DARPA. By September 1982, he had driven out the highest-ranking hard-core supporters of missile defense, the directors of the Directed Energy office, Tanimoto and Pike. As for industry, Wallop formally asked John Tower, as chairman of the Armed Services Committee, to call a set of industry witnesses, put them under oath in order to free them from any pressures from their military customers to tailor their testimony to support only present programs, and then ask straightforward questions about what, regardless of the military's wishes or regulations, their companies could do to produce antimissile weapons to defend the country. The companies would not be asked to advocate or "sell" anything but merely to present what their raw technical capacity would allow them to do, or not to do, so that Congress could then make responsible decisions about what to buy and not to buy. Tower denied the request thus:

> As you know, the Armed Services Committee has a long-standing policy of refraining from calling upon outside witnesses whose personal or corporate interests might in any way be construed as impeaching the objectivity and validity of their testimony.[23]

This answer obviously assumed that the testimony of the military, various groups within the Department of Defense, the national laboratories, and "outside experts" such as Richard Garwin and Kosta Tsipis, is not affected by "personal or corporate interests." No one takes this seriously.

In fact, the exclusion of industry from congressional testimony on military matters is a result of the confluence of the political left's interest in cutting down expenditures on military forces with the military's interest in dominating its relationship with the defense industries. Since the late McNamara era, this domination has been complete, and industry has long since ceased to rebel at the Pentagon's inflated requirements and time-and-money-consuming procedures. If the government wants to pay money for paper-shuffling, industry will put it in the bank just the same.

From the beginning, because Wallop's strategy had been to put the choice of whether or not to have antimissile defenses before the public, he had tried mightily to get industry to deliver the simple message: "We can do it now. Do you want it or not?" After all, *industry*—not the military, nor any university laboratory—builds weapons and satellites. Industry, then, is the final authority on what can and cannot be done. But even when speaking privately with senators, representatives of industry are acutely conscious that their customer, the military, demands that they do neither more nor less than support the programs that the military have proposed and not so much as mention the possibility that these programs could be done under different procedures or on different schedules. For industry nowadays to talk with Congress in ways that might lead the Congress to adopt programs that the military does not want is simply unheard of. So accustomed are aerospace executives to this discipline that they factor their customer's favorite assumptions and procedures even into private conversations, often even into their own thoughts. Thus, unless in a safe setting—and unless they are prompted—industry executives factor the armed forces' wasteful procedures, assumptions, and schedules into every answer. How quickly can you do "X"? one might ask. The answer, strictly in terms of materials and labor, might be three months. But the executive will tend to factor in his customer's administrative proclivities, and answer three years. Since he could not set up a proper hearing to force industry to speak, Wallop tried to cajole it—without much success.

The closest Wallop ever got to getting what he wanted was a meeting he arranged on a spring morning in 1982 between Henry (Scoop) Jackson (D-Wash.), John Warner, and the aerospace vice president widely regarded as perhaps the industry's foremost satellite builder. This gentleman, close to retirement and responsible for much of the design and all of the production of the KH-11, had instant credibility. He strongly believed that he had more than enough technology in hand to build a space-based laser: "The technology is so ripe, it's rotting," he said. Scoop Jackson was rightly the most respected member of the Senate—a serious man whose presence dominated the Armed Services Committee. Wallop wanted Warner to be there as the satellite builder laid the option of "missile defense now" before Jackson.

The gentleman did that clearly enough, and Jackson was duly impressed. But then Warner asked: "Now, Dr.———, as you know, the technologies you have been speaking of are dealt with by the president's budget. Would you clarify for us whether you and your company support or oppose the president's budget?" The aerospace veteran flushed and began to stammer. "Of course we support the President's budget. . . . but . . ." At this point Warner said, "So do we all," and went on at some length about how fully present plans fulfill the technology's potential. Then it was time for the senators to go. As the thoroughly flustered technologist left he rued that he had lacked the presence of mind to say "I'm not here to support or oppose anything. That is your job. Mine is just to tell you that if you really want a missile-killing laser badly enough, I can deliver it." But the world is not ruled by afterthoughts.

Two other attempts to have industry "speak up" also illustrate the problem. At one point, Fred C. Ikle, undersecretary of defense for policy and nominally the number three official in the Pentagon, wrote a letter to the president of a major aerospace company asking him to describe in detail—and wholly abstracting from current procedures, programs, and policies—his company's capacity for building several antimissile devices. Three *months* passed before he received a one-page reply informing him that the company works under contracts overseen by the military services and the undersecretary for research and engineering, and that surely these sources would be able to answer the undersecretary for policy's question.

Finally, just before Christmas 1982, at the end of a day's briefings with the Lockheed Missiles and Space Company, as its president Dan Tellep was explaining to me why his company could never "get ahead of the customer," I asked: "What would happen if the president of the United States were to go on national television, declare that antimissile defense is our nation's top priority, and invite industry to submit its best view of how the job could be done? Would you then send *him* a statement of what you could do, unconditioned by the bureaucracy's expectations?" "No," answered Tellep. "But why not; is he not your customer?" I replied. Tellep then dotted the "i's" and crossed the "t's": "No. My customers are the colonels who sign my checks."

Three months later, on March 23, 1983, President Reagan did go on national television and spoke much as every advocate of antimissile defense would have wished him to speak. But he was speaking as the head of an administration whose leading members were unwilling, or perhaps unable, to master or to bypass a bureaucracy and an advisory system that is profoundly hostile to defending against missiles. Even as he prepared to tell the American people that they ought to have a defense, Ronald Reagan was agreeing with advisers who were telling him that the entire idea ought to be treated as an open question, to be turned over for judgment and for implementation (if any) to the regular bureaucracy—the very customers that industry is so eager not to "get ahead of." Dan Tellep proved wise in the ways of his environment.

Thus on March 23, 1983, after some four years of fighting the bureaucracy to build up antimissile programs and to put the issue of ballistic missile defense on the national agenda, Wallop and his staff could raise one cheer: Their issue had made it to the top, all right. But, it was no longer their issue. The president was putting the whole matter of antimissile protection into the very hands from whom Wallop had sought to take it. The issue would certainly get a lot more publicity than in the past, but its essence—the question, shall we build this and that and that now—would be blurred.

That became unmistakable when, on July 15, 1983, as the Senate debated the Armed Services Authorization bill for fiscal 1984, Wallop proposed to give to the Army the mission to defend the country against ballistic missiles and the mandate to actually build certain antimissile weapons. This time the opponents, Tower and Warner, were so confident that they would not have to engage in a substantive debate that they did not even attempt to bargain with Wallop. On the floor, they merely said that they, like Wallop, fully agreed with President Reagan's resounding speech of March 23. They noted that a panel—under James Fletcher of NASA—composed of the best and brightest technologists (many from the Defense Science Board) that had been summoned pursuant to the president's call, was sitting to define a plan of action and that Senator Wallop's praiseworthy amendment was premature. Wallop got only 24 votes.

To vote in favor of the FY 1984 Wallop amendment, a senator would have had to be convinced that, as Wallop was arguing and the president's rhetoric notwithstanding, the panel was defining the Soviet offensive threat and the technical requirements for a defense in ways that would make a defense infeasible by definition. Even though the Fletcher panel had been sitting for only a few weeks, enough of its biases were evident[24] that this conclusion was a safe bet for knowledgeable people. But these were in short supply. Most observers would not accept this radical proposition until it was proved correct by events. That would not begin to happen until the spring of 1986.

5 / *The Best and the Brightest*

Yet, in holding scientific research and discovery in respect as we should, we must also be alert to the equal opposite danger that public policy could itself become the captive of a scientific-technological elite.

—Dwight Eisenhower, farewell address

Not, surely, that the men involved lacked intelligence or patriotism, but the workings of the system consumed and paralyzed them.

—Charles de Gaulle, *War Memoirs*

Verba fugent, facta restant.

—Old Latin proverb

After March 23, 1983 the question Are you for or against building antimissile weapons? became Are you for or against the SDI? But while the first proposition speaks for itself, the meaning of SDI is not self-evident. Conventional wisdom has it that pursuant to President Reagan's call, the nation's best and brightest scientists started a program to build the antimissile system called SDI. The press conveys the image that the SDI program is not one of many possible options that a panel acting pursuant to the president's speech might have outlined, but rather that "it" is the only conceivable way to go about providing an antimissile defense for the United States. Many even believe that SDI is a "thing" in the way that, say, a Boeing 747 is a thing with whose design one can fiddle but that one can buy or not buy. Just about everyone believes that the President is trying to acquire this "SDI system" for the country. More sophisticated observers know that SDI is only a research program. But even these typically believe that the SDI research program, as constituted by the president's panels after March 23, 1983, is the indispensable first step in finding out whether "it," that is, the SDI approach to ballistic missile defense—whatever that is—will work.

In fact, however, the SDI, like the research program established a generation earlier as an alternative to deploying Nike Zeus, is a research program fashioned with the specific intention of not building any antimissile devices whatever in the foreseeable future. Most important, therefore, the SDI program is not the only possible way in which one might follow up a commitment to remove the threat of ballistic missiles. Indeed, the SDI program, as defined by those put in charge of defining it, shunts an inherently practical task of military engineering onto a theoretical track that stretches out to infinity. As such, the SDI program is not the solution that any normal human being would conjure up if asked to defend the U.S. against ballistic missiles. Rather, it is the nonsolution conjured up by a mentality that is nonetheless narrow and curious for being so widespread among those in charge of innovation in the Pentagon.

In fact, far beyond Reagan's knowing or caring, the definition of the SDI program that followed March 23, 1983, was similar to the recommendations of the Defense Science Board panel that Harold Brown had rejected in 1980 as being too antidefense. Thus, when it started the SDI, the Reagan administration, unbeknownst to itself, delegated control of antimissile defense to the stand-pat element of the defense scientific bureaucracy that had been losing control near the end of the Carter administration. That element determined the content of the Fletcher Panel's report, founding document of the SDI. That document—completed almost six years prior to the time Reagan must surely leave office—features statements to the effect that any decision about whether or not to build any antimissile device could properly be made only *after* the president who commissioned the report went out of office. Hence, the first act of the SDI program was to delegitimize any possible inclination Ronald Reagan might have had to actually build antimissile defenses.

Pursuant to the Fletcher Panel's report, the SDI research program has been built on a set of very peculiar assumptions that make the task of ballistic missile defense seem impossibly complex. Much as the technical bureaucrats of the early 1950s delayed American missile programs with needless inflation of technical requirements, and their successors in the 1960s stymied the ABM system of that epoch, the "best and the brightest" who took complete charge of the American SDI program after March 23, 1983, have "gold-plated" the requirements for performance of antimissile devices and inflated their estimates of the sophistication of the Soviet missile threat that American defenses would have to face. Of course, this technical mismatch results in a clear prescription: research forever; deploy never. The SDI program, then, is based on the planted axiom that any and all current technology is insufficient for the job, and literally not worth bothering with. Moreover, by stating plainly that even these inflated requirements are subject to being increased further solely to take account of the bureaucracy's evolving notions of what might be required, the bureaucrats of the SDI have insulated their preference for perpetual research from any and all developments in the real world.

The public debate on the SDI, thus, is literally unreal. On one side are the official proponents of the SDI who argue that the technology is advancing by leaps and bounds and that, not now, but in a decade or so, they will be able to decide if the technology will be sufficient—according to their standards—to defend the nation against their conception of what the Soviet missile threat might be around the year 2010. On the other side, the opponents of defense argue that they, for their part, do not have to wait a decade and spend $26 billion to decide that—by *their* standards and according to their conception of the Soviet threat in whatever year—there can never be enough technology to defend against ballistic missiles. Yet these two positions are closer than they might seem at first glance. Both oppose building any antimissile device. Both deal in coin whose worth cannot be tested against reality. One can see how close these two positions are by comparing them to the position of those who began to promote defense in the late 1970s—namely, build what defenses can be built now against the threat that exists now.

To understand both the opponents and proponents of the SDI we must look at the program's very foundations.

On Friday, February 11, 1983, Ronald Reagan met with his secretary of defense, with the Joint Chiefs of Staff, and with his Deputy National Security Adviser Robert MacFarlane on how to deal with the declining strategic position of the United States vis-à-vis the Soviet Union and, even more pressing, how to deal with declining domestic support for offensive missile programs. The focus was a prospective presidential speech to revive that support. The men in the room batted around several alternatives. It was not clear whether the subject on the table was how to deal with a public relations problem, with a strategic problem, or with both.

A proposal for a combination of space-based and ground-based antimissile defense had been on the front page of the *Washington Post*'s "Outlook" section the previous Sunday,[1] so the idea came up, but simply as one thought among many. Reagan seized on it. Admiral Watkins, chief of naval operations, supported it on moral grounds. Bud McFarlane, formerly an aide to John Tower and now deputy national security adviser, said that talking about defense would be good for the administration politically. Reagan indicated that he wanted to go in that direction, but as usual was not specific. It is not clear whether at that meeting President Reagan intended that henceforth his administration would only *talk* about antimissile defenses or would actually acquire some. Given Reagan's normal tendency to equate speech with action, the question might not even have risen in his mind.

However, it is clear that the military chiefs had endorsed the president's talk as a political maneuver rather than as a weapons program. That is because, when it came time to draft the text of the president's remarks, high-level officials in the Pentagon, including several of the military chiefs, argued very strongly against early drafts and succeeded in having them toned down. Presumably they would not have done this if the president had only expressed a desire for a research program whose main fruit was to be public relations. Or perhaps they just wanted to make sure that whatever the president had or had not meant, the speech would not wind up disturbing their budgets. Thus it is not clear whether Ronald Reagan intended SDI to be a P.R. program, or merely accepted that formulation of it when it came through "the system."

The final draft of the President's remarks was drafted by Bud McFarlane, who had worked for Henry Kissinger while the latter was fashioning the ABM Treaty, as well as for John Tower, and who has never been accused of being in favor of the U.S. having antimissile defenses. At any rate, President Reagan's speech of March 23 called not for deployment but for research and development. So, while the news media wrongly assumed that the president was endorsing the movement toward defense that had been gathering steam since the 1970s, MacFarlane, Keyworth, and Robert Cooper were naming the Fletcher panel and drafting instructions to it that struck off in the opposite direction.

Those instructions were to develop a long-term (twenty- to thirty-year) research plan that would explore "the fundamental limits of technology." The panel was not to consider concretely how any technology might be applied because, Keyworth stated axiomatically, "there is no technical basis yet for systems definition," and "the time scale is the next generation." Hence any solution to the strategic problems posed by present-day Soviet missiles would be irrelevant because, by the next generation, Soviet offensive forces could be expected to have responded to our search for a defense. We should only consider technologies that could leapfrog such problems. Thus Keyworth, MacFarlane, and Robert Cooper stipulated that the panel was to survey all of science and technology and identify those areas that hold promise for doing this "responsive" job.[2]

These instructions pushed the panel's members further in the direction they were already inclined to go. Science and technology, *not* weapons engineering, was to be the order of the day. Hence the panel did not organize itself to evaluate proposed weapons systems, or strategic schemes, but to do a survey of the technologies that might to applicable to defenses in the twenty-first century. So the panel did not organize itself to study, say weapons "A," "B," and "C" or boost-phase defenses, midcourse defenses, and terminal defenses. Rather according to its report, the panel organized itself to study the following subjects: "surveillance, acquisition, tracking and kill assessment," "directed energy weapons," "conventional weapons" (later called kinetic energy weapons), "battle management, C^3 [Command, Control and Communications] and data processing," "systems concepts," and "countermeasures." The last topic included problems regarding the relative vulnerability of enemy missiles and the vulnerabilities of various conceivable defensive devices. The panel studied all these topics generically, for the purpose of finding the scientific limits of the technologies involved. It is worthwhile reiterating that the panel's agenda was not the only possible way of approaching the subject. Indeed, had the panel had the remotest interest in providing a defense, it would have organized subgroups to pull technology elements from several of these categories into individual engineering projects, or at least into individual engineering studies.

Here, it is important to note the important differences between the way that, on the one hand, scientists/technologists and, on the other hand, engineers approach the world. Scientists/technologists tend to think about how far a principle will be applicable, and about advancing the state of the art. Thus, if a problem requires the use of data processing, they prefer to develop superior processors in order to solve the problems in the most elegant and advanced way conceivable. The engineer, however, is trained to get a job done, and consequently to "make do" with the tools at hand. A program structured according to the engineering mentality would be too busy trying to "make do" to worry about advancing the state of the art per se.

One could well imagine an engineer who was working on the data-processing part of a pointer-tracker trying to convince his supervisor that if he were given just a year and a few million dollars more, he could provide a much better component. The supervisor would surely tell him to file his interesting ideas, because the overall product was due in six months. On the other hand, one does not have to imagine how technologists on the Fletcher Panel greeted suggestions that, say, pointer-tracker technologies were good enough to be used. "Don't bother with that," would be the reigning reflex. "Our job is to see how much better we can make them." Taken exclusively, these approaches either rob the future for the sake of the present, or rob the present for the sake of the future. The Fletcher Panel, by inclination and assignment, recommended robbing the U.S. for the rest of the 20th century, for the sake of the 21st century—maybe.

The Fletcher Panel's penchant, as well as its organization for technology rather than producing weapons, led to a set of recommendations that ironically reinforced the popular misconception that the administration had in mind "a system," and that a program was being laid out to built it. In brief, both the classified and the unclassified versions of those recommendations begin with the standard explanation that to do a good job of defending against ballistic missiles, one must attack those missiles throughout all phases of their journey. But to justify its core recommendation that the SDI program should consist *exclusively* of improving the state of the art and eschew building such devices as the present state of the art would permit building, both versions of the panel's report gave the unmistakable impression that the end product of the SDI program would indeed be a fully integrated system comprising weapons and sensors working against missiles during all phases of flight.

The panel made clear in its recommendations that it was not ready to choose among the many "candidate technologies" that were "in the race." It specified that the "race" would be long, and indeed that at the end of the "race" there would be not weaponry but rather a development program. The panel made even clearer its determination to channel research into those technologies it determined were crucial if "the system" was ultimately to perform as the panel wished it to—that is, destroy 90 percent of the targets during each of the four phases of missile flight, for an overall effectiveness of 99.9 percent. Because these tasks were difficult and the technologies for performing them nonexistent, the panel termed them the "long poles in the tent." The essence of the panel's recommendations was that the only decision worth making was not whether it was worthwhile to build this or that antimissile device, but rather whether to pursue an abstract "highly effective system" by researching the "long poles." The panel was confident that a decade's worth of research that focused on the "long poles" would provide a future president and a future Congress with a positive indication about the theoretical possibility of a "highly effective system," and that only then could a rational decision be made about whether to pursue that system by selecting specific "technology paths" for further development.

How does one resolve the logical contradiction? On the one hand, the panel was oriented to a "system" specific enough to include set standards of performance as well as to warrant concentration on "the long poles." But, on the other hand, the panel reserved judgment about the future to the point of refusing to consider whether or not to use any old or current technology. One explanation may be that virtually everyone on the panel was in the business of researching and developing rather than using technology. Also, perhaps only three out of the panel's fifty-two members favored antimissile defense at all. Absent were those who had fought for ballistic missile defense since the 1950s. This intellectual bias was important. Nevertheless, we should note that the panel was also biased in terms of the interests its members represented.

The panel was led by four people, in addition to NASA's Fletcher,[3] whose past careers were in offensive weaponry and would be furthered by making sure that any money flowing from the president's speech would be spent according to the priorities of the organizations they represented rather than by a new organization that would build weapons. The panel's working groups, in turn, were made up of a representative sample of the U.S. government's R&D establishment, and its clients. By far the largest representation was from the Los Alamos, Sandia, and Livermore National Laboratories, and "Beltway Bandit" study mills such as Sparta, Inc., Physical Dynamics Inc., Science Applications, Inc., Institute for Defense Analysis, Research and Development Associates, etc. There were also eight individuals who were one-man consulting firms. Of course, there was heavy representation from the headquarters of the Army and the Air Force.

Was the panel so constituted because its members were the people most expert in the new technologies of antimissile defense? No. None of these people and organizations had developed any part of the technologies that had set the Congress and the press clamoring for antimissile defense. Indeed, if those clamors had led to a large weapons program, the entities represented on the panel would have lost money. Not surprisingly, all of these people had a common interest in preserving and advancing such of their programs and contracts as might possibly be rationalized as fitting into the new initiative. Therefore, it is not surprising that the programs they defined turned out to be neither more nor less than their ongoing programs, *but redefined to make sure that these programs would remain under their control for the foreseeable future— rather than be shifted to an operational command hell-bent on building weapons.* Ideology and interest make a powerful combination.

It must be reemphasized that without the notion of an overarching, highly effective overall "SDI system" to be deployed all at once or not at all, it would have been difficult for the panel to so completely preclude discussion of whether or not to build this or that antimissile device. The image of the "SDI system" then, effectively served to legitimize long-range research and to delegitimize any consideration of weapons whatever, while at the same time giving the impression that there existed a well-thought-out plan, the first step of which was to provide the "long poles" for the rest.

Let us now briefly review the panel's substantive recommendations and take a closer look at these "long poles." To understand fully how and why these "poles" are "long," however, we will have to keep in mind that the panel fully subscribed to the notion of the "responsive threat." Whether it did so principally because of interest, ideology, or habit is immaterial.

Surveillance, Acquisition, Tracking, and Kill Assessment

The working group concentrated on laying out a research plan for dealing with the problem of identifying missile warheads in midcourse while they are cold and surrounded by many cheap decoys as well as debris. It was easy work to point out how hard it is to do this without resorting to imaginary reasons. The panel also spent much time defining the need for better sensors for the terminal phase, which was more difficult to do, because many terminal sensors exist. But given that the problem of surveillance and tracking in the boost phase is obviously simple and well within the capacity of current programs, justifying turning these programs into research programs was most difficult and required much reference to the "responsive threat."

Midcourse discrimination may be the longest "pole" of all, especially as the panel defined it. The problem, says the panel's report, is not merely to provide throughout the midcourse phase the kind of very fine look at the "threat cloud" of warheads and decoys that the ground-based Cobra Dane intelligence radar now gives us for the last minutes of midcourse. Nor, is the problem merely to place a very fine heat sensor—such as the Air Force's space infrared experiment, completed in 1981, or the homing overlay experiment sensor, the first version of which was completed in 1984—within the range of the threat cloud. This would indeed provide detailed differentiation on the basis of the different thermodynamic characteristics of the decoys and warheads. Nor would even laser-quality optical images of the objects in the threat cloud do. The problem, according to the panel, is to account simultaneously for every object in the threat cloud from the time it comes into existence to the time it is surely destroyed, either by defensive action or by burning up in the atmosphere. To do this, says the panel, it is not enough simply to have one of the kinds of sensors producible by current technology available to monitor the entire midcourse phase. Rather, it is necessary to have at least three kinds of sensors, and to have all of them compare notes about each and every piece of debris, decoy, or warhead just to make sure. To make triply sure, especially against hypothetical Soviet "responsive" decoys, the panel thought it would be good to prepare to hit every object in the threat cloud, either with continuous-wave laser power or with particle beams, in order to make it possible for the several kinds of sensors to notice how each object would react to being heated and/or to being struck. If an object reacts slowly rather than quickly to a particle beam, or if it has enough mass to absorb more than less heat from a continuous wave laser, then it's a warhead—especially if fine laser pictures show that neighboring objects' thin skins have been torn up by the particle beam.

Doing all of this would be enormously difficult. Building the individual sensors would be demanding enough. Radars, especially ones that can see fine details far away, are necessarily big and require much electrical power. To reproduce a dozen copies of the huge Cobra Dane on U.S. soil would be a nontrivial expense. But to design, produce, and orbit a dozen radar imaging devices of a quality superior to Cobra Dane's and to supply them with power in space is to talk of sums of as-yet unknown dimensions.

Laser-imaging devices are inherently much smaller and consume a tiny fraction of the power that radars consume. However, given the inevitable increase in the diffraction (spread) of laser beams as the distance to the target increases, designers of such devices face the nasty choice between designing the laser receiving mirrors large enough to gather enough returning light to make a fine image, or to simply prepare to make dozens of sensors. Today's infrared heat-reading sensors are well enough advanced to pick up subtle differences in characteristics, even of cold targets. Nevertheless, a serious improvement in present infrared technology would be required to make such sensors good enough to deliver very sharp images at long distances while instantly analyzing changes both in the motion and in the thermodynamic properties of those images.

To fulfill the panel's vision, it is also essential to develop the computer programs to compare the "take" from each kind of sensor. But in order to do this one must have a mass of radar, infrared, and laser imagery data about warheads and decoys as a basis for comparison. That mass of data has yet to be gathered. Then there is a logical obstacle. If this multidisciplinary sensor analysis is *necessary* because the panel assumes that we will confront a "responsive threat" different from the one that now exists, writing the computer comparison-and-recognition guides to govern such analysis is *impossible* for the very same reason. Finally, in order to carry out this scheme it would be essential to very precisely determine and control each sensor's orbital location and to make sure that each was oriented very precisely on three axes. This would be necessary to make sure that all sensors could have common reference to the same target objects. The practical problems of such precise station-keeping are significant. Hence the case for why these projects require research is self-evident.

The panel, however, does not explain how the midcourse problem might be dealt with by less sophisticated means. Especially, it does not explain how useful for the task at hand might be a set of current state-of-the-art infrared sensors in orbit.

The terminal sensor problem, according to the panel, also requires improvement in the state of the art. The Army's new commanding officer at Huntsville, Major General Eugene Fox was ready with the school solution: A fixed terminal-imaging radar must be developed de novo. This would save the jobs of the legions who had been working on big, fixed radars. The Army's flying infrared sensors (AOA) get praise but also get sent back for improvement. This was fine with Huntsville, which did not want to lose a project just because it had logically left the research stage. The panel did not discuss why the U.S. should not simply use the technology of current radars (e.g., Cobra Dane) for acquisition, and the Navy's Aegis radar for local battle management, or, if need be, modify them rather than develop wholly new ones. Nor did it explain why it was necessary to put off the availability of the AOA for almost a decade to improve its coverage. The logic of the panel's approach, however, supplies an answer to these and other detailed questions. If we are going to put off building any weapon until the longest "poles" come along, then why not turn even short poles into long ones?

Nowhere is this clearer than with regard to sensors for the boost phase. The well-known current Defense Support Program (DSP) satellites, embodying the technology of the early 1970s, may already be good enough, to provide any defensive battle stations in low earth orbit information about the location and track of rising missiles. With such approximate data, each of these stations could turn its own on-board acquisition sensors toward its respectively appropriate cluster of targets. The current DSP satellites are not equipped to transfer their data in this way, but so equipping their successors would be a trivial matter.

Indeed, the successor satellite to DSP that had been in engineering development since the late 1970s would have had the ability to stare down at areas whence Soviet missiles might be launched, and to track the missiles accurately. Only the on-board data processing would have been necessary for this DSP follow-on to do the job of boost phase acquisition. The panel instead recommended a major R&D project aimed at producing a boost surveillance and tracking system (BSTS) that would do precise three-dimensional spatial location of rising missiles, and whose feasibility, by definition, was doubtful. Five years later, BSTS was more doubtful than ever. But surely in its name Robert Cooper had destroyed DARPA's capacity to build a true geosynchronous staring sensor and no move had been made to give DSP the ability to sort and deliver information for boost-phase battle management.

Battle Management and Computers

The panel's key point here was that hand-off of information about each and every target from boost phase and post-boost phase through midcourse and terminal phase to a central computer is absolutely essential. The dogma is that every bit of information from every part of the system must, in principle, be transferable to every other part of the system, as well as to a single battle-management center.

Writing the "creative software" to do all that would require the development of new "expert systems" able to instantly write new programs was needed. This would involve "improved techniques such as programs and design slicing, attribute generation analysis, symbolic execution, and forward-effect tracing and analysis." Software and hardware design would combine to allow the "system" to operate in space for ten years without maintenance in the presence of high doses of nuclear radiation, and even despite catastrophic failures in major subsystems.

Moreover, according to the panel, the software must be written so as to provide, to the maximum extent of human capacity, for human involvement in decisions all the way through the battle-management process. So, as a prerequisite for writing the software, the program called for testing how quickly human subjects could comprehend situations and make decisions. Of course, formatting information to produce displays comprehensible to human beings, and then providing the computer links that would allow human judgment to interface with individual machine-made decisions regarding any of the four layers of the battle is no small task in itself. It looms even greater, however, since the panel superimposed this chore on one whose size is already staggering: to provide "arbitrary connectivity between any pair of points."

Could this be done? What would it take? The report judged that perhaps 10 million lines of software code would do. This is a very big program, but only one-fifth the size of the software that runs the U.S. telephone system. Since then, however, a variety of computer experts have claimed that to do the kind of battle management the Panel asked for, at least 100 million lines would be required, if indeed software of such complexity could be written at all.

In the summer of 1985, in an effort to resolve such questions, the SDIO commissioned a panel of computer experts known as the Eastport Study Group, under Danny Cohen of the University of Southern California, to estimate just what it would take to do the job that the Fletcher Panel had described. In sum, the Eastport group concluded that there are "inflexible limits" in the complexity and reliability that software can achieve, and that it makes little sense to make massive software development efforts which butt up against those limits. Rather, the group concluded that "the trade-offs necessary to make the software task tractable are in the system's architecture." Specifically, the group saw no reason why anyone would *want* to have a battle-management system as dependent on tight coordination as that implied by the Fletcher

Report, and indicated that a much more decentralized approach would not only be unquestionably feasible but would also enjoy the advantages of robustness and simplicity.[4] Nevertheless, in the field of battle management as well as in others, the Fletcher Panel had set in motion both the programs and the public debate on them.

Is battle-management feasible? That depends on one's definition of battle management. No small number of computer experts will point out that the programs set up to achieve the original standards are a long way from bearing fruit. Others point out that it would be no problem at all to write simple software to reasonably connect defensive sensors and weapons *within* each defensive layer. The answer, then, is that—as the panel has defined it—battle management is highly problematic, but, that on the other hand, more than enough computer technology exists to accomplish battle management if battle management is defined differently.

But since there is no plan to build any given kind or number of defensive weapons, it is impossible to correctly define a battle-management task. Only once one has decided to build a given set of weapons can one ask: What degree of coordination would current data-processing technology allow us to give to these particular weapons? So, once again, the indecisiveness of the whole SDI program vitiates each of its parts. It is obvious, however, that in the field of battle management, as in others, the Fletcher Panel simply started from the wrong end of the task—that is, by defining the biggest problem conceivable.

Directed-Energy Weapons

"The Fletcher panel places chemical lasers in idle while accelerating shorter wavelength devices."[5] Thus did the Defense Department define the thrust of the panel's recommendations in the field of directed energy weapons. This meant that what Robert Cooper had been fearful of saying to the Senate Defense Appropriations Subcommittee in the fall of 1982 the Fletcher Panel openly made into national policy a year later. That policy is not to have a space-based laser weapon as quickly as technology would allow. Rather, that policy is, *by choice*, to slow down the laser weapon's arrival on the scene. The rationalization for this was twofold, but of the same stuff: First, according to the panel's conception, it would be useless to have a laser for boost phase all by itself, because other parts of the system would not be ready. According to the dogma, no weapon makes sense except as part of the overall, multi-tier system. But, by its definition, such a system would have to include midcourse discrimination and integrated battle management. That would take at the very best twenty years to put into place.

But note well: the panel did not recommend building this and other components and storing them in wait for the day when the "long poles" would be ready, say twenty years hence. That is because—and this is the second point—according to its view, twenty years hence the Soviets would have responded by making their missiles resistant to this particular laser weapon. Hence, the panel strongly recommended that priority be given to developing short-wavelength lasers that would be able to pierce these "responsive" Soviet missiles of *circa* the turn of the millennium.

How "responsive" could these Soviet missiles be? The panel adopted a standard of 75,000 to 100,000 joules/cm^2—existing missiles self-destruct once they have received 80–800 Joules/cm^2. The hypothetical missiles would withstand up to fifteen times the amount of radiant energy that exists on the surface of the sun—indeed, fifteen times as much as the ablative coverings on ballistic reentry vehicles experience during reentry.

The panel never explained how it chose those figures. It acknowledged that the nation urgently needed more and better data about the actual and possible resistance of missiles to various kinds of lasers, to particle beams, and to impact-projectiles as well. Of course, it stipulated that data would have to be gathered within the constraints of the ABM Treaty. It certainly did not suggest that the U.S. build any of these "responsive missiles," so that we could conduct realistic tests. So, in the absence of the space-based laser that the panel was recommending against, and in the absence of the "responsive missiles" that the U.S. was most certainly not about to develop and to fly, and given the determination not to carry out a realistic confrontation between these missiles and lasers even if they were available, this "urgently needed" data was not about to arrive. The panel nonetheless recommended a research program. But in the chronologically long and uncertain shadow of that program, its assumption of missile hardness would continue to be the high, unchallengeable hurdle that all "candidate" directed-energy weapons would have to prove they could pass before they were allowed into full-scale engineering development.

The chemical laser had already been flunked peremptorily. Nevertheless, the panel held out hope that the power of individual chemical laser battle stations might be increased manyfold by "ganging" a dozen or so chemical laser generators, so that all in each gang might feed their beams into a single phased-array of mirrors. As we shall see later, it is a patently silly idea to try to make up for any real or imagined lack of laser power in a defensive station by increasing that power rather than by proliferating the number of lower-power laser stations, because proliferating the number of stations cuts the distance between each station and its eventual missile targets.

By similarly bright lights, the panel put great confidence in several directed-energy weapons that twenty years hence might thwart the "responsive" threat that the panel conceived in 1983. The panel gave "major emphasis" to large, ground-based excimer and free-electron lasers. *If* these could be made to generate short-wavelength beams with very great power (say, 25 megawatts), *and if* most of the power in those beams could be projected through the atmosphere, *and if* the atmosphere did not diffuse the beam too much so that the mirrors stationed at geosynchronous orbit (22,300 miles away) that caught such beams would not have to be outrageously large, *then* those geosynchronous mirrors *might well* be able to focus enough power onto "mission" (or "fighting") mirrors to overwhelm these "responsive" missiles.

This was faith multiplied by faith. First the panel assumed that the new lasers' internal mirrors could be made reflective enough not to be penetrated and destroyed by these very penetrating beams. Neither then nor since has any mirror ever stood up to a high concentration of visible laser or ultraviolet laser power for more than a fraction of a second. Then the panel had faith that the excimer lasers and linear-accelerator lasers could actually turn out megawatts of power. There were and are basic scientific unknowns about that. Then the panel assumed that by constantly (thousands of times per second) modifying the shape of the lasers' primary mirror in response to changing atmospheric conditions, it would be possible to ease the path of a stream of light through the atmosphere—literally to "take the twinkle out of the star"—so that little divergence and dispersion of energy would occur. This would be essential since the normal atmospheric "twinkle" if not corrected creates so much divergence as to make it necessary to make the geosynchronous relay mirrors "acres and acres" in size. Too much dispersion and the advantage of having a shorter wavelength would be overcome by having too little power left. Hence, "taking the twinkle out of massive laser beams was absolutely essential. But, like the rest of the panel's articles of faith, it was based on little but faith.

The panel's confidence in regard to nuclear-driven X-ray lasers was based on two underground nuclear tests, which may have shown that when the "short" X-rays of a nuclear detonation strike the crystalline molecular structure of certain heavy metals, these structures vibrate so as to emit "long" X-rays. But no one knew how to narrow these emissions into beams usable at long ranges. To this day no one has argued to this author that anyone knows how.

Neutral particle beams, the panel said, "require demonstration of the basic elements of high brightness sources, the first stages of acceleration and beam-direction sensing before scale-up to high energy is warranted." Therefore it recommended demonstrating in the laboratory the flexibility of components that might reduce the size and weight of the basic accelerators by roughly a factor of 5 while actually increasing the concentration of energized particles at long ranges by a factor of 1,000 over the largest current accelerators. The National Laboratories have been in the business of making and improving accelerators for over a generation. Not surprisingly, they made sure that if the SDI produced nothing else, it would give them some new accelerators.

No one looking at the panel's survey of "advanced" directed energy technology could have been surprised at its reluctance to order immediate "weaponization." But given that survey, many were surprised at the panel's optimism that weaponization might begin as soon as ten years thence. Also, all too few realized the most important fact about this optimism about the unknown: It was the flip-side of the panel's preemptive dismissal of any practical antimissile device whatever.

Conventional Weapons

Since everyone recognizes that a multilayer defense must include ground-based interceptor missiles, since the U.S. has approximately eighty Spartan and Sprint antiwarhead interceptor missiles "mothballed" in warehouses, and since no one contends that there is any secret about what it takes to build such interceptors, one might reasonably have supposed that the panel—which was charting a path to a ballistic missile defense—would recommend that the old interceptors be reactivated and new ones built. To rebuild the launch and test equipment for these missiles that was destroyed long ago would cost—but not like pushing forward the frontiers of science. But cost was not the point! In fact, the title of the panel's working group, "Conventional Weapons," precluded even considering the old interceptors because these carried nuclear weapons. The panel made it an article of dogma, not to be discussed, that only nonnuclear means would be used to defeat nuclear weapons. In the SDI's jargon, then, the term "conventional weapons" does not mean relatively old-fashioned things, but rather another reason to reject what we have today in favor of things that we may not have tomorrow.

Nor was the working group particularly impressed that the guidance systems of the early 1980s allow reasonable confidence of successful interception on the edges of the atmosphere with a conventional high explosive warhead. Rather, the panel was clearly interested in developing the technology to kill warheads without even conventional explosives simply by direct-impact (otherwise known as kinetic energy) kills. The Army's homing overlay experiment (HOE) program was already producing hardware to accomplish this at very high altitudes, that is, where there is well over a minute for the sensor to align its path with that of the warhead. The panel simply decided to push the technology applicable to the kinetic kill approach across the board. So, in this subfield, too, the peremptory rejection of nuclear, and even of large conventional, explosives disqualified on-the-shelf technology and made necessary an R&D program.

Nevertheless, on-the-shelf guidance technology was close to satisfying the hit-to-kill requirement for ground-based high endo-atmospheric interceptors even though there are only a few seconds for aligning the guidance systems. Of course, the HOE program had long since satisfied it for ground-based exo-atmospheric interceptors, and several Air Force missiles, the Phoenix, Sparrow, and Maverick have guidance systems useful for space-based interceptors. Hence the programs that flowed from the panel's recommendations separated efforts to develop technology applicable to each of the three kinds of weapons from the development of "test beds," that is, rockets, on which this technology might *or might not* be tested.

At no point in these "concept definition" programs would there be a weapon that someone might decide to deploy. Hence the "test bed" program for the high-endo defense interceptor (HEDI) was to validate the requirements for guidance, provide a means for testing the effects of countermeasures, and thus to evaluate the technological alternatives being developed in a parallel program. The HEDI program had already developed a guidance system that would have made unnecessary carrying a nuclear warhead. But the program had another objective: building a fast rocket. Because HEDI would fly at 18 thousand feet per second, three times faster than our fastest current homing missile, that program had the ambitious goal of finding a way for the missile's guidance to receive very precise radar and short-wave infrared energy through a plasma of air molecules created by the interceptor missile's own very great velocity. Without this unnecessary goal of ultra-high speed, the rest of the technology development would have been easy; with it, it would be hard.

The technology development for exo-atmospheric interception, however, had already gone a long way. A reasonable person might suggest that because a set of hardware (HOE) existed that was about to be tested against an ICBM warhead, that any program in this field prepare for the possibility that the test would be successful and prepare to mass produce the results. But no, the panel decided that the technology program in this field should stress investigation of possible countermeasures. The parallel exo-atmospheric test-bed program put off a functional technology demonstration until 1990 while it was stressed that mere performance in the tests should not determine whether the device to be tested (later named Eris) should be bought or not. This line of argument goes back directly to Robert McNamara's comments to Congress on Nike Zeus. There is an additional complication, however. As the HOE program became Eris, the range and capacity for distinguishing real warheads decreased, because the program managers assumed that the space surveillance and tracking system would come into existence by the time Eris was deployed. But SSTS turned out to be an overly ambitious project. Thus Eris, if and when it is deployed, will be less useful than it might have been had it been less "coordinated."

As for space-based interceptors, the panel justified limiting the program to mere technology development by declaring that the Air Force's existing antisatellite rocket (which no one denies could find and hit a ballistic missile booster far more easily than it can find and hit satellites) should be thought of not as a weapon but as a technical "baseline," a point of departure for an R&D program. The Air Force anti-satellite program's current "tomato can" guidance system weighs 15 kilograms and has a circular error probability of 1 to 2 meters, and, together with the rocket, costs $6 million per shot. The standard for the R&D program should be something that costs $200,000 per shot, weighs 1 to 2 kilograms, and has an accuracy of half a meter. No current devices such as the guidance systems of air-to-ground and air-to-air missiles (e.g., Maverick and Phoenix) that could probably fit the bill with little if any modification, need apply.

Indeed, nothing shows the spirit of the best and the brightest regarding these matters better than a request for proposal for a space-based interceptor that DARPA sent to the aerospace industry while the Fletcher Panel was sitting. DARPA wanted something that would hit not just any part of the missile but only the very tip. It was not content with the fact that millions of foot-pounds of energy applied to any part of the missile would splinter the whole, or with the fact that once the booster ceased to exist, the warhead would not reach its target. DARPA wanted to smash the tip. But it required that the tip be hit not just as the missile was on a normal ballistic trajectory but also in case the missile was tumbling. Never mind that the whole art of missilery consists of stabilizing for accuracy's sake, that no one has ever seen a tumbling missile, and that if such a thing ever came to be, it would not be a weapon. Cooper's DARPA wanted to make sure. In short, Boeing proposed a ten-year multimillion dollar R&D program that would produce a "miniature" vehicle weighing some 3,600 pounds. Of course the proposal went nowhere. But it served its purpose: to generate a daunting definition of a space-based KKV.

Logistics and the Future

The panel stressed—as well it should have—that for its systems requirements to be met, the U.S. would have to be able to put enormous amounts of equipment into orbit. But by 1983 the U.S. had made a total commitment to relying on the space shuttle for launching all civilian and military payloads into orbit. This was done in order to spread out the cost of the shuttle's development to all American civilian and military users of space. By 1983 the shuttle's manifest was booked for a decade ahead. It would seem that a decision to substantially expand the use of space would logically call for scrapping the United States' shuttle-based policy regarding access to space and making a new one. Specifically, the expansion of the need for launch services took away the only argument (and a flimsy one at that) that there ever had been for using the expensive wonder that is the shuttle for the mere task of lifting payloads. Now the shuttle would be needed for other tasks, tasks worthy of its capacity—assembling, refueling, and refurbishing weapons and sensors, changing modules, performing checkout procedures, etc. Now the nation's needs for space launchers, far in excess of the capacity of four shuttle orbiters, must clearly be met by building a fleet of the cheapest possible launchers with the leanest possible bureaucratic infrastructure.

This was obviously not a technical challenge. After all, the U.S. had gone to the moon fifteen years earlier, and had used a reliable series of heavy lift-launch vehicles to do so. The plans and tools for those vehicles were still there—although scattered in warehouses and museums. The expensive R&D had been done long ago. This at last was an unambiguously old-tech task—an approach to launching payloads inherently much less costly than the shuttle. Alas, the panel acted as if the old, proven, cheap, no research technology of the moon program did not exist, and made logistics, too, into an R&D project. The first part of it was to be the *identification* of brand-new technologies to be used in a brand-new logistical system. Then, *circa* 1990, after weighing alternative logistical architectures, would come the decision of which launch technologies to create. In other words, NASA's James Fletcher wanted to reinvent the wheel. As a result of this approach, while the United States had routinely lifted 150 tons at a time into orbit in the 1960s, in the 1980s, the U.S. would agonize over just the right way to put 100 tons in orbit by the turn of the century! Clearly, the America of the SDI program could not compete with the America of the 1960s—much less with the America that had won World War II.

Finally, the best and the brightests' simultaneous rejection of the practical, and their embrace of dalliance in the name of the fantastic, led to the recommendation that in order to protect U.S. space assets against the "responsive threat," something like a *million tons* of armoring material would be needed, and that it might be cheaper not to try to lift it all into orbit from the surface of the earth but rather, to go to the moon or even to the asteroid belt and mine and manufacture in space. As for weaponry, the panel pointed out that the most elegant solution to the missile problem lay in hitting the missiles with little antimatter particles (products of collisions in super accelerators), each of which would turn the matter it struck directly into energy. The formula $E=MC^2$ would surely guarantee a big bang. But no one need hold his breath for the time when we will be able to carry antimatter around like ammunition, put it into antimatter guns, and fire it.

That, of course, was the point. If ballistic missile defense was pursued according to the Fletcher Panel's approach, there would be deferral of the good in favor of the theoretically better without logical end—especially since the "responsive threat" is defined as "a reiterative process." In this context, the panel's recommendation that the program contain "near-term demonstrations," intended to show the public that "progress" was being made, was self-defeating. By stressing that these demonstrations should not be of any usable weapon or component of weapons, the panel's recommendation, intentionally or not, would give opponents of ballistic missile defense solid grounds on which to argue that the demonstrations are nothing but "sleazy stunts" contrived to get more money, but proving that the U.S. government is still far from being able to provide any protection whatever.

Thus did the Fletcher Panel construct a highly peculiar set of gold-plated definitions of what is required for ballistic missile defense that distills and puts into one place all the faults of modern American military R&D.

The October 1983 report of the Defense Technologies Study Team became the SDI program that was presented to Congress in February 1984 as part of the fiscal 1985 Pentagon budget. As far as the program is concerned, the parallel Future Security Strategy Study under Ikle's appointee Fred Hoffman, with its emphasis on protecting offensive missiles and U.S. forces in Europe in the relatively near term, might as well never have happened. The SDI program proposed spending $26 billion over five years, but delivering no protection in five years, or perhaps ever. By November 9, 1983 when Richard de Lauer testified before the House of Representatives, the message he delivered had already sunk into the Congress and the attentive public: Each of the SDI technologies presents a challenge "greater than that of the Manhattan Project" that invented the atom bomb. Even if each and every one succeeds, the task of putting them all together would be staggering. Finally, said deLauer, "You will be staggered by the cost."[6] Of course this was patent nonsense. The atom bomb involved demonstrating the basic relationship of energy to matter, and the project involved such enormous undertakings as gaseous diffusion of uranium isotopes. But deLauer's statements accurately reflected that the establishment viewed antimissile defense as something to be put off.

Why should anyone want to buy into a program thus conceived? Besides, the SDI was an obvious challenge to the ABM Treaty and to the United States' approach to dealing with the Soviet Union. But President Reagan presented it along with fulsome promises that the program would scrupulously respect the treaty, and with his own promise to share the fruits of the SDI technology with the Soviet Union. The American people were asked to pay plenty, with the assurance that they would receive no returns for at least a generation except for greater Soviet hostility. After enduring it all, they might still get nothing. In short, the SDI might or might not produce a revolution in weaponry, but for the foreseeable future it would produce costs and trouble.

The SDI program submitted to Congress was a reshuffling and

relabelling of preexisting programs. The total budget request, $1.7 billion, was not "new money," but rather roughly the amount that would have been requested for the sum of all of the programs had they not been labeled "SDI." The final appropriation, $1.4 billion, represented a cut somewhat larger than the sum of the cuts that the program would have sustained had they not been labeled "SDI." Hence from the beginning, a program pledged not to produce began to lose support. As time passed and the seeds of self-contradiction grew, it became clear that the program as formulated had never had a chance to run the three-stage course that the Fletcher Panel had sketched for it. One may speculate that this did not terribly upset the officials who had given the panel its charter.

The Fletcher Panel, however, should not bear the final responsibility for making SDI what it became. The panel only recommended; Caspar Weinberger and Ronald Reagan both appointed the panel and accepted its recommendations. They appointed and approved without knowing well enough (or perhaps caring enough) that the reason why the U.S. needed an antimissile defense at all is the very reason why it needs one *now*, not in the 21st century. But Reagan was not like John Kennedy when he made the decision to put a man on the moon in the 1960s. Reagan did not have it in him to answer the bureaucrats' caution by telling them that if they did not answer the nation's needs, he would find those who would. Reagan, instead, was content to see "his" bureaucrats redefine the United States' urgent need for antimissile defenses as an open question that only they themselves were qualified to answer—and that would not be answered on his watch.

6 / *The Empty Core*

SDI is now the very core of U.S. strategic policy.

—Caspar Weinberger, to the Congress.

The nightly news, the headlines, no less than the Department of Defense's annual posture statements, portray SDI as the foremost, indeed the central pillar of American strategic policy. Also, the SDI is surely the political showpiece of the Reagan administration's military policy. Candidate Ronald Reagan gladly accepted the challenge to make the 1984 election something of a referendum on the SDI. In October 1986, rather than endanger the SDI, President Reagan turned down the Soviet Union's offer of eliminating all offensive ballistic missiles from the face of the earth by 1996. Although the SDI program represents almost exactly one percent of the U.S. defense budget, it is the subject of more attacks by domestic and foreign opponents and of more defensive maneuvering on the part of the Reagan administration than the remaining 99 percent of the budget combined. In 1988, anyone who was asked On what do the hopes of American strategic planners rest? could give only one answer, namely, the SDI.

But in fact, the SDI, as formulated and pursued by the Reagan administration, cannot be an answer to anything, because it is itself an open question. Indeed the SDI program explicitly precludes an answer for decades. SDI cannot be the core of any serious policy because five years after March 23, 1983, the SDI has not provided the means to protect against even one solitary warhead, and contains no commitment—never mind plans—to do so, ever. Thus SDI cannot be the pillar of anything except illusion. Hence, while high U.S. officials and official documents explain convincingly that antimissile devices are essential if the U.S. is not to concede strategic superiority to the Soviet Union for the indefinite future, the hard fact is that the need cannot possibly be met by the SDI program's products: documents, speeches, experiments, expense vouchers, and favorable public opinion polls for the president. None of these things will stop missiles.

The primary reason why, notwithstanding its insubstantiality, the SDI is the very core of U.S. strategic policy is that the policy has no other core. Within the Pentagon, the White House, the Congress, and the think tanks, no one is propounding a set of military suggestions for dealing with the United States' strategic problems that competes with the option of building ballistic missile defenses. The fact that after March 23, 1983 the option of ballistic missile defense was reformulated as an open technical question has only obscured the reason why the option was chosen in the first place: there are no other attractive ones. Be it ever so hollow, the SDI is indeed inescapably, by default, the core of U.S. policy.

By the time Ronald Reagan met with the Joint Chiefs of Staff on February 11, 1983, the lack of options was clear and present. Reagan had been elected in 1980 by criticizing his predecessor's lack of plans for closing the "window of vulnerability," that is, the vulnerability of American missiles and other military forces to Soviet disarming "counterforce" strikes and the subsequent vulnerability of the U.S. population to threats by Soviet reserve forces.

This prospect had haunted the U.S. military since the 1960s. Avoiding it had been the prime mover behind the SALT I Treaty of 1972, which was supposed to prevent the emergence of counterforce missile forces in exchange for giving up plans to defend against missiles in flight. By the time President Carter took office, the existence of Soviet counterforce missiles and warheads many times the number that the U.S. had tried to forestall through SALT I was a foregone conclusion. But Carter's secretary of defense, Harold Brown, did have a plan for dealing with the Soviet counterforce problem. As Brown's military posture statements for fiscal 1980 and 1981 outlined, the U.S. would purchase 200 MX missiles with 10 warheads each and base them somewhat deceptively to give them a greater chance of surviving a Soviet first strike. Most of these 2,000 MX warheads would survive and be targeted to destroy the Soviet Union's reserve missile forces—the forces that the Soviet Union would be holding back to use to coerce a disarmed U.S. So, reasoned Brown, since the U.S. would have the intention and the ability to place at least one high-quality warhead on each Soviet reserve missile silo, the Soviets would realize that their strategy of disarm-and-coerce would not work. Hence the Soviets would be deterred. This is the program that candidate Reagan in 1980 depicted to the American public as wimpy.

But, once in office, President Reagan confided military matters to his secretary of defense, who in turn saw himself as the collector and presenter of the military service chiefs' programs. Weinberger's desire to please as many of the services' constituencies as possible simply made impossible even the semblance of an attempt to improve on Harold Brown's plan. At the urging of the dominant wing of the Air Force, Weinberger committed the U.S. to buying 100 B-1 bombers and to spending even more billions on development of the Stealth bomber than had Brown. In addition, he committed the U.S. to funding an ambitious improvement in the Air Force's command, control, and communications that had been started by Brown. If Weinberger had then also merely tried to maintain Brown's commitment to 200 deceptively based MXs— much less had he tried to increase their number or improve their survivability—he would have had to devote to the Air Force a disproportionately large share of the defense budget. This was, arguably, a wise option. But Weinberger did not seriously consider it, not because he disliked it on its merits but because taking it would have forced cutbacks in the Navy's plans for 600 ships and in the Army's drive for better equipment. Had he wanted to fund all these projects while maintaining or improving Harold Brown's strategic plan, he could have asked for much more money for the Pentagon. As it happened, he felt he could not ask for more. But the fact that his resources were limited did not relieve him from the responsibility of formulating some reasonable plan for using the money he had. If he did not think that such a plan was possible, he should have declared his inability to do his job under a given set of financial constraints and resigned. But Weinberger did none of those things, because he apparently saw his responsibility as adjusting the services' competing claims rather than making hard decisions about how to fight wars.

Such hard decisions are what strategy is all about. Whatever the substance of his final decision, the decision maker must choose an instrument and be able to explain to himself and others just how he proposes to use that instrument to actually achieve his goal. Agree with him or not, Harold Brown had such an explanation for his proposed 200 MXs. But Caspar Weinberger did not have a plausible argument for his 100 B-1s and his 100 MXs (later he and Ronald Reagan meekly agreed with Senator Nunn to limit MX to a maximum of fifty in fixed, vulnerable silos). The sole strategic argument the Reagan administration put forth for cutting the MX force from 200 to 100 was that the smaller number would not be so threatening to the Soviet Union! Weinberger did not argue that Brown's strategic objective was wrong, because he operated from bureaucratic imperative rather than from strategic reasoning. His posture statements for fiscal years 1982–1984 simply stopped describing a concrete military strategy. Rather, they concentrated on touting, on the one hand, "the Soviet threat" and, on the other hand, "improvements" and "modernizations" in U.S. forces that did not specifically overcome the Soviet threat. Critics rightly asked to what end American forces were being improved. What could they do for the American people *after* they were improved that they could not do before?[1] Weinberger's Pentagon gave no answer and regarded the question as impudent.

Since the only real changes that the Reagan–Weinberger "strategic modernization plan" of October 1, 1981 proposed over the Carter–Brown plan was the substitution of 100 B-1s for 100 MXs (the other elements, among other things the Trident II submarine-launched missile and the small ICBM by 1992, etc., had been part of previous programs) that plan hardly excited popular support. By early 1982, the Democratic Party, looking for issues for the midterm elections, and no longer bound to support the policies of its "own" at the Pentagon, violently attacked Reagan as a warmonger, even as the Soviet Union's hoary old Communist fronts, like the U.S. Peace Council and a broad spectrum of leftist organizations, pushed the same theme under the banner of a "nuclear freeze." By the fall of 1982, Reagan had become convinced that he was so bereft of support for *maintenance,* much less modernization, of the United States' strategic forces that he felt compelled to purchase some support from the foreign and defense policy establishment by appointing a bipartisan commission headed by former National Security Adviser Brent Scowcroft, and including Harold Brown.

Months before the Scowcroft Commission released its report in April 1983, however, it had become clear that the commission would speak not in the language of military strategy but in a way that would put even more pressure on the Reagan administration to follow the arms control policies of the previous decades. Hence the commission would support MX merely as an adjunct to arms control. As it happened, the brief report mentioned arms control sixty-two times without ever mentioning how the MX might be used to save American lives. Not much was needed to grasp that this approach to strategic forces would mean the end of major strategic force improvement. Whether or not the Reagan administration saw this event as a military problem, it surely saw the report's confirmation of its failure to do anything about "the window of vulnerability" as a blow to its own political standing. After all if the Scowcroft report was correct—and Reagan was committed in advance to accepting it—Reagan's own campaign against Jimmy Carter's and Harold Brown's approach to the MX and arms control had been a dangerous fraud on the American people.

Hence, by early 1983 any American official looking for a fruitful way of employing U.S. strategic forces had few choices. Returning to the Carter–Brown strategy was not among them. By 1983 the Soviet Union's strategic rocket forces were obviously on the edge of deploying road-mobile and rail-mobile ICBMS. Clearly, within a few years, any Soviet ICBM that had not been used in a first strike would not be in locations known by U.S. satellites. Those satellites had been conceived in the '60s and perfected in the '70s in the context of two ruling assumptions. First, the world would be characterized not by Soviet attempts to prepare to fight and win wars but by arms control; hence, the satellites' primary task would be to monitor arms control agreements. Second, the Soviets' ICBMs would be few, immobile, and silo-launched. Hence the satellites were made to take relatively few high-quality pictures of relatively small places already known to be interesting, rather than to follow moving targets around the vastness of Eurasia. By 1983, anyone who looked had to conclude that in order to revive Harold Brown's strategy for using nuclear weapons, the U.S. would have to reverse the intellectual assumptions of a generation and develop and procure a whole new generation of intelligence satellites. This was not about to happen, least of all given an administration that was adverse to criticizing the intelligence bureaucracy.

How about trying to build a mirror image of the Soviet force, and thereby threaten the Soviet Union with a counterforce duel? Given the inefficiency of the American system for procuring strategic weapons, it was literally unthinkable to try to reach the Soviet figure of 6,000 counterforce warheads. Even 200 MXs with 2,000 counterforce warheads had already proved too expensive for the Reagan administration.

What then about revamping MAD, the policy of mutual assured destruction? Surely the Reagan administration's penchant for letting budgets drive policy tempted it—as McNamara and Richard Nixon's Secretary of Defense Melvin Laird had been tempted—to designate a certain number of Soviet targets, maintain the capability of destroying them, and declare this sufficient for deterrence.

After all, the fuzzy reassuring term "sufficiency" comes from the Nixon administration in the era of SALT I. But no. Since 1974, under Secretaries of Defense Schlesinger, Rumsfeld, and Brown the U.S. government had made an intellectual "long march" away from that way of thinking. The Reagan administration was neither willing nor able to reverse it. Besides, one of the principal "driving factors" of the strategic situation in the 1980s is precisely the Soviet Union's increasing ability to use its own counterforce missiles to limit more and more the number of Soviet targets that *we* could count on hitting in retaliation. Moreover the Soviet antimissile defense system was expanding.

So, even if we very much wanted to engage in MAD, by 1983 it was clear that Soviet offensive and defensive forces would soon be able to reduce very drastically the number of arriving U.S. warheads and make it impossible for the U.S. to do truly devastating damage. If we wanted to make sure that just a few warheads would produce huge casualties, we would have to load them not with nuclear weapons but with bioengineered germs of supercontagious, incurable diseases. Naturally, carrying out such a retaliatory strike would be absurd. So, if we really wanted our preparations for such a monstrous event to have a deterrent effect we would have to institute a kind of "launch on warning" that could not be interfered with by human reason in order to convince the Soviets that the strike would take place despite its idiocy. Thus the option to be serious about MAD in the 1980s and 1990s was literally unthinkable.

Thus, in 1983, President Reagan had two choices. He could continue trying to sell the "strategic modernization program" of October 1981, but admit that the Soviet Union's effective military superiority was going to continue to grow unchecked. Nevertheless, the opposition to his program would continue to call him a warmonger, and its power was growing. Ironically, he would be suffering slings and arrows for the sake of programs that left him open to the charge of having failed to redeem his campaign promises. That is, if he stayed the course he would be open to a double-barrelled charge of militarist evil *and* of military incompetence. In 1983, turning into a pacifist was not an option. The only other option was to try to reverse the situation through absolutely the only means of doing so: an American ballistic missile defense. The president chose to talk about defense on March 23, 1983.

In political terms Reagan was a smashing success. Overnight, he dispossessed the "nuclear freeze" movement of the moral high ground in the strategic arms debate. Overnight, the greater promise of safety for the American people erased the fact that Reagan had not tried (or if he had, he had failed) to keep his lesser promise to close the "window of vulnerability" with strategic forces more muscular and better conceived than Carter's and Brown's. Overnight, Reagan laid claim to restoring America to military preeminence. Yet he did so arguably as a peacemaker by proposing weapons incapable of killing human beings.

The political relief, however, was brief. By November of 1983, Reagan's Undersecretary of Defense for Research and Engineering Richard de Lauer was telling the Congress that the SDI was a staggeringly expensive pipe dream about the next century. Moreover, almost instantly the Soviet Union, its sympathizers, and all of the "progressive" organizations influenced by them; and consequently every "progressive" organization in the world began to beat out the theme: the SDI is the chief danger to world peace. Thus, the Reagan administration was soon back on the defensive. To its old problems—the lack of credible policy for dealing with Soviet strategic forces in war—it had added a new one, defending a program that was obviously expensive, that obviously protected no one, that substantial numbers of people said was a danger to world peace, *and* a program that on its face contradicted a treaty whose purpose is antithetical to defense but that the administration was committed to publicly praising, because it is the jewel and keystone of the arms control process. In other words, by adopting the SDI as it did, the Reagan administration put itself in the uncomfortable position of contradicting itself, and therefore of discrediting itself.

The core of the administration's policy problem is that all of the arguments that it makes in favor of the SDI are willy-nilly arguments for the U.S. having antimissile weapons ready for use. Inevitably, such arguments are discredited by the administration's obviously sincere insistence that it is not interested in acquiring such weapons, and that it is not preparing to acquire them. Moreover, the direct clash of two sincere and deeply felt courses of action leads logically to the suspicion that the administration *cannot* be sincere about either one, and is therefore engaging in some kind of deception. Let us look at some of these arguments.

One of the administration's staple arguments for the SDI is the existence of a Soviet antimissile defense program. For example, on March 8, 1984, the administration's first witness before the Senate Armed Services Committee's first hearing on the SDI program was the CIA's Lawrence Gershwin, national intelligence officer for Soviet strategic forces. In a forty-minute, top-secret briefing, Gershwin explained the basics. Here is a sanitized abstract.[2]

The ABM system around Moscow is a potent thing, whose high-altitude interceptors can knock down warheads that pass over the Moscow area on their way to a broad swath of the country as well as the warheads coming into Moscow itself. The high acceleration interceptors near Moscow may be as reloadable as semi-automatic rifles. The Moscow system, were it alone, could be overwhelmed—though at high cost. But the Moscow system is the tip of the iceberg. It is the training ground for what looks like a larger, nationwide system. The USSR is ringed by six [since then the total has risen to *nine*] large Pechora class phased-array radars. These are bigger, more powerful, and more capable than our best ABM radars ever were and better suited to ABM work than anything the U.S. has built. They are the indispensable battle-management network of a nationwide antimissile system. The other components of that system, smaller radars, as well as interceptors are all in full production. Since all are small enough to be moved by trucks, we do not know how many the Soviets have produced, or where they are. If the Soviets were producing these components seriously, and were storing them with a view to deployment, only a few months would pass between the time when the U.S. could notice that open deployment had started and the full operational capability of a very serious nationwide ABM system.

Then Gershwin talked about how the Soviet SA-12 surface-to-air missile system has effectively blurred the distinction between an antiaircraft interception and an antiwarhead interceptor. Each unit of the SA-12 consists of a truck that carries a state-of-the-art small phased-array radar able to see incoming warheads some 200 miles away and some fifty miles up, a truck that carries the generator to supply the radar's power, and one or more trucks carrying the interceptor missiles themselves. If the SA-12 radar is told where to point by one of the larger battle-management radars, or if it is simply guarding a corridor likely to be used by attacking American missiles, an individual SA-12 unit can probably launch soon enough to intercept a handful of attacking warheads at altitudes of between ten and twenty miles, and some forty to eighty miles from the target.

Each SA-12 unit's coverage is geographically small—say a radius of 50 kilometers—and the coverage can be saturated. But the existence of many hundreds of mobile SA-12 units would pose enormous problems for the U.S. That is because, normally, the number of warheads assigned to any one target is very small. However, any target that might be defended by a single SA-12 unit would have to be assigned many warheads to provide a good chance of penetration. Assigning a high number to any target would drastically cut down by a factor of perhaps 5 the number of targets the U.S. could threaten. But since the U.S. could not know *where* the SA 12s would be, or how heavily they would be concentrated, the U.S. might have to assume that certain targets would be protected by several units of SA-12s. Hence, the existence of the SA-12 alone, never mind any nationwide ABM system, would press U.S. targeting personnel to leave much of the Soviet target base untouched, in order to really concentrate their fire.

Then, of course, Gershwin discussed the Soviet Union's work in the field of directed-energy weapons. Even the U.S. government's darkest drawers do not contain a full account of what the Soviets are doing in this field. It is clear, however, that the Soviet directed-energy warfare program, like other Soviet military programs, and most unlike our own, is in the process of turning out not just technology, but primarily weapons. No American really knows what these weapons will or won't be able to do. But U.S. intelligence has some idea of what they are. The intelligence community has long expected a Soviet high-energy laser device in space during the 1980s.[3]

The intelligence community's official explanation of that expected Soviet device is that it will be an antisatellite weapon. But it is very clear to anyone who knows anything about laser weapons that, in all respects but one—power—it is inherently more difficult to build an antisatellite laser than it is to build an antimissile laser. So, certainly the Soviet Union's near-term laser device will have some—but no one can know how much—"residual" antimissile capacity. Since Soviet weapons come along in an evolutionary fashion, the Soviet Union's space-based laser weapons will become better and better as the 1990s draw to a close. At any rate, the Soviet directed-energy weapons program is "three to five times" larger than the American program and, unlike the American program, is oriented to production as well as to research.

Gershwin finished with a summary evaluation: On balance, taking account of our advantages and theirs, the Soviet Union is really ten years ahead of the United States in antimissile weapons.

Then Robert Cooper and Undersecretary of Defense for Policy Fred Ikle presented the budget request for the SDI: $26 billion over five to seven years for research. Then, if the research is judged successful, another, more expensive development program would be required before a decision were made on whether or not to deploy, and on what to deploy.

The Armed Services Committee, liberals and conservatives, Republicans and Democrats, unanimously thought this a silly idea—

though for different reasons. All seemed to agree that because there is nothing in the SDI program that would produce anything like what the Soviets are producing, the Soviet Union's antimissile program cannot be a logical reason for SDI. All agreed that if, indeed, the Soviet Union is ten years ahead of us in the antimissile field, after ten years of our SDI program they are sure to be precisely twenty years ahead. But they differed on whether or not this was something to be worried about. Some thought that if, indeed, it is important to have antimissile weapons, and if the Soviets, as it seemed, are in the process of acquiring them, then the U.S. should also acquire them. But in that case, they argued, the SDI program as presented makes no sense.

Others, were willing to concede that the Soviets were ten years ahead, but they believed that, in the nuclear age, antimissile weapons can never really affect the balance of mutual deterrence. Hence they concluded that the Soviets are ten years ahead in a wild goose chase, that they are wasting their money, and that the U.S. should not join them. Besides, they argued, those who crafted the American SDI program obviously do not really think that the Soviets are on to something important, because, if they did, they would have proposed building antimissile weapons. Since the president is not proposing to follow the Soviets' example and build antimissile weapons, he must not take Soviet activities seriously. Hence, his worried talk about the Soviet Union's activities in this field must be as an excuse to spend money for a politically showy program.

The senators were telling the Reagan administration that its attempts to sell the SDI on the basis of the Soviet antimissile program are self-contradictory and self-discrediting. Nevertheless, the Soviet program is a staple of Reagan rhetoric. "The Soviet Union is the only country in the world with a functioning ABM system," President Reagan is fond of reminding his audiences. In innumerable forums, administration spokesmen have followed the president and delivered approximations of Gershhwin's opening shot to the Senate. And innumerable times, those presentations have been met with the observation that if the president and his Pentagon really and seriously thought that the Soviet Union was doing something militarily important, they would be proposing to do similar things—or at least would be proposing to acquire *some* antimissile capacity. But since the president and the Pentagon are doing no such thing, it must mean that they really believe that the Soviet preparations are meaningless, that they can be easily overcome, and that the administration's talk is merely insincere salesmanship in the service of some sort of partisan game-playing.

The Reagan administration's charges that the Soviets have violated the ABM treaty are made of the same stuff. Beginning with its report to Congress of January 1984, and innumerable times since, the Reagan administration has said that the Soviet Union has built a large Pechora class radar near Knasnoyarsk in direct violation of the ABM treaty. Opponents of the administration (e.g. the Stanford arms control center) counter that although the radar regrettably is a technical violation, it is militarily insignificant in itself. The Reagan administration has routinely replied that Krasnoyarsk is only one of nine such radars, and has listed all the other things that the Soviets have done in violation, circumvention, as well as within the bounds of the ABM treaty to produce antimissile devices. Perhaps the most comprehensive argument of this kind was the Arms Control and Disarmament Agency's report of February 1986. But, from all these facts, the Reagan administration's report concluded only that "the Soviet Union *may be* preparing" (emphasis mine) an antimissile defense of its territory.

In other words, having charged that the Soviet Union has violated the *letter* of the ABM treaty the Reagan administration solemnly declared that it had no idea why it has done so, and that, for practical purposes of U.S. force planning and of U.S. politics, we must continue to give equal value to the possibility that the Soviet Union really does mean to abide by the *purpose* of the treaty. This, however, shocks common sense.

Any reasonable person listening to this argument naturally senses that the only important question involves not technicalities but strategic intentions. The plain intent of the ABM treaty is that both sides shall remain perpetually vulnerable to ballistic missiles. Now, does the Soviet Union, in the U.S. government's view, share that intention, or is it—by hook and crook—trying to protect itself against ballistic missiles as best it can? That is the question. The Reagan administration's recitation of facts about Soviet antimissile activities and violations of the ABM treaty leads so ineluctably to the conclusion that the Soviet Union *is* defending itself—and effectively to boot—that any reasonable person is led to wonder why the administration has repeatedly stepped back from saying so plainly. It is anything but clear what else the U.S. government would have to know before making such a judgment. The administration's reticence in the face of its own evidence cannot be explained in terms of the evidence itself. Of course it can be explained easily in terms of the Reagan administration's incompetent indecisiveness. But most of the public, who are not aware of the situation, can be excused for concluding that the administration never did believe that the Soviets were hostile to the spirit of the ABM treaty, but was making mountains out of molehills for its own partisan purposes.

In fact, the Reagan administration effectively began to discard its own charges of Soviet ABM treaty violations in the very act of making them. It is important to remember that the Reagan administration, could not *and did not* bring itself to charging the Soviet Union with violating the ABM Treaty or any other arms control agreement. The data regarding Soviet violations was well known within the administration. But those who wanted to formally charge "violation" were always overruled. The administration prepared its first "violations report" for release in January 1984 *only* pursuant to a legislative requirement enacted by the Congress the previous year. Once the law was passed, the Reagan administration had no choice but to say either that certain Soviet activities are violations or that they are not. In the interagency working group that hammered out the report, the State Department and the Joint Chiefs of Staff succeeded in limiting the number of declared violations to the most undeniable seven. Some thirty other sets of facts were relegated to the category of "possible or probable." Yet it is essential to note that no one on the working group had the authority to discuss the question of the Soviet Union's *intention* with regard to the *purpose* of any treaty. Much less did representatives to the interagency group have clearance from their own cabinet secretaries to raise the issue of what should be *done* about the violations.

Indeed, as the report reached Capitol Hill so did loud and clear signals from the secretary of defense that under no circumstances should the violations be made the occasion for raising questions about the appropriate allocation of funds in the defense budget. So, the administration's spokesman on the hill echoed Senator John Tower: "We've got a budget to get through." In other words, the Reagan administration, rhetoric aside, never did take Soviet violations seriously.

Now, it is clear to everyone who deals with defense matters that the United States' military budgets have been constructed on the assumption that the Soviets would abide by the arms control treaties they have signed. Logically, the discovery that the budget's very basis had been miscalculated would demand a reordering of priorities. Nevertheless, whenever anyone from Capitol Hill or the press called the White House to ask what might be the appropriate response to the violations that the President had formally charged, the response they received was: "Steady as she goes." U.S. defense budgets *by definition* take all possible contingencies into account. In other words, the Reagan administration never considered the Soviet Union's behavior with regard to the ABM treaty serious enough to warrant questioning the complex set of interservice and intraservice budgeting by which the Pentagon is ruled.

Just as important, the administration did not take the violations seriously enough either to try to compel, *or even to consider the question of how one might compel,* the Soviet Union to live up to the ABM treaty. Instead, it further wrapped itself in knots over how *the U.S.* should observe the *letter* of the treaty but never allowed any of its officials to publicly question whether the *spirit* of the treaty—that is, there shall be no defense—is a good thing or not. Indeed President Reagan has gone out of his way to speak well of the treaty, calling for reestablishing its "integrity." He has even offered to give up for ten years the United States' right, clearly established in the treaty, to withdraw from it on six months' notice.

Given all of this, reasonable people can be forgiven for not having taken seriously Ronald Reagan's protestations about how "seriously" he views Soviet violations of the ABM treaty and about how "worrisome" the Soviet Union's defensive buildup is.

What then, is the Reagan administration's strategic policy? There is none—either good, bad, or indifferent. There is certainly much rhetoric about strategic matters, and in that rhetoric references to the SDI are paramount. But even in the realm of rhetoric, the Reagan administration is not persuasive, because despite all of its passionate hints that the United States is in a grave strategic predicament, it cannot bring itself to admit that this predicament is grave enough to warrant actually forcing the military chiefs to form some plan, *any* plan to get out of it. During its first years, the Reagan administration was immobilized by a kind of reflexive, worshipful attitude toward senior military leaders. In its later years, whatever Secretary Weinberger might have learned about the generals' inadequacies, the administration has felt increasingly constrained to justify its own record of adherence to strategic nonplanning. Especially in the later years, for the Reagan administration to discuss the United States' strategic predicament meant to discuss its own failure. Hence the Reagan administration's rhetoric on strategic problems has been more abstract than any of its predecessors'.

Every year the secretary of defense submits a budget request to the Congress that customarily contains the administration's best thinking on the subject. These are the documents in which in the 1960s Robert McNamara proudly explained the policy of mutual assured destruction, in which during the early 1970s James Schlesinger confidently explained how the United States' possession of "limited (non-MAD) nuclear options" enhanced the deterrent effect of the United States' (then) invulnerable MAD forces, and in which, during the late 1970s, Harold Brown explained how the increasingly vulnerable American missile forces could still deter superior Soviet power by the addition of 200 Mxs targeted against Soviet reserves. But in the "posture statements" for fiscal 1987 and 1988, Ronald Reagan's Caspar Weinberger could not bring himself to describe any connection between strategic doctrine and planned hardware. Indeed, the gap between the two was so wide that Weinberger's strategic talk was entirely abstract. Thus, Weinberger's posture statements come close to saying that the U.S. is in dire strategic straits, that antimissile defense is the only way out, and that the Soviet approach to strategic weaponry is better than the approach that the U.S. has followed for many years. But the statements do not cross the threshold, nor do they put forth any sort of plan. Accordingly, they leave the reader with the sense that their author was not exercising the responsibility of his office.

The 1987 document[4] admits that the conceptual tools that have ruled and continue to rule the Pentagon's approach to strategic policy, namely "nuclear deterrence, extended deterrence, escalation control, strategic stability, offense dominance, flexible response, counterinsurgency, limited war, and escalation ladders" are now obsolete. They had been developed during the 1950s to deal with a world characterized by a decisive American nuclear advantage. But, says the document, that era has vanished. Today the U.S. is struggling to "ensure parity in military power." The author does not say what the Soviet Union could *do* for itself with its sharply increased forces. That would oblige him to say something about how, concretely, the U.S. would stop the Soviets from doing it. Since the U.S. has no plans for stopping them, this nakedness would be embarrassing. But the author of the 1987 posture statement removes the next-to-last garment when he says that while our forces may appear to be the equivalent of Soviet power, "they are not equivalent in their capabilities." The author leaves it at that, and does not dare describe the United States' predicament. But, says this posture statement, because things are bad and getting worse, and, by implication, nothing at hand will make them any better, we are compelled to "reach out for new ideas," the boldest of which is the SDI. The author goes on to argue that deterrence by threat of attack on civilians is incredible and obsolete.[5]

Weinberger goes on to chide the Congress for having approved only 74 percent of the previous year's request for the SDI. But he cannot say how much better off the American people would have been had the Congress approved 100 percent of the plan, or any strategic plan. Again the author chides the Soviet Union for never having accepted "mutual assured vulnerability" and for having built up armed forces that "reduce the vulnerability of their country." But does the author say that the Soviet Union did something useful for itself or that it wasted its money? Did it do something morally right, or did it do something morally wrong? Did it do something the U.S. should have done, or something the U.S. should be glad it did not do? The document does not say. It is never clear whether Weinberger is saying that the U.S. should deal with the existence of this Soviet approach to strategic weaponry by emulating it or by doing something else. The only thing that is clear from the U.S. Secretary of Defense's posture statement for FY 1987 is that while there is a Soviet plan for surviving, fighting, and winning a major war, there is no U.S. plan. Nor is it clear why there is not.

This confusion is even more obvious in the posture statement for fiscal 1988.[6] It describes in even greater detail the mixture of offensive and defensive forces on which the Soviets count to limit damage to their country in case of war. But then it says, "We may not agree with the assumptions on which the Soviet strategy is founded. . . . but, we must pay attention to it" (i.e. the Soviet strategy). But what does paying attention to the Soviet strategy's existence mean? It means granting the Pentagon's budget requests. But why? Because, although *"We* don't believe in it. . . ." the Soviets do.

At this point the reader is baffled. Did not the posture statement's rhetoric about SDI just imply that *we* would try to limit damage to *our* country and to our allies in case of war? So it did. But if that is so, then, it must be that we fully share the practical assumptions of Soviet military strategy (apart from aggressive intention). But if we really shared those assumptions, then why are our offensive and defensive programs so very different from those of the Soviet Union? Specifically, why is the U.S. not building any antimissile devices? The Reagan administration's posture statements avoid dealing with such questions by pounding away at the truism that we do not have to match the Soviets "weapon for weapon." But the reader is compelled to ask, again and again, "If you don't plan to do the job *this* way, then how *are* you planning to do it? If you don't believe in the Soviet strategy of damage limitation through offensive counterforce plus strategic defense, and you don't believe in Harold Brown's counterforce strikes on strategic missile reserves, and you don't believe in MAD, what do you believe in? What forces are you buying with our money, and what would you do with them?"

The Reagan–Weinberger posture statements say that American strategic weapons are targeted to do unacceptable damage to the things that the Soviet leadership cares about most, and lead one to believe that these are Soviet military forces, the Soviet leaders' own lives, and key structures dear to the Communist party. Thus the Reagan–Weinberger posture statements seem to express beliefs a little like Harold Brown's and a lot like McNamara's. That is, there is a finite, fixed set of objects the threatened destruction of which will deter the Soviets. But unlike their predecessors, they contain no numbers arguing that U.S. forces might, thus-and-so, reasonably achieve the goals set for them. These posture statements mark a failure to come to grips with the chief problem by giving the impression that U.S. forces are growing into radically new capabilities that are at once secret, and highly effective. But of course these forces do not exist, and the U.S. has made no decision to procure them.

At the core of Ronald Reagan's strategic policy, then, is resolute indecision. It seems that at the outset of his presidency Ronald Reagan simply decided to allow the various parts of his national security bureaucracy to pursue their own departmental or personal ends, and to draw political benefit from all of them. There is a constituency in the bureaucracy that favors arms control. Hence, Ronald Reagan speaks well of arms control, and furthers the arms control process. But there is a constituency in the country demanding that he speak up about Soviet violations. Since this constituency is not seriously represented in the bureaucracy, Reagan could satisfy it with rhetoric while at the same time satisfying the arms control constituencies with both words *and* deeds. There are many constituencies for ongoing military programs, and Reagan speaks much of the need to spend a great deal on the military and indeed has allowed the various military constituencies free rein to share the defense dollar as best they could. But the constituency for antimissile defense exists only in the country—not in the bureaucracy. Hence Reagan has spoken much about the SDI but has never tried to force antimissile defense—*or any other strategy*—on the various military constituencies. These constituencies, in turn, divided as they may be by their desire to nuzzle further into the budgetary trough, are united in their opposition to the one thing that would upset their daily lives—a serious American strategic plan, whether based on antimissile defense or on anything else. That is why Ronald Reagan, faithfully reflecting his bureaucracy, has gone out of his way to crush any and all efforts to fill the empty void that is the core of American strategic policy.

In 1984, for example, as the Republican national convention was meeting in Dallas to draw up the platform on which Ronald Reagan would run for reelection, Reagan's national security advisor, Bud MacFarlane, stationed his deputy, Donald Fortier, in Dallas to make sure that the Republican party's platform would not call for actually building an antimissile device. In fact, during the months prior to the convention, the drafting committee had come up with precisely such a call. This commitment by the way, was so strong that it deliberately used the phrase "as soon as possible" twice in the same sentence! At the convention, Senator John Warner, speaking as he said with the authority of the president, the secretary of defense, and "this nation's senior military leaders" told the platform committee that a commitment to antimissile defense was at best premature and certainly subversive of the nation's military structure. His impassioned speech asked any delegates who might have been swayed by the messages that Senator Wallop and Congressmen Kemp and Courter had sent them to consult with the real expert—the president's man, Fortier—and to vote against the platform plank's commitment to build antimissile devices.

Despite all that, the plank passed overwhelmingly. Late that evening, however, in a move that was as telling as it was unusual, President Ronald Reagan called Congresswoman Marjorie Holt (R-Md.), cochair of the platform committee, to ask, as a personal favor, that she delete the platform's commitment to actually building antimissile devices. Mrs. Holt, in her familiar gentle-but-firm grandmotherly style, told the president that the favor was not hers to give, but that perhaps the committee, as a personal favor to the president, would agree to change one word of its statement on antimissile defense from "build" to "achieve."

Nor was this an isolated instance of Reagan's personal intervention to head off antimissile devices. In 1985 and 1986 Ronald Reagan intervened personally to defeat Senate amendments sponsored by Senators Pete Wilson (R-Calif.), Don Quayle (R-Ind.), and Malcolm Wallop to reserve one-third of the SDI budget for actual development of actual antimissile devices. Finally, in January 1987, Ronald Reagan explicitly stated that, in the two years remaining in his term as president he would not make any decision about development. In effect, he had decided to reaffirm the status quo. There would be no missile defense on his watch.

Obviously, the "best and the brightest's" definition of the SDI turned out to have suited Ronald Reagan very well. It provided him a way of appearing forceful, peaceful, and forward-looking at the same time but did not require him to fight any constituency within the U.S. government or in the country. Even to the devotés of arms control, Reagan presented the SDI as something that would help them attain their favorite goals. And indeed, the SDI could be all things to all men—unless and until it actually set about turning out weapons. That would be the time for uncomfortable choices about strategy, budgets, and arms control. But that would be someone else's watch.

If we were to judge Ronald Reagan's strategic policy on the scale of British history, we would not compare it to Winston Churchill's or even to Neville Chamberlain's. These men made their choices and lived with them. We should rather compare the policy to that of Conservative Stanley Baldwin who, in Churchill's words, delivered up the mid-1930s for the locusts to eat.

7 / *The Menu*

The slothful man roasteth not that which he took in hunting but the substance of the diligent man is precious.

—Proverbs

Conventional wisdom has it that technology, rather than any possible failure in the judgment of U.S. officials, is responsible for the emptiness at the heart of U.S. policy. Both those in charge of the SDI and most of their opponents agree that the question facing U.S. policy makers in the 1980s is whether or not to have faith in the technology of the year 2000. Both agree that it would be somehow inappropriate for U.S. policy-making to consider what to do with the technology at hand. Yet common sense counsels that what to do with what we have today this is the only real choice—ever. Conventional wisdom is divided on whether the "stuff in the labs" is or is not terrific enough to overcome what many consider to be the "absolute" character of nuclear weapons. However, both proponents of the SDI and their opponents explicitly agree to judge the worthiness of future defensive technology against a standard of offensive proficiency that is constantly redefined to be "responsive" to defensive measures. In other words, regardless of their different motivations, both those in charge of the SDI and their opponents agree that the U.S. has no good strategic options at the present time—a present that stretches out indefinitely.

Caspar Weinberger most succinctly stated this position when he parried the suggestion that the U.S. use "off the shelf technology" for BMD: "There is nothing on the shelf."[1] Naturally, no one, especially someone who touts the Soviet Union's antimissile program, can mean such a statement literally, any more than teenage girls mean it literally when they look into their closets and cry, "I have nothing to wear"! Yet common sense counsels that to get at the truth of the situation, it is as wise to inspect Caspar Weinberger's shelves as it is to examine the closets of the complaining adolescents. So let us look at those shelves, and see what technology we have, what it would do against ballistic missiles, how long it would take to turn the technology into weapons, and how much it would cost to do so. In other words we are going to answer the question: What can we do for ourselves? We will start with the top shelf, where, figuratively, are the tools useful for boost-phase defense.

Boost Phase

Everyone agrees that it is most advantageous for the defense to destroy a ballistic missile as its engines are pushing it beyond the atmosphere and into its trajectory. A missile destroyed in boost phase is destroyed regardless of where it is headed. The missile destroyed in boost phase might as easily have been headed for the Bremerton submarine piers, or for NATO headquarters near Brussels, or might have been a missile whose malfunctioning guidance would have sent it to Quebec or New York! Hence to destroy it is an act of *area defense,* not to say of global defense. Each missile destroyed in boost phase means that no defensive station on the ground anywhere in the world need worry about it. Any missile destroyed in boost phase also means *leverage* for the defense, because the missile never gets a chance to deploy its three to fourteen warheads and possibly its dozens of decoys. Of course, midcourse and terminal defenses function better the fewer warheads and decoys they must face. Hence boost-phase defenses perform an important *thinning* function. Finally, boost-phase kills are most important strategically because they are inherently *indiscriminate.* That means that someone planning an attack that must pass through even rudimentary boost-phase defenses likely to take only a small toll of missiles cannot know *which* missiles he will lose. Thus, even if the offensive planner expects the toll to be small, he must take into account the statistical possibility that the toll will be disproportionately concentrated on the missiles he is sending to destroy "must" targets. He must disproportionately increase the number of missiles and warheads devoted to "must" targets to make up for the uncertainty. As the expected effectiveness of a boost-phase defensive system rises, and as the stock of offensive warheads would have to be increased geometrically, the attack planner quickly ceases to be able to count on success.

Everyone also agrees that, during boost phase, missiles are more visible than at any other time during their trajectory, due to the emission of plumes of exhaust gases that reach temperatures of 2300°C. No one disputes that decoying such things is infinitely more difficult than decoying the inert, cold, 4-foot-long conical bodies of warheads. Big missiles can't be decoyed with small rockets of equal acceleration because the intensity of the plume that accelerates a much lighter object must be much inferior. Only a high-thrust engine can match the plume of a high-thrust engine. But, attached to a smaller rocket, a big engine produces a very different acceleration than if it were part of a big missile. In addition, everyone agrees that it is easier to destroy missiles during boost phase than to kill warheads as they are reentering the atmosphere. That is because the bodies of missiles are physically weaker than those of the warheads—designed as these are for the stresses of reentering the atmosphere. Were it otherwise, every missile would have to be engineered like the space shuttle. Missiles must be light and have a high thrust-to-weight ratio, or they tend not to go very far.

Hence, as we have seen, the idea of defending against missiles during boost phase dates back to the very beginning of the missile age. When, in 1962, the first American spacecraft performed an orbital rendezvous, that is, "saw" another spacecraft and guided itself to physical proximity with it, it became undeniable that one rocket, based in space, could get near another rocket as it was being launched into space and destroy it. By the early '60s, the U.S. had long been using heat-seeking missiles to home in on aircraft exhausts. Since missile exhausts were far more obvious than aircraft exhausts, there was never any doubt that the guidance systems of air-to-air missiles could home in on the heat of ballistic missile targets in space. But since the relative speed at which the interceptor and its target would approach each other in space was so much greater than in the air, it was clear that the imperfection in the interceptor missile's guidance system and in the timing devices that set off the interceptor's warhead would guarantee miss-distances of hundreds of meters. That is why early plans for boost-phase defense would have placed nuclear warheads on space-based, heat-seeking interceptor rockets. So, as far back as the 1960s, the only difficulty in the scheme was to make sure that the interceptor rocket was fired in the right place at the right time to accomplish the intercept.

So, the technical elements for the endgame of one form of boost-phase defense were on the shelf back in the 1960s. Of course many economic and managerial factors argued against making use of the strictly technical capabilities we had. In the intervening twenty years the *technology* available for this kind of boost-phase endgame intercept has improved. But as we shall see, it has not and cannot remove the basic problem involved with this kind of defense: putting the interceptor rocket in the right place at the right time to make the intercept. The problem, however, has a neat solution. In a word, quantity. Let us see why a great number of space-based rockets would be needed.

The problem stemmed—and continues to stem—from the fact that rockets are relatively slow things. Even where there is no atmosphere to slow them down, the outer limit of a rocket's speed is set by the speed at which gases from burning chemical fuels can escape out the rocket's rear end. In space, the best modern rockets may produce a velocity (over and above the orbital velocity at which they were traveling before ignition) of perhaps 6 kilometers (four miles) per second. This is about the maximum velocity of ICBMs, and also roughly minimum orbital velocity. Thus, a space-based interceptor could travel some 12 kilometers per second while its target travels at half that speed. But in order for the interceptor to catch up with the missile during the approximately 250 seconds between the time the missile is detected and the time when the missiles' engines stop burning brightly enough to make it unmistakably visible, an interceptor that is traveling only twice as fast as the missile must be relatively close—no more then, say, 600 miles. In order to cover the earth evenly with rocket-bearing satellites that are only 600 miles apart would take some 800 satellites. Supposing for a moment that each of these satellites carried twenty interceptors. Then the total number of rockets in orbit would be 16,000. Principally because of the fuel they would need to reach high speeds, each rocket would have to weigh perhaps 1,000 pounds, including the rocket fuel, the guidance system, and the warhead. This would mean that 16 million pounds of interceptors plus perhaps another million pounds (for satellite structures and sensors) would have to be put into orbit. One gets the idea of the magnitude of the enterprise from the fact that 20 million pounds amounts to 300 flights of the space shuttle. Putting this amount of weight into orbit was certainly a daunting logistical prospect in the 1960s, and remains so.

In the 1980s the technology available for space-based interceptor rockets has improved. As we have said, guidance systems especially have improved to the point of making nuclear or even conventional warheads unnecessary. Moreover, the weight of guidance systems has come down almost to the point of being a negligible factor. Nevertheless, even if the weight of all of the interceptor rocket's components except fuel were eliminated, the irreducible requirements for rocket fuel alone would ensure that placing a rocket interceptor system in orbit would be a very large logistical enterprise. The U.S., however, does not lack any technological element for such a "smart bullet" defense.

Some have argued that this is due to the remarkable Delta 180 experiment of August, 1986, in which an optical sensor aboard one Delta rocket tracked the booster of another Delta rocket precisely enough so that the guidance system attached to that sensor would have been able to smash into precisely the point where the ultraviolet part of the booster's plume met the booster. But that is an exaggeration. No one with a nodding acquaintance with physics should have been surprised that exhaust gases at 2000°c produce strong ultraviolet emissions. No one acquainted with the Maverick guidance system used in that experiment should have been surprised that it functioned, once again, very well. Rather, whenever it occurs, such talk of technological "breakthroughs" is a political trial balloon.

What about the technology for managing and coordinating the work of, perhaps, 800 satellites? Is that available? The basic requirements are simple: to alert the orbital rocket-bearing stations that the Soviet Union has launched a missile attack, that the missiles from that attack are coming roughly through a set of geographic coordinates, and that when individual stations approach those coordinates, they should be ready to launch their rockets. This is well within the bonds of the technology now being applied to our early warning satellites.

Then each station must be able to identify and roughly track each of the tens of Soviet missiles within its own rather narrow field of view at any given time (which field of view would be adjusted to overlap somewhat with the field of view of neighboring stations). Each station would have to prioritize the targets for itself in relation to its own knowledge of the position of other stations, assign individual missile targets to individual interceptors, and send them on their way. The former function would require the power of a modern business computer. The latter function would not even require that. As the satellite stations moved along their orbits, the ones that had first come into range of the Soviet missiles and had fired their own interceptors would move out of range of the Soviet launch areas, while others would come up behind them to join in the battle. The battle-management problem for the oncoming stations would be the same as for the ones that had preceded it.

How useful would such a smart-bullet network be? No one can deny that a missile in boost phase struck by an interceptor rocket would cease to exist. The chances are very high that an individual rocket, *when fired in range*, would actually strike a missile. If the shock from the impact on the booster or the explosion of its remaining fuel did not disintegrate or incapacitate the warhead (as it almost certainly would), the annihilation of the booster and post-boost vehicle would necessarily deprive the warheads of the thrust and the guidance they would need to get to their targets. Since the warheads would never reach the top of their intended ballistic arch, chances are also that they would never even be armed to explode.

How many missiles thus would be rendered harmless? Obviously, more rather than fewer satellite stations, and more rather than fewer interceptor rockets in orbit would result in more missiles being killed. The ratio however is not one to one. That is because Soviet missiles are not going to be launched evenly spread out over the earth's surface. Rather, Soviet ICBMs are based primarily in a band of territory running most of the length of the Trans-Siberian railroad. The Soviet Union's missile-launching submarines are likely to be concentrated near the edges of the polar icecap. Of course they could be almost anywhere in the earth's oceans. Hence the U.S. must spread its defensive satellites over the entire globe, while concentrating them on Siberia and the Arctic by making the orbits pass over the earth's poles.

Now, given the severe limitations on the speed, and therefore on the range of the interceptors, a total of no more than perhaps one-eighth of the satellites would be in range of the missiles during boost phase. That means that out of a hypothetical 800 satellites, only 100, carrying a hypothetical 2,000 interceptors, would ever get to fire. To increase effectiveness one would have to increase the number of satellites and interceptors, realizing that necessarily, at any given moment, some seven-eighths of the satellites would be "absentees."

Still, even if the U.S. were to place enough satellites in orbit to make sure that only, say, 1,000 interceptors were in position to fire on boosting Soviet missiles, this number would be quite enough to make impossible any militarily reasonable Soviet plan. Such a plan at the unreasonable extreme, might involve firing of all of the Soviet Union's 1,400 silo-launched missiles, some 820 of which presumably carry multiple warheads. But even though such an extreme launch would already be too great for rational military purposes, the 1,000 interceptors in position to fire would cut in half the number of missiles getting though the boost-phase defense. This would mean that the Soviet Union could be sure that half of its multiple warhead carriers, the cream of its force, would be nipped in the bud. Only 3,000 warheads would have a chance to go on against subsequent layers of American defenses. But where would these 3,000 surviving warheads be targeted? The Soviet Union would not know. But it would know that even if the subsequent layers of American defense were even minimally effective, the attack that would arrive on American forces would be small, ragged, and militarily unproductive. Of course these 1,000 interceptors could not prevent the Soviet Union from launching its entire missile force against American cities, leaving itself at the mercy of U.S. forces that would be essentially whole. But a hypothetical 2,000 interceptors in the right place at the right time would put a serious crimp into even such a masochistic plan.

How much would it cost to put some 10- or 20-million pounds of interceptor missiles into orbit? If we take the space shuttle's price of *circa* $4,000 per pound as our guide, the total is between $40 and $80 billion for the transportation alone! But surely the space shuttle should not be used as a standard for cost. Earlier in the space age the cost per pound in orbit had been cheaper. Anyone looking to lower the cost of placing objects in orbit should not be under the illusion that application of new technology would necessarily help. For example, it would do virtually no good to drastically increase the fuel efficiency of the space shuttle, or of any given rocket, because the fuel itself is an almost insignificantly small part of the cost of a space launch.

Surprisingly enough, the cost of the launch vehicle itself is also a relatively small part of the equation. Nevertheless, the application of common sense can help cut the cost of launch vehicles.

After the destruction of the Challenger Shuttle in January of 1986 investigative reporters swarmed over the Morton Thiokol company, which had produced the solid booster rockets whose failure apparently caused the accident, looking for wrongdoing. But these reporters failed to notice something about the way Thiokol produces rockets that was right before their eyes and that, although it is anything but illegal or unethical, nevertheless is quite harmful to the United States. That flaw is a kind of structural inefficiency. Rather than producing the boosters in an industrial assembly-line manner, each piece goes through various processes in widely separated parts of the company's huge compound. The process works with all the efficiency of a cottage industry. Thiokol's management knows this and would not in the least object to doing things differently. Either Thiokol or its competitor, the Hercules Corporation, would gladly produce shuttle boosters, or any other solid fuel rocket, on an assembly-line basis *if* the U.S. government made the commitment to buying the large volume of rockets that would justify the capital expenses necessary for setting up an assembly line.

The production of solid fuel rockets, by the way, lends itself to mass-production techniques. The body of the rocket is almost always a cylindrical cocoon wound of synthetic string impregnated with graphite. The cylinder is then filled with a gooey paste of fuel that later solidifies. Since the fuel is explosive, the manufacturing process is more dangerous than making sausages, but it is not wholly dissimilar. At any rate, such savings as can be made in launch vehicles will come when the government makes it possible for rocket contractors to make the twin commitments to quantity and simplicity.

By far the largest part of U.S. space-launch costs, however, is the management structure that has grown up around the U.S. space business. Unless drastic reductions are made in this structure, even heroic cost reductions for equipment will have barely perceptible effects on costs. Some 12,000 people, and a correspondingly large set of secondary and tertiary activities, are involved in the management of the shuttle's operations. This "standing army" at Cape Canaveral, Huntsville, Houston, and Vandenberg Air Force bases, plus the bureaucratic dinosaur that is NASA headquarters add something like a billion dollars a year in direct overhead costs to the space-launch programs it handles. These standing armies also interfere with one another and with the contractors involved in ways that complicate and delay—while people must be paid. This bureaucratic-industrial complex is also capable of pressing ahead unwisely primarily because the responsibility for the outcome of events is so diffused.

As responsible officials who may be contemplating launching into orbit large numbers of interceptor rockets recoil at the cost of doing so, the worst thing they could do would be to continue to research the launch cost problem as if technology could *ever* bring a solution. No doubt, it is possible to make more sophisticated launch vehicles. But any savings dearly bought in regard to materials can be overwhelmed by the slightest inattention to management. The Strategic Defense Initiative Organization (SDIO) projects a hypothetical launch system for space-based rockets that would rely on MX boosters and would cost $1,500 per pound. The U.S. government might well fail to meet that cost target, or it might well do much better. Only one thing is certain: whether or not it does, the outcome will depend primarily on what is done with regard to management, and secondarily with regard to *industrial* engineering. Aerospace engineering and science are only tangentially involved. There is reason to hope that the cost of placing one pound in orbit might be brought down to a few hundred dollars, or even to less than one hundred. But one will never know whether this is possible until the U.S. government decides to try it outside the managerial constraints that clearly make it impossible.

It is also very difficult to estimate the cost of manufacturing thousands of interceptor rockets and hundreds of satellites to carry them—or almost any other military equipment. That is because since the 1960s, the proportion of the price of military equipment that is due strictly to materials and labor has declined while the proportion due to the way the individual program is managed has risen. Tales of Pentagon-procured toilet seats that cost $600 and coffee brewers that cost $7,000 do not indicate that government contractors filched millions of dollars. Every penny of these outrageous costs is fully accounted for by the amount of time that contractors' personnel were assigned to the program. The allocation of manpower and facilities, in turn, is fully accounted for by the regulations and program directives that the contractor received. So, when proponents of using space-based rockets cite cost estimates of $1.5 million for each rocket interceptor, "based on independent studies by three contractors and the Department of Defense,"[2] the knowledgeable reader realizes that the estimates consist largely of assumptions by all about how the program would be managed—how many stops and starts and re-scopings and de-scopings, and how many key decisions would be required. The actual cost could be lower, and it could be higher.

This is even truer of the satellites that would carry the rockets. Fifteen million dollars of production costs, as estimated by proponents of the idea, seems low even for a simple satellite. But even if such a satellite could be built for so little money, it is all too easy to imagine the Pentagon rerunning the saga of the Bradley Fighting Vehicle, which, with a decade's delay, was transformed from a $115,000 armored car into a multimillion dollar, high-technology problem.

Finally, the advocates of space-based rockets cite figures of $1 and $2 billion respectively as the cost for surveillance satellites in low orbits[3] and in geosynchronous orbit respectively. The moment one begins to arm a satellite with the ability to maneuver and to put out decoys, one incurs costs in the tens of millions. Those figures indeed are roughly in line with the costs of existing high-tech surveillance satellites. But it is easy to imagine the requirement for the performance of surveillance satellites, for their survivability, and even for their number, being raised so high as to make the cost soar.

All of this is not to say that the semi-official projections of the SDIO that a large-scale deployment of some 10,000 space-based rockets would cost $68 billion are unreasonable. Our point is two-fold: On the one hand, unless the Pentagon changes the wasteful way it approaches its normal functions, never mind ballistic missile defense, such figures would quickly be dwarfed. On the other hand, if the Pentagon were to abandon the procedures governing research, development acquisition, and procurement that have grown up since 1961, there is no reason why space-based rockets could not be put into orbit for less.

When could the rockets begin to go into space? The unofficial SDIO position is 1994, or seven years after a decision to do it. But this estimate is a managerial, not a technical one. If the U.S. were at war, the first satellite might well be in orbit nine months after a decision to put it there. On the other hand, there is no limit to the delays that the "normal" workings of the system might impose. We mean to emphasize that the choice is not simply between "business as usual" and what the Pentagon calls "streamlined procedures." Even in today's Pentagon there are a variety of ways of doing business. Some so-called streamlined procedures are more streamlined than others. A few "black" (i.e. supersecret) programs in the intelligence field enjoy few layers of management and are the most streamlined of all. But compared to the way that airplanes or, for that matter, the atomic bomb, were developed during World War II the most "streamlined" of today's Pentagon procedures are bad jokes. How quickly the United States could be defended by space-based rockets would depend primarily on how much we wanted this item on the menu.

The Space-Based Laser

It was always clear that if a defensive satellite could strike a missile at the speed of light, it would not matter how far from the satellite the missile was. If one satellite could thus "cover" a wide area, only a few satellites would be needed to cover the earth. Laser satellites can use the time they are "in view" of missiles far more efficiently than could rocket satellites. While a rocket satellite might carry twenty interceptors, the number of missiles that a laser satellite could kill would equal the number of seconds that the satellite was "in view" of the missile, divided by the number of seconds it took to kill each. Thus the number of potential kills per satellite climbs into the hundreds.

As noted, interest in using space-based lasers for boost-phase antimissile work arose when two sets of facts converged: Ballistic missiles (even solid boosters) are relatively fragile things that do not resist 1,000 joules/cm^2 of radiant energy, and chemical lasers of well-known characteristics could project a missile-killing dose of radiant energy some 3,000 kilometers. Senator Wallop and DARPA put the item on the nation's menu. Let us examine it more closely.

Laser energy is released when highly energized atoms undergo a rapid loss of energy. Electrons that had been pushed away from the nucleus snap back, releasing energy somewhat like a stretched rubber band when let go. Atoms may be "excited" and "lased" in a variety of ways. The tiny lasers that read out prices at supermarkets, for example, are produced by inducing vibrations in the molecular structure of crystals with tiny amounts of electricity. However, the first direct-energy device to be built with the power sufficient to destroy missile boosters at long distances is the chemical laser.[4]

This device is more like a rocket engine than an electrical instrument. Two fuels (e.g., hydrogen and fluorine, or oxygen and iodine) are mixed and ignited in a combustion chamber. The resulting compound, very hot, and with its outer electron orbits barely attached, exits the chamber at hypersonic speeds through special nozzles. As it does, it cools radically and its outer electrons "snap back" releasing energy in the form of light. This light is collected, shaped, and directed by a series of mirrors. The power of a chemical laser depends on the number of molecules that can be "lased" at any given time. That means that to increase the power one needs but to burn more fuel and build more nozzles. The laser's efficiency depends largely on the speed at which the hot molecules exit. That, in turn, means that the purer the vacuum that draws out the hot molecules, the better the laser runs. On earth, the vacuum is produced by huge steam pumps or by elaborate chemical absorption. In space, chemical lasers run at top efficiency, gratis. Moreover, since their power comes from the chemical fuel they burn, chemical lasers require no large sources of electricity.

The building of chemical lasers and their optical trains involves hard-nosed engineering of gas dynamics and of adaptive optics, but no new science. The TRW company built a hydrogen fluoride laser at its San Juan Capistrano facility in the late 70s based on linear banks of nozzles that yields 2.2 million watts (megawatts) of continuous wave laser power. That laser was used in 1978 to destroy antitank missiles in tests. The same company designed and built a chemical laser with nozzles in a cylindrical array under the Defense Department's Alpha project. The original design—a cylinder about 5 meters by 1 (3 feet by 15 feet)—would have yielded 5 megawatts. Fitted with improved nozzles developed in 1980– 81, the same design would have yielded 10 megawatts.

The chemical laser, like any other directed-energy weapon, must be pointed accurately, like a gun, so that when its beam is turned on, it will shine on the target, and follow the target as it moves. Such a pointer-tracker was designed—and the basic elements of it built—between 1979 and 1983 under the Defense Department's Talon Gold program. The device was to consist of two telescopes. The first would have focused the rough images from the hot ex-hausts of Soviet missiles onto an array of electro-optical detectors. Once the battle-management program had chosen which of the missiles should be engaged first, the telescope would move itself (and the laser gun to which it was attached), so that the image of the missile was at the center of its own theoretical "cross-hairs." Then control over the movement of the pointer-tracker (and of the laser gun to which it was attached) would pass to a second telescope. This would shine a low-power, shortwave, accurate laser beam onto the missile, receive the reflected beam onto its own set of electro-optical detectors, and move so as to keep that reflec-tion "locked on" to the center of its own "cross hairs." In the laboratory, the elements of this device showed the ability to point and follow with an accuracy of .05 microradians as early as 1981. This is roughly equivalent to hitting a grapefruit over Los Angeles from a satellite over New York, and quite good enough for antimis-sile work.

A laser beam, however, must be focused onto the missile by as large a mirror as possible, in order to diminish as much as possible the natural tendency of light beams to spread out as they travel long distances. By 1980, under the Defense Department's LODE program, Kodak and Perkin Elmer developed the technology for building large laser-quality glass mirrors out of segments. This makes it possible to produce fine mirrors that are both very big and transportable. United Technologies did the same using seg-ments of composite materials on which gaseous silicon had been evenly deposited, molecule by molecule. Lockheed developed tiny computer-controlled push-pull devices for the backs of the mirrors. These devices make sure that the edges of the several segments are constantly aligned with one another. They also correct for tiny imperfections on the mirror's surface and enable the mirror to shine its beam onto different targets without moving, just by changing its shape. By 1982, the companies involved were saying quite clearly that although production of large numbers of such mirrors—say 10 meters in diameter—would require substantial investment in tools, it required no further development of technology.

In sum, then, despite deliberate de-scoping on the part of DARPA in 1982–84, and despite the SDIO's deliberate near-destruction of the space-based laser program from mid-1985 until late 1986, the elements are very much at hand to build a 10-megawatt chemical laser with a 10-meter mirror, and an accuracy to hit a missile 3,000 kilometers away. At that distance, such a laser would deliver about 1,200 joules per square centimeter onto the target—enough to destroy a solid-fueled booster in about one second, and a liquid-fueled one in much less time than that.

What could such lasers do for us? Suppose, for the sake of argument, that a single 10-megawatt chemical laser with a 10-meter mirror happened to be right over the middle of the Soviet Union's belt of SS-18 silos just at the time when the whole SS-18 force was being launched in a counterforce strike. If the Soviets wanted their RVs to *arrive* simultaneously at widely dispersed American targets from their own widely dispersed launch points, they would have to stagger the timing over perhaps 250–300 seconds and delay the arrival of some warheads by sending them on high ("lofted") trajectories. The boost phase of an individual SS-18 is also 300 seconds. Thus the time between the first missile becoming vulnerable to the last missile's engines cutting out would be little less than 600 seconds—for sake of argument, 500. During that time, this hypothetically well-placed laser could kill one missile with one-second shots. Indeed, given the softness of the liquid-fueled SS-18, less than a second's attention by such a powerful laser would be needed. Moreover, from thousands of kilometers, the angular distances between missile targets would be tiny enough to require computer modification of the mirror's shape rather than movement by the whole mirror. Hence, the laser would probably average much less than a second between shots. But even if it averaged a full second, it would kill 250 out of the total 308 SS-18s. Thus a single laser of this kind, if it happened to be at the right place at the right time, could prevent some 2,500 out of 3,000 SS-18 warheads from ever reaching their targets.

Of course, because the earth turns under satellites as they revolve in their orbits, in order to have just one laser station optimally located with regard to Soviet silos would require nine lasers, spread over three orbital paths. The one laser station that this deployment would surely put into the battle would be taking a big enough bite out of the Soviet Union's ability to carry out a counterforce strike as probably to deter that strike.

Suppose, then that the number of American lasers in orbit grew to sixteen, distributed on four separate orbital paths, or rings, crossing both poles of the earth. This would put at least four over the Soviet ICBM launch areas at any given time. That would mean that some 1,000 missiles—if the Soviets were so foolish as to launch them into this defense—would never make it beyond boost phase. That would not only make nonsense of a counterforce strike but would practically annihilate it in boost phase. With these lasers in place, it would become conceivable to protect the U.S. population against the collateral effects of such a counterforce strike.

If the U.S. then brought the number of laser stations to thirty-two, it could count on having eight lasers in the battle against Soviet ICBMs, plus several at all times over any possible ocean area whence Soviet submarines might launch their missiles. This would give the U.S. the theoretical possibility of destroying all of the Soviets' missiles in boost phase, even if the Soviets, for some purpose unfathomable by human reason, chose to launch them all just to do some indiscriminate damage to the U.S.

How much direction and battle management would laser stations need from above? The SDIO's R&D project for a Boost-Phase Surveillance and Tracking System (BSTS) is based on the correct assumption that if individual directed-energy weapons (or, indeed, satellites carrying interceptor rockets) are told precisely where to look, they will be able to "lock on" to their targets more quickly. Moreover, a good BSTS would be good enough to make sure that where the coverage of any two stations overlap, the two don't waste any of their capacities on the same targets. A good BSTS would assign each target to each weapon, figure out which had been killed and which needed continuing attention by other defensive elements.

In fact, however, the minimum requirements for external support is simply that of alerting the stations that some enemy missiles are going to cross the stations' fields of view, and that the stations are authorized to shoot. The stations would not lose much by having this degree of independence. The extra time required of each station to find and prioritize targets on their own would not exceed a second or two. Also, merely by virtue of knowing where the other stations are at any given time, each station's computer could manage to judge correctly whether it or its neighbors could most efficiently engage any given missile. After all, each station would "know" that every other station would prioritize targets in the same way. Each would know every other station's location and would communicate directly with its neighbors. Any small loss of efficiency would be overshadowed by the inherent resistance to damage that such a decentralized battle-management system would possess. If, in the course of an attack, the enemy succeeded in disabling one station, he would not thereby have hurt the battle management system significantly. Moreover, disabling a satellite that is itself designed for serious combat would prove harder than disabling a mere surveillance "bird."

This brings us to the question of the ability of laser satellites, or any other kind of satellites, to survive attempts to destroy them. Conventional wisdom has it that every object in space is necessarily highly visible to radar and to heat-sensing equipment, that objects in space are flimsy sitting ducks, and that therefore one can expect them to survive only so long as no technically advanced enemy wants to kill them. We have already seen, however, that this is not necessarily the case for the warheads spawned by ballistic missiles because missiles can also put out cheap tin foil balloons in the shape of warheads. It is possible for radar and heat-sensing equipment to tell the real warheads from the tin foil imitations, but it is not easy. In similar ways, the location of satellites can be hidden by producing very many cheap, inflatable tin foil copies of the satellite. Perhaps these decoy copies could be supplied with heat sources to simulate the heat put out by the real satellite. Meanwhile the real satellite might change its radar "signature," change its thermal "signature," and maneuver to another location. Stealth need not be confined to airplanes, or to warheads, or to space mines.

Makers of radar and infrared sensors are well aware of how easy it is to make large things appear small and small things look large to these sensors. This is not to say that technical puzzles thus made cannot be solved. But it does take time, energy, and ingenuity to try. Hiding and finding is a contest of detail. In that contest, the advantage goes to objects that are big enough and expensive enough to carry large bags of tricks. Hence, the advantage is with those who would hide defensive satellites rather than with those who find them. Finally, laser satellites (and, indeed satellites carrying interceptors) have the option of shooting at any interceptor that appears to be maneuvering after them, or at any "space mine" that they wish to avoid.

None of this is to suggest that laser battle stations are invulnerable. No doubt, one laser station will fall to another that sees farther, understands better, shoots more accurately and more powerfully, is better armored, and stays in better working order. But to do justice to all the factors involved in space combat—including electronic countermeasures—would require a separate, elaborate discussion.

How much would a set of chemical laser satellites cost? The cost of transporting them in orbit would not be trivial. As designed in 1981, a 10-megawatt laser station with a 10-meter mirror would weigh 65,000 pounds. The station was designed to the maximum dimensions and carrying capacity of the space shuttle's cargo bay. The station's fuel pod would take up another full cargo bay. Thus thirty-two laser battle stations would require sixty-four flights of the space shuttle, or thirty-two flights of the old Saturn V. (Incidentally, the newest Soviet space launch vehicle could do it in only sixteen trips!) As we have said, for good or ill, the cost of space transportation is quite plastic. Thus the bill for putting thirty-two laser stations in orbit could range from $30 billion if the space shuttle were used, to one-hundreth of that, if one were to adopt the rocket—and the management plan under discussion in the SDIO in 1987. The actual cost would be the result of managerial rather than scientific decisions.

The cost of building the laser stations themselves is almost as plastic. DARPA's estimate in 1980 was for 2.3 billion for the first copy, and one billion for each copy thereafter. Again, no one acquainted with the Pentagon doubts that the price could skyrocket. Indeed, in 1981 the Department of Defense had set the cost of the Talon Gold pointer-tracker, a key part of the laser station, at $400 million, with the first flight to take place in 1984. But after funding cuts, fifty-four "de-scoping" and "re-scoping" actions during one fifty-two week period, and a bitter jurisdictional struggle between the Air Force Space Division, the SDIO, and DARPA, the program was reduced to a one-telescope laser radar experiment, delayed to 1991, and its cost rose to $1.2 billion. Then it was canceled, renamed, reduced to a one-telescope tracking experiment to be carried on the shuttle in 1987 (six years after the Soviet Union had performed a similar experiment from its Saylut 7 space station). But the Challenger's accident canceled shuttle flights for over two years, pushing this program into limbo and its budget into unknown regions.

Had DARPA's 1980 option for an accelerated program been taken, the first copy of an American space-based laser might have been in orbit in November 1986. But when the government rejected fixing an early date on which the weapon must come into existence, there vanished the possibility of imposing discipline on the tendency of the R&D bureaucracy to add, subtract, quarrel, delay, and raise costs. In late 1986, as part of a tentative interest in the possibility of "early partial deployment," the SDIO's leadership showed renewed interest in chemical laser battle stations. But whatever it did pursuant to its new interest, it apparently did not curb the bureaucracy's natural tendency to plan for new, improved features (i.e. a device for reducing the wavelength of the laser beam after it is generated is rumored to be part of the new design). Moreover, since the SDIO did not fix a constraining, early due date, it is impossible to say when the SDIO's renewed interest might bear fruit, or at what cost.

If, however, the U.S. government were to order space-based lasers with a sense of wartime urgency, there is every reason to believe that the first copy might be ready between three and four years thereafter, at a cost of between $4 and $5 billion. Production of subsequent copies might well be prepared during this time. Since such things would be more like KH-11 cameras than aircraft carriers, the time required for fabrication of each copy might be on the order of nine months to a year. Each copy might cost between $1.5 and $2 billion.

Of what, then, should a boost-phase defense consist—rockets or lasers? As we have seen, each kind of weapon has its peculiar advantages. Common sense would suggest that a judicious combination of both would be optimal—especially if the Soviet Union did not know what the nature of that combination was. Rockets, for example, would make excellent guards for laser stations. The enormous kinetic energy of collision at orbital speeds would unquestionably destroy any defense-suppression missile, or space mine, without the laser station having to devote precious time and fuel to burning through whatever thick thermal shielding these devices might have. Having the ability to increase the "mix" of rockets in orbit would also help to insure against the possibility that the Soviet Union would go through tremendous expenses and, sometime in the future, succeed in fielding missiles that are substantially laser-resistant. Nothing could resist a rocket's impact at orbital speeds.

Lasers, on the other hand have the advantage of greater range, of near-instantaneous kill, and therefore of greater flexibility of targeting. Since a much higher percentage of laser stations would be able to take part in the defensive battle than would rocket-launching satellites, and since an individual laser might be expected to account for far more missile kills than would a rocket satellite, each individual laser station would make a bigger contribution to defense. Because of the lasers' relatively high kill rate, each laser station added to the defensive constellation would make it less and less advantageous for the offence to try to launch its missiles all at once. Also, the lasers would surely be far more efficient over areas whence few Soviet missiles would be fired—e.g. the oceans—and, hence, where a thick blanket of rocket satellites would be largely wasted.

In sum, it would appear wise for the U.S. to place into orbit as many missile-killing devices as possible as quickly as possible with priority given to orbits that maximize the number of satellites over the Soviet ICBM fields and over their Arctic paths. Given a rush, rocket satellites might win the race by perhaps two years. By the time that a significant number of laser stations were in orbit, say a dozen, there might already be 150 rocket satellites in orbit. It might then be wise to stop increasing the number of rockets and to assign them as bodyguards and assistants for those laser stations most heavily engaged over the Soviet Union. The rockets would be best for short-range protection, while the lasers would be best at long-range destruction of missiles.

There is no such thing as an optimum number of boost-phase stations. The more there were, the better they would function, the easier the job of subsequent defensive layers would be, the more protection would be available to those whom the Soviets might wish to attack, and the less reasonable such attacks would appear to the Soviet Union. A note of caution is essential: an American boost-phase defense would have to be proportionally much heavier than a Soviet one, because the U.S., unlike the Soviet Union, does not have a serious *pre* boost defense—that is a large number of counterforce ICBMs. Hence an American boost-phase defense, unlike its Soviet counterpart, would not be facing an enemy missile arsenal sharply reduced by first strike. For America, the boost-phase layer would be the first line of defense, and would have to bear the brunt of an attack.

Postboost

After a missile's main engines shut off on burnout in space, the nose cone opens up, revealing a postboost vehicle (PBV) that contains the warheads. The PBV is powered by a smaller engine that maneuvers it on various tangents to the main trajectory. On each precise maneuver it releases a warhead (and/or decoys) in the direction of a separate target. This postboost phase may last longer than the boostphase itself—400 seconds. During this phase, the PBVs' engines—although not as dazzlingly bright as the main engines—are still visible to on-the-shelf uncooled heat sensing devices. Also, although no comprehensive tests have yet been carried out, the PBV is probably as vulnerable as a missile booster, although in a different way. Finally, although the PBV loses warheads as the minutes of the postboost phase tick away, and thus becomes a decreasingly vulnerable target, destroying a PBV would result—on the average—in destroying half of the warheads that the missile had carried originally. Hence striking PBVs in postboost phase is almost as important and almost as easy as striking missiles in postboost phase.

On-the-shelf technology is almost as useful for postboost as it is for boost phase. The sensors on the Air Force "tomato-can" antisatellite weapon, designed as they are to home in on cold targets, are more than sufficient to intercept a moderately hot PBV engine. The terminal sensors that were tested on Delta 180 would probably have to be within 200 miles of the PBV to "see" its plume. But the effective range of the rockets that would carry them would not be greater than that anyhow. Of course the PBV would be shattered by the impact from the interceptor rockets. Any and all decoys remaining on board would surely cease to exist. Although one cannot be absolutely sure that the same would happen to all of the warheads, it is almost certain that the destruction of the PBV would keep them from being dispensed and armed. This means that any set of rocket-bearing satellites that we put into orbit as a boost-phase defense would also pay serious dividends in the postboost phase.

The vulnerability of PBVs to lasers is complex. On the one hand, because the PBV—unlike the missile itself—is not primarily a fuel casing under great stress, a laser would probably have to put more energy on it before the PBV's fuel explodes. On the other hand, the PBV is a mass of fine electronic equipment. Even if the equipment were protected by a heavy armored shell, the PBV must open up as it releases warheads and decoys. This would allow even small amounts of laser energy to do great damage. Of course, since the PBV would already be in a ballistic trajectory, it would be difficult to know how much damage the laser had inflicted unless the fuel tank ignited.

But this uncertainty would cut more heavily against the Soviet perpetrator of a first strike than against the U.S. If the U.S. had in orbit a boost phase defensive constellation of thirty-two laser stations, and perhaps some rocket satellites, it could be certain that eight or more stations would be in range of the Soviet PBVs. Because of the difference between the stations' orbital speeds and the speed of the Soviet ballistic missiles, the stations in range of the PBVs would be different from the ones engaged in the antimissile battle. Hence the U.S. could be certain that our defensive laser stations could shine their beams on just about every PBV that had gotten through the boost-phase defense. How much this would do would be significant but uncertain. But a Soviet strike planner would have to assume the worst.

There is no way for the Soviets—or ourselves for that matter—to disguise postboost vehicles. In May 1987, the American Physical Society published a report on directed energy weapons which claimed that PBVs could use "cold gas thrusters" to foil heat detectors.[5] But this makes no sense. Cold (that is, compressed) gas yields so much less energy than gas produced through combustion that in order for a PBV to run on it, that PBV could not carry any load. The same report contends—without any evidence—that the hot exhaust from PBVs could be masked by "shrouds" i.e. skirts that would extend out from the PBV itself. But the antidefense physicists who wrote the report do not explain how, given the principle of conservation of energy, the heat of the engines exhaust could be kept from heating the shrouds to the point that they themselves would be detectable.

All of this is to say that although it is impossible to guarantee the results of a defensive battle in postboost phase, current technology could guarantee that large amounts of laser power or rockets would strike most, if not all, Soviet PBVs.

Midcourse

To intercept a warhead during midcourse, almost regardless of its destination, is to protect a very broad area from that warhead. Also, because an attacker cannot predict which warheads will and will not be killed during midcourse, he cannot distribute his warheads among enemy targets with confidence that "n" warheads will arrive at target "A". Any midcourse defense that follows a boostphase and postboost-phase defense triply compounds an attacker's problems. However, midcourse defense (except in its last stages) is genuinely difficult today because no directed-energy weapon on today's menu can deliver enough energy from sufficiently far away to efficiently overcome the warheads' tough heat shields. Hence midcourse defense must rely largely on intercepting warheads with kinetic kill vehicles. As we have maintained, guiding such vehicles to intercept is no problem. "Seeing" the warheads and discriminating between warheads and decoys is even more difficult. It is manageable to some extent when the "threat cloud" comes into range of large ground-based radars and high-altitude infra-red telescopes. Regardless of what may happen in the future, as of today these tasks are best accomplished by instruments based primarily on the ground. Hence the midcourse defense on today's menu must be essentially a great extension of terminal defense.

This is not to say that space-based assets cannot play some role in midcourse defense. Individual space-based laser stations, after having passed over the areas where missiles were in boost phase, would surely pass near concentrations of warheads and decoys. The lasers' sensors would not be up to discriminating. But the lasers would almost surely have enough fuel left (most would be fully fueled) so that it would not be wasteful for them to put their beams on targets within, say, a thousand kilometers (the lasers' uncooled sensors probably could not pick them up farther away) for perhaps five seconds each. Even if only one of every twenty targets they hit were a warhead, the lasers would surely eliminate a goodly number of decoys!

The ground-based midcourse defense could begin with over-the-horizon backscatter radars (OTHB). The DSP satellites provide information on the attacking missiles' initial tracks. Since the OTHB's are imprecise, they could not contribute much to the DSP's information. But they could find the "threat clouds" that have escaped the postboost-phase defense, and pass on confirmation on their general location and heading to large phased-array radars (of the Grand Forks or Cobra Dane class). Nothing prevents the U.S. government from building six powerful radars of this kind, in addition to the one at Grand Forks, around the periphery of the United States. The great power of these radars would be essential for performing preliminary discrimination at great distances. This in turn would be necessary to allow the ground-based interceptor rockets (of the Eris class) to be launched just as soon as possible, so that the intercept can take place as far out in space as possible. That is important because the higher the altitude of intercept, the larger the area that is potentially protected.

The U.S., or the Soviet Union, or France, for that matter has no shortage of rockets that can reach up into deep space. The terminal guidance package that would consummate the intercept can be put on top of almost any modern long-range missile. It is useful to remember that the original HOE interceptor used a Minuteman missile as a vehicle. If the large radars can do some discrimination and compute the point at which the intercept should take place, they can give the long-range interceptor a good initial heading. Thus common sense dictates that the U.S. build this network of powerful ground-based radars. True, the space-based multidisciplinary, interactive midcourse discrimination devices that exist in the SDIO's research program would do a much better job. But they exist nowhere else.

While the interceptor missiles were already on their way to the point in space where the radars had calculated that the intercept would take place, the Airborne Optical System (AOS) would be at work. Mounted on a high-flying Boeing 767 aircraft, the AOS features a bank of heat detectors that would weigh the differences between the infrared signatures of the various incoming objects. The AOS would add its judgments on the discrimination of warheads and decoys to the judgments already made by the radar. As the "threat cloud" got closer, the AOS' infrared analysis might conclude that in this or that case the radar had made a mistake. Thus the AOS would redirect this or that interceptor somewhat to another part of the "threat cloud." However, the guidance package atop the interceptor itself would be the final instrument of discrimination. When the interceptor got close enough, its own terminal sensors could not mistake the difference between a decoy and a warhead. It is easy enough to program an interceptor not to make a final homing maneuver against a decoy but to go on past it. Hence, even if the interceptor was misdirected both by the ground-based radar and by the flying optical sensor, its own onboard sensors would give it a chance to hit whatever warhead might be traveling through its field of view. This is not to deny that, even up close, the infrared detectors could make mistakes. Certainly the Soviets could try to insulate the warheads to mask their infrared signatures. But this would make them "stand out" to the radars. Moreover, to add insulation to a warhead is to interfere with the precise release that is essential to accuracy. All of this is to say that late mid-course interception would be far from useless.

Literally no new technology need be involved in this rudimentary mid-course defense. Suggestions by some that the Airborne Optical System would require a new kind of "laser radar" that must somehow await further development[6] mistake administrative hurdles for technical ones. The laser radar was part of the AOS until 1984, when it was removed because some in the Defense Department thought that not to do so might be construed as a violation of the ABM treaty. The Eris interceptor rocket is under development. But, as we have pointed out, the key to its functioning is not the rocket propulsion system, but its terminal homing package, which was tested in one usable form in 1984, and has since been refined to a form that is even more usable. To state, as many do, that development—without—deployment of Eris must continue until 1992 or 1995 or whatever date is to state a preference rather than necessity.

How quickly could such a midcourse defense be built? It takes a minimum of three years to build a large modern phased-array radar once one has settled on the design and allocated the money. Of course if the Pentagon follows standard, or even standard "streamlined" procedures for settling on designs and allocating money, this period stretches out indefinitely. The AOS could have its laser rangefinder component reintegrated in about one year. The Boeing 767 aircraft would be available immediately to have a new equipment dome fitted. Two years after a serious decision, a fleet of perhaps twenty AOSs could be flying. As for the Eris interceptor, the engineers who actually work the program are confident that they could begin to tool up immediately for mass production, and that they could deliver an acceptable product to the production people within six to nine months of a serious decision. Within perhaps two years the U.S. would have a stock of some 3,000 Eris interceptors. Within three years, the total could be close to 10,000.

The costs would not be low. Large phased-array radars are inherently very expensive. The U.S. would need seven, for no less than $1 billion each. The AOS aircraft would cost about as much as the Airborne Warning and Control Systems (AWACS) aircraft whose function so resembles theirs—that is, some $350 million. The Eris type interceptors themselves have been advertised at $1.5 million apiece for early versions and $1 million apiece for more advanced versions. All of this is to say that the entire midcourse layer would cost somewhere in the neighborhood of $30 billion, not counting the pay of the people who would operate it. It makes little sense to count such costs, because if the people involved were not taking up their share of the "operations and management" account performing this function, they would be taking it up doing something else. Again, if the Pentagon does business as usual, the cost would rise.

For this money the U.S. would purchase an uncertain leverage.

Out of a nominal 10,000 Eris-type interceptors, stationed in perhaps 100 locations, each of which would theoretically be able to cover most of the U.S., how many warheads could we expect to destroy? There is no way of knowing. The existence of a boost-phase layer would already have made a coordinated counterforce strike nonsensical. If the Soviet Union meant to increase the likelihood that a significant number of warheads would get past the boost-phase layer, it would have to use up the vast majority of its warheads without being sure what would land where. But even in that case, the midcourse layer would be facing only a few thousand warheads and perhaps 30,000 decoys. In other words, a Soviet attack reaching our midcourse layer—if it got there at all—would confront that layer with only about four times as many objects as we had interceptors. Assuming that we could have no discrimination whatever, the mere existence of 10,000 accurate interceptors would impose roughly a 25 percent attrition on the warheads, as well as the decoys. But no one suggests that discrimination would be totally ineffective. On the other hand, it might be quite effective. If discrimination were, say, only half effective, half of the warheads would be intercepted, as it were, on purpose, while roughly one-fourth of the rest would be destroyed at random as the remaining interceptors smashed indifferently into decoys and warheads. Any reasonable level of discrimination would cut the maximum conceivable number of warheads coming through a midcourse layer to the hundreds.

Terminal Phase

The infrastructure for midcourse—the large phased—array radars and the AOS aircraft—would also be the infrastructure for the terminal-phase defense, because the radars and the aircraft would automatically create electronic files on the objects that had *not* been destroyed by the ERIS-type interceptors. The radars and AOS aircraft would sort these files according to destination, and transmit them to terminal-defense units. This would at the very least tell the terminal-defense radars where to point, and at best would transfer individual track files, individually recognized.

Today's technology allows terminal antimissile defenses to be mobile. Nowadays they should be mobile. Only arms control—not any military considerations—argues against mobility. Mobility gives to terminal defenses something of the attack-confounding *unpredictability* possessed by boost-phase and midcourse defenses. If an attacker cannot know how strong the terminal defenses around any given target are, he cannot know how many warheads it would take to overwhelm these defenses. On the other hand, because the defender knows where his terminal units are at any given time, terminal defenses are *predictable* insurance from his viewpoint. Other defensive layers may well have eliminated all of the warheads that the attacker ever intended for target "A." But the defender can be confident that even if a few warheads are still coming there, "A" will survive because *he* has devoted a unit of interceptors specifically to protect "A."

Terminal defenses depend primarily on radars. Any terminal-defense radar does not have to work hard to discriminate between decoys and warheads, because by the time the "threat cloud," or what remains of it, reaches an altitude of fifty miles (*circa* 200 linear miles from the target) the outermost fringes of the atmosphere have begun to slow the lighter decoys, or to destroy them outright. A terminal radar must locate the several warheads coming into its sector, keep track of them, and direct interceptors to them very accurately, because the interceptors will have very little time to adjust their course.

At the beginning of the missile age, separate radars were required for search, target acquisition and classification, tracking, and missile guidance. In the 1960s, as we have seen, the application of phased-array technology to the missile defense problem allowed the numbers of radars to be shrunk to two. By the 1970s it became possible to do the job with one. By the 1970s miniaturization also made it possible to pack into one small radar the capacity to do more than many large ones could previously have done. Hence, while the Air Force's space detection and tracking radar, built between 1962 and 1969, contains 5,184 transmitting elements on a 72 by 72 foot antenna, the Navy's Aegis radar, whose development began in 1973 packs 4,480 transmitters into an octagonal antenna that measures a mere 12.5 feet across.[7] Each antenna covers a full 90° of azimuth—meaning that it does not have to be accurately pointed to do its job. With its agile data processing, the Aegis radar can detect some two dozen small objects more than 200 miles away. Individual pencil-thin beams within Aegis' main beam can follow and track each object individually, while other beams individually follow and direct the interceptor rockets toward their targets. Aegis was developed to defend ships against airplanes and cruise missiles. But since its radar is competent against ballistic reentry vehicles, it makes sense to physically repackage it to ride on trucks, and to use it for terminal antimissile defense of land targets.

The Aegis radar however must be accompanied by a competent interceptor missile. The missile it normally uses, the Navy's SM-2, was designed for other purposes and is simply too slow. Making a fast missile, however, is not a high-tech challenge. Beginning in the 1960s, the U.S. developed Sprint. It is still the fastest interceptor in the world. No one contends that it is not fast enough. Sprint missiles could surely be mass-produced immediately for deployment along with Aegis radars. But a better missile is available—the 1987 version of the High Endoatmospheric Defense Interceptor (HEDI). If the HEDI program's technology were "frozen" and simply used, the U.S. would have a missile about as fast as Sprint but much more accurate. HEDI could use the Aegis radar's command guidance during its own midtrajectory. For the endgame, HEDI's own guidance computer would be able to work from the radar signals that its own active radar had bounced off the warhead as well as radar energy that the Aegis had bounced off the warhead. The HEDI guidance computer would also work from the substantial amount of heat that the reentering warhead would radiate. Thus the current model of HEDI would probably be accurate enough to do without a nuclear weapon.

The main drawback associated with "freezing" the HEDI technology would be that the speed of the rocket would have to be reduced from the level originally planned for it. That would be necessary to prevent the rocket's nose cone from creating a hot gaseous plasma as it pushed through the air. The principal technical difficulty in the HEDI program has been that at the speed specified for the rocket, such a plasma would be created and would hinder sending and receiving of precise guidance signals. Hence, the need to slow the rocket down if the program is to yield immediate fruits. Slower rockets cannot protect as wide an area as faster ones. But that can be overcome by stationing the rockets all around the area to be protected. Each of the near-term HEDI rockets might well intercept warheads at slant ranges of 60 miles, and at altitudes of 15 miles or so.

A terminal-defense unit would consist of at least three trucks. One would carry the Aegis radar. Another would provide the radar with electrical power, and the third would carry two HEDI missiles. There would be a practical limit of some twenty interceptor missiles per radar. Most units would carry perhaps ten interceptor missiles. By parking the rocket-carrying trucks in a pattern perhaps 10 miles away from the radar, one would increase the unit's coverage and make up a bit for having rockets slower than one might wish.

Most units might be assigned the task of providing insurance to cities. Unlike boost-phase defenses, which most certainly would be used in case of attack, any given terminal defense unit would probably never see action. First of all, the upper layers of the defense would have destroyed warheads regardless of their destination, and thus would have entirely eliminated the threat to some targets. Second, we would want to defend more places than the Soviets would want to attack. For example, cities are not and are not likely ever to be on the Soviet Union's target list. The danger to cities comes from their proximity to strategic targets— e.g. Washington D.C.'s proximity to the Pentagon and the National Signal Intelligence system's headquarters at Ft. Meade; Maryland; San Diego's, Oakland's, New London's, Seattle's, and Norfolk's proximity to submarine ports. Some cities such as Little Rock, Arkansas; Omaha, Nebraska; and Cheyenne, Wyoming are close to bases of the strategic air command.

In other words, a few centers of population must be insured against collateral damage, while most others (ranging from New York City to, say, Moline, Illinois) would require insurance only against stray rounds. Nevertheless, because regardless of why it got there, a warhead that landed in New York or Chicago, or Philadelphia or Los Angeles would cause great human suffering, several units would probably be located near such places. Surely some units would also be located near the San Diegos, Little Rocks and Cheyennes of America because even though the boost phase and midcourse defenses would probably have eliminated nearly all the warheads going to the strategic installations in their areas, and therefore would have much reduced the chances that a warhead would land downtown, still these centers of population are the ones that would be most endangered by an attack on the U.S. and should receive the bulk of terminal defenses. The Cheyennes and Little Rocks of America could be confident, however that even as a massive attack on the U.S. left Siberia, it could not have contained more than a few warheads that had a statistically significant chance of landing downtown. The chances of those few warheads surviving serious boost-phase and midcourse defenses would not be great. It would hardly be conceivable that, after all that, enough warheads would appear in the skies above Little Rock or San Diego to overwhelm a local defense unit.

Some terminal defense units would be used to ensure the survival of especially important American military assets. It would probably be a waste to try to terminally defend missile silos. On the one hand, the number of Soviet warheads that would be sent against ICBM fields would be so great that some would be likely to get through. But on the other hand, this would not be strategically significant because the boostphase and mid-course layers would already have thinned any attack to the point that it could not significantly cut down our retaliatory forces. It would make sense, however, to order some terminal defense units to accompany any mobile offensive missiles the U.S. might have acquired—e.g. a rail-mobile version of the MX. The chances of even a few enemy warheads finding such mobile forces would be small. Hence it would be all the more worthwhile to make very sure of their survival by attaching a small terminal-defense units to them. It would also make sense to put terminal-defense units with those military units on whose survival the nations's military power would most depend—aircraft wings, military ports, and certainly major ground-force units in Europe.

Just as there is no magic sum of dollars for which one should insure one's life or one's vital assets, there can be no "right" number of terminal defense units. A nominal 1,000 units, each armed with ten missiles, however, would allow perhaps one-third of the land mass of the United States to be provided with individual insurance against any warheads that leaked through the two defensive layers that would be covering the United States. Those areas would be chosen because of special risk, because of high population density, and because of strategic importance.

How much would a terminal layer cost? By far the most expensive part would be the Aegis radars. Mass production might reduce the cost of each unit to $25 million and, hence, the total for 1,000 units to $25 billion. The missiles are currently quoted at $3 million apiece, but might well be reduced to half of that for a production run of 10,000. Trucks and facilities would push the cost of a terminal system to at least $50 billion. Again, as we have mentioned, the Pentagon could make the costs prohibitive.

The total cost for the boost, postboost, midcourse, and terminal layers might be somewhat less than $200 billion over perhaps seven years. This is a lot of money, but roughly as much in constant dollars as the U.S. air defense system cost in the 1950s. It is also roughly as much as the life cycle cost of the 100 B-1 bombers the American people have just bought. But the defense on today's menu would provide a greater return to the taxpayer.

None of this could purchase a guarantee of absolute protection against any and all vagaries of chance, or against nutty acts such as the concentration of the entire Soviet missile force on ten American cities and its instantaneous salvoing. But any Soviet leader who, facing an undefended America, had found attractive the thought of a disarming first strike against the U.S. followed by coercion of the American people would surely discover that the boost phase, midcourse and terminal systems that we have described had removed any thought of an attack from the category of the arguably rational to that of the insane.

Filling the Shelves

As we have noted, Secretary of Defense Caspar Weinberger claimed that we have nothing on the shelf. He was correct in the sense that the U.S. does not even have a unit of the armed forces whose mission it is to intercept missiles or warheads, much less has the U.S. purchased any equipment for such a unit. Indeed, as we shall see, the Pentagon's position is that such a mission should not be assigned. The shelves are empty in this sense, then, because of this attitude. To see how true this is one need only imagine the state of our shelves if McNamara had approved Nike Zeus in 1961–62. The seventy Zeus batteries would have been deployed by about 1965. By about 1970, the Zeus missiles would have been upgraded into Spartans and would have been supplemented with Sprints. The infrastructure for Zeus' various radars would have served large phased-array radars like the ones that today ring the Soviet Union. In 1974–77, the mobile SAM-D antimissile system probably would not have been killed but would have been assigned to the Zeus units. The command responsible for these units would have appropriated the HOE and HEDI technology. By about 1980 the entire defensive system would probably have shed its nuclear weapons. In addition, by the time of the Wallop amendments of 1980–82, the command responsible for the Zeus system would have taken over responsibility for developing space laser weapons. This command would have been pressed from inside the executive branch to pursue the option that Robert Fossum outlined in his letter to Senator Culver in 1980 and by 1987 the first of the first-generation American space lasers would have been in orbit.

Because the United States defensive shelves would have been occupied it would have been natural for them to accept new technology as it came along. As it is, confusion between the availability of technology and the availability of defense helps to keep America undefended. On the one hand, so goes the argument, we need not fear for our defenses because our technology in the laboratory is superior to the Soviet Union's. On the other hand, we cannot employ our superior pieces of defensive technology because no one can show how well it would work in a given set of imagined circumstances.

8 / *The Numbers Game*

A staff officer renders no service to the country who aims at ideal standards and thereafter simply adds and multiplies until impossible totals are reached.

—Winston Churchill, *The Second Word War*

Life does not run by the numbers. If it did, the nerds would own the world.

—A contemporary sage

Conventional wisdom is replete with contrasting claims, often expressed in terms of numbers, about the effectiveness of "the SDI System." A wide variety of groups—including the Pentagon, the National Laboratories, the Office of Technology Assessment, the Union of Concerned Scientists, the Soviet Academy of Sciences, and the American Physical Society—have published papers purporting to calculate the effectiveness of SDI. There is near-universal agreement that no defense can be 100 percent effective. On the other hand, not even the most avid opponents of the SDI deny that modern antimissile devices could destroy *some* missiles in flight. So the debate over American strategic policy has come to consist in substantial part of sterile assertions about whether this or that hypothetical system would be 35 percent or 85 percent or only 10 percent effective, or by what percentage a particular countermeasure might reduce the system's effectiveness.

In fact, however, all the figures bandied about are worse than incorrect. It is all too easy to predict what damage nuclear bombs of a certain yield would cause to structures of a certain hardness if exploded at a certain distance. However, the very notion that it is possible to calculate a priori how an unknown number of missiles of uncertain hardness launched under unknown conditions will be affected by defenses of hypothetical performance is presumptuous to the point of being self-deceptive.

The widespread use of numbers in the debate gives the impression that there is at issue a question of science rather than one of public policy. But in fact, although the number-crunchers are often scientists, the numbers are the direct products of assumptions about how many and what kinds of offensive missiles would be employed, about how they would be used against what targets, about what kind of defensive devices would be available, about what orbits they would travel, as well as about how well various countermeasures and counter counter-measures would work. Such analyses are exercises in policy reasoning dressed in pseudotechnical cloaks. Unfortunately, the cloaks are thick enough to confound policy makers as well as the public. When anyone who reads such analyses comes across the words "if," "nominal," or "assuming," he is well advised to hold onto his intellectual wallet.

Yet the numbers are anything but useless in and of themselves. They can help to clarify the relationship between various factors affecting the possible battle between offensive missiles and antimissile devices. Thus, they can help to answer questions like What happens if they do this and we do that? For example, would we be better off increasing the power of our lasers or increasing the number of lower-power lasers? Or, more important, *does it make any sense at all to wait to deploy laser weapons until we can make them more powerful?*

Let us then look at the numbers game to get some notion of the many ways in which technical possibilities, quantities of defensive deployments, as well as tactics and circumstances may combine to produce vastly different answers to the question, How well will "it" work? Our point is that through the curtain of numbers it is easy to see two facts; that actual circumstances give the U.S. a chance to achieve substantial but uncertain protection against ballistic missiles; and that, given the many permutations of technical and tactical possibilities in this field, there is a tremendous premium on taking the initiative.

The Effectiveness of Battle Stations

The most often-debated point is also the most crucial. How effective would boost-phase defense be? By far the most important factor in this regard is the relationship between the amount of power per unit area (flux) that a laser can put on a missile, and the resistance of that missile to laser flux. For example, in their "studies," the Union of Concerned Scientists (UCS), the congressional Office of Technology Assessment (OTA), and Livermore Labs assumed that the lasers available to the U.S. would be able to put 24,000 watts per square centimeter on a missile at a range of 1,000 kilometers, and 8,000 watts per square centimeter on a missile at a range of 3,000 kilometers, (that is, a "brightness" of 2.4×10^{20} watts per steradian). But the UCS assumed that the missiles would be resistant to 20,000 watts per square centimeter per second, while the OTA and Livermore Labs assumed that they would be resistant to half that figure. From what we have seen, these figures for laser flux are roughly 2 to 4 times higher than what the U.S. can now comfortably achieve, but these figures for missile hardness are 10 to 20 times higher than any missile built or designed. Hence any calculation of effectiveness using these figures begins with an error of a factor of 2 to 5. Our purpose here however is not to quibble with the details, but rather to see what effect various assumptions have on estimated results.

At any rate, assuming a laser brightness of 2.4×10^{20} watts per steradian, and missiles resistant to 10,000 joules per square centimeter, Livermore Labs calculated that it would take sixty-five satellites to destroy 1,400 Soviet ICBMs launched from their present launch areas if these missiles had a boost phase that lasted a total of 400 seconds. But if one changes only one of Livermore Labs' assumptions, the one about missile hardness, and accepts the Union of Concerned Scientists' assumption (which happens to be double Livermore's figure), the number of satellites required to do the job simply doubles to 130. Of course, if one uses the actual figures for the hardness of solid-fueled missiles and laser power, the number of stations required drops into the teens. If the rest of Livermore's assumptions remain constant, and if one assumes that the Soviet missile force is—as indeed it is—composed preponderantly of liquid-fueled missiles, which are from 1/10th to 1/4th as resistant to lasers as are solid-fueled missiles, the number of satellites required to kill 1,400 ICBMs drops even further. Of course, current lasers are not as "bright" as those assumed by these studies. So if one decreases one's assumptions about the flux that the laser could deliver to match the capabilities of the once-planned 10-megawatt/10-meter mirror laser, the number of stations required would rise to about 32. However, if—again all assumptions but one remaining constant—we were to assume that the missiles would be as resistant to lasers as the Fletcher Panel assumes they may be someday, i.e., 100 kilojoules, the number of satellites would climb into the many hundreds. All of this is to say that different assumptions yield different results.

In fact, even the above-mentioned assumptions are not enough to define a hypothetical situation. That is because even assuming a certain level of missile hardness, laser satellites of a certain brightness, and a certain number of satellites the performance necessarily depends in large part on how the satellites would be distributed in orbit. That includes the orbit's altitude, the orbit's inclination in relation to the earth's equator, and the number of satellites on each orbital path. These factors are important because they affect how far any given satellite would be from its missile targets at any time. The distance of any laser satellite to its missile target is almost as important to the outcome of any engagement as is the hardness of the missile targets. Whether additional satellites would be clustered with ones already there, or would be used to fill in the spaces between satellites would also affect the *average* distance of engagements, and hence would affect the performance of any group of the defensive satellites.

The satellites' orbital altitude is important because, *optimally*, it must put them, as often as possible, where they can most easily destroy the largest possible numbers of boosting missiles. The satellites must be just high enough to be able to destroy the farthest boosting missile they can see without keeping their beam on it so long that they let closer and more vulnerable targets escape. Hence it is clear that optimal altitude depends not just on the altitude at which the target missiles' engines stop boosting but also in part on the relationship between the capacity of the lasers and the hardness of the missiles. Given any relationship between these three quantities, there is an orbital altitude that maximizes the efficiency of the laser satellites. In any case, given the (unrealistic) relationship between laser capacity and missile hardness mentioned above, how many satellites would it take to totally negate an attack by 1,400 ICBMs available to laser satellites for a total of 400 seconds? The answer seems to be 70 satellites if the height of their orbits were only 250 kilometers or 85 satellites in 500-kilometer orbits, or 120 satellites if these were in 1,000-kilometer orbits.

But that assumes that the orbits would be inclined 90° to the equator—that is, that they would pass directly over the poles. Such polar orbits make sense because Soviet ICBMs would travel over the Arctic. But in fact for most of them the direct route to their targets would take them "over the top" a bit south of the pole. It is also important that the Soviet Union's ICBM launch areas are located in a wide band of territory near 60° latitude. Hence, Livermore Labs' calculations show that orbits inclined 60° are more efficient—given all their other assumptions.[1]

Discussions of the number or the capacity of satellites required to kill a given number of missiles often include hidden assumptions about the range at which the engagements take place. One of the most striking analyses of this phenomenon is Gregory Canavan's,[2] with regard to the "study" by the Soviet Scientists Committee for Peace Against Nuclear Threat (sic). The Soviet committee's paper, first circulated to American opponents of ballistic missile defense at Dartmouth College in Spring 1983, was written specifically to discredit the proposal that Senator Wallop had made in *Strategic Review* in 1979. Canavan says that the Soviet study

> assumes that all engagements take place at their maximum range of 5 [thousand kilometers], which is actually the average distance between lasers in the 6 × 3 satellite constellation they discuss. This choice of range would have one laser ignore nearby targets to shoot at ones directly beneath another laser the maximum range away. The range to a target halfway between them is 2.5 [thousand kilometers]. Moreover, on the average many targets are at much closer ranges; the effective engagement range on the Soviets' kill-time analysis should be about 2.5/(2)1/2 = 1.8 [thousand kilometers]. Because the laser flux scales inversely as the square of the effective range, the 30w/cm^2 on the target estimated by the committee from the 5-megawatt, 4-meter mirror they assumed, should be increased by a factor of (5/1.8)^2 = 8 to 240 w/cm^2. *This rate, in contradiction to the committee's statement is adequate for the threat for which the 6 × 3 constellation of near-term 5–4 platforms was proposed.* [Emphasis ours.] Current boosters burn out in about 400 seconds; Mirv deployment takes another 300 seconds. Near-term boosters and buses can withstand about 500 j/cm^2 as *assumed by the committee* (emphasis ours). Thus the kill rate is about 240/w cm^2/500 jcm2 = 0.5 kill/sec/satellites. With 2–4 satellites in the battle this would give (2–4 sat) × 0.5 kill/sec/sat × 700 sec = 700–1400 missiles killed, *which is appropriate for the current threat for which this 6 × 3 constellation was proposed.*[3] [Emphasis ours.]

Thus we see that a semi-hidden assumption that all satellites would fire on targets at extreme ranges only, rather than on the targets closest to them, plus neglect of the simple statistical formula that approximates the optimal distribution of targets for each satellite were enough to make the original proposal for U.S. laser satellites, that otherwise appears as a serious defensive scheme, appear to be a nonserious one.

Now consider the same numbers game from a slightly different perspective. Suppose that the Soviet missiles were as laser-resistant as the Fletcher Panel stipulates—that is, 100 times the hardness of current solid-fueled missiles and 1,000 times the hardness of liquid fueled missiles. Whatever one considered the effectiveness of current lasers against current missiles to be, how could we change our defensive system to cope with these harder missiles? If we were to follow the Soviet committee and the Union of Concerned Scientists, we would have to increase by 100-fold the lasers' ability to deliver flux on a target. That requires not just a hundred-fold increase in power but also a much larger main mirror. In other words, such an increase in flux is a job requiring much technical innovation. But note. Since a laser's ability to deliver flux on a target decreases by the square of the distance to the target, it is much easier to arrange to deliver more flux on a target by putting the laser closer to the target than by leaving the distance unchanged and increasing the brightness of the laser.

So, if one wished to destroy a given number of missiles whose hardness had been multiplied by 100, the easiest thing to do would be not to wait for the technical innovation that would increase the brightness of lasers 100-fold, but to quickly multiply the number of current satellites by 10. By the same token, if those missiles were of the same hardness and launched under the same conditions as before, the same multiplication of the number of current satellites by a factor of 10 would be enough to destroy *100 times* the number of enemy missiles.

As we have seen, it is essential to note that simply increasing the number of satellites does little good unless they are distributed *evenly* in orbit so as to decrease the distance between the lasers and the missiles at which they must shoot. This simple lesson of the numbers game seems to have escaped the Office of Technology Assessment—and indeed of the SDIO. These organizations have approached the problem, (real or imaginary) of increasing the amount of flux deliverable on enemy missiles by planning to increase the number of laser generators in orbit. But their approaches are literally self-defeating because they involve *clustering* in relatively few locations in orbit many satellites (in the case of OTA) or, in the case of the SDIO, clustering many laser elements to form one satellite—which amounts to almost the same thing. If the number and hardness of the offensive missiles to be defended against remains constant, a tenfold increase in the number of satellites (assuming they are clustered) would indeed result in a tenfold increase in effectiveness. But suppose the enemy missiles had been hardened by a factor of 10. A tenfold increase of identical satellites, *without an increase in the number of orbital locations*, would result in no net gain at all in the destruction of targets. A hundredfold increase in the number of satellites under the same conditions would result in only a tenfold increase in effectiveness, and so on.

Of course all of the above calculations assume that during an attack, Soviet ICBMs would be evenly distributed above the broad geographic area where Soviet ICBM silos are located. This is an unavoidable assumption. But in fact, the actual distribution of Soviet ICBMs at any given moment during an attack is entirely unpredictable. Which Soviet missiles, located where, would be launched when, is a decision that only Soviet attack planners could make. At any given moment at any given location, the distribution of the attack might be more favorable or less favorable to the efficient utilization of defensive satellites than the hypothetical "even" distribution.

A secondary but not negligible effect of unpredictable geographic distribution of the missiles actually launched at any given time is that it is impossible to predict accurately the angular distances that each satellite's mirrors will have to move as they aim first at one and then at another missile. At a distance of 1000 kilometers, the distances between missiles coming out of a given field would be on the order of five hundredths of one degree. The time necessary for such small angular displacements are well below a second. But a satellite whose hypothetical fifty missile targets were widely dispersed within its field of view might have to make shifts of up to one degree. During an antimissile battle lasting 300 seconds this satellite might lose 25 seconds in retargeting that it would not otherwise have lost. On the other hand, a satellite whose targets were bunched would have somewhat shorter retargeting angles and thus make more efficient use of its time. All of this is to say that whenever the numbers game is played, the geographic distribution of the missiles actually launched at any given time is another uncertainty that is routinely covered over by making convenient assumptions. There is simply no way of dealing with such uncertainties a priori.

Countermeasures

Since we are on the subject of geographic distribution, let us note, as many have already done, that one of the most effective ways of drastically reducing the efficiency of any constellation of defensive satellites covering the earth would be to concentrate the launch of offensive missiles at a single place on the surface of the earth at a single instant in time. By definition, that would render useless all but one of the constellation of defensive satellites, because they would all be someplace else. But the one satellite that would be at the right place at the right time could do relatively small damage to the entire attack. As we have mentioned, a single 10-megawatt laser with a 10-meter mirror might be able to kill one missile per second. If all the Soviet Union's 1,400 ICBMs were salvoed from one spot, and there were, say, thirty-two such lasers in orbit, all the missiles would be vulnerable to just one laser for only the length of the boost phase of one missile. Hence the Soviets would lose no more than about one-fifth of their attacking force.

On the other side, however, one should note that to concentrate hundreds of ICBMs onto a single spot of the earth is an enterprise whose cost is exceeded only by its strategic stupidity. Never mind the fact that the Soviet Union has spent untold hundreds of billions of rubles to set up the present, widely distributed network of hardened ICBM launch sites. To duplicate this feat in one location would duplicate the expense. But above all such a move would make it possible for the United States' few counterforce missiles to do much more serious damage to the Soviet missile force than they can now do. After all, there is a reason why the missiles were dispersed in the first place. Of course this "move" would take many years and could not be secret. To try to concentrate the missiles secretly, just prior to the launch of an attack would mean doing so without the protection of shelters. If such a move were discovered, the entire force would be exposed to easy destruction by U.S. missiles. Even the relatively punchless (but plentiful) American submarine launched missiles could do *that* job. But the U.S. would not even have to use offensive means to counter such a move. Those who speak of concentrating missiles on the ground seem not to have noticed that it is much easier to shift the orbits of satellites to cover the bunching of missiles on the ground than it is to actually bring about such a concentration over roads and rails.

Suppose, however, that the Soviets were to develop a race of fast-burn missile boosters that would do their work very quickly, shortening the time during which boost-phase satellites could attack them. By how much would this reduce the satellites' effectiveness? How many satellites would one have to add to negate this countermeasure? Gregory Canavan argues persuasively as follows:

> Fast-burn boosters have leverage in connection with point launch; much less by themselves. Going from 1400 200-sec. missiles to 100-sec. missiles in distributed launch requires 160 − 105 = 55 additional defensive platforms, or an exchange ratio of missiles to satellites

of 1400:55 = 25:1. Going to still faster 50-sec. missiles requires 250 − 160 = 90 additional satellites, or 16:1, which is still highly favorable. But then taking that 1400 50 sec. − missiles, or 28/sec. and concentrating it in a point launch requires an increase in satellites of 960/250 = 3.8, dropping the exchange ratio to 1600:960 = 1.5:1. So with point launch, fast burn has leverage; without it, the difference between 100- and 50-sec. missiles is 250/160 = 1.6, just another 60 percent correction.[4]

In other words, introducing fast-burn boosters by itself cannot seriously degrade the effectiveness of space-based lasers. If the U.S. responded to the introduction of fast-burn boosters by increasing the number of its laser satellites, it could maintain a favorable ratio between satellites in orbit and missiles killed by making relatively small increases in its force. Why is this so? As one adds satellites (always assuming they are distributed evenly) the distance between any given satellites and any given missile drops. Because each satellite is shooting at closer range, each satellite makes kills much faster. Hence, the doubling of defensive satellites would be more than enough to negate the Soviet Union's halving of the time that boost-phase missiles are available to satellite-borne lasers. On the other hand, if the Soviet Union were to cut its missiles' boost time drastically *and* were to become able to secretly concentrate them all at any point on the earth for instantaneous launch, it would become prohibitively expensive for the U.S. to cover the earth with satellites thickly enough to guard against that eventuality. But that prospect is far wilder than science fiction.

What then do such figures mean? In and of themselves they mean nothing. The lasers that are factored into Canavan's calculations don't exist. Neither do the 100-second boosters—much less the 50-second boosters that also figure in those calculations. As we have seen, there are serious engineering obstacles to building such things, and good military reasons not to build them. So the only useful service that such quantitative exercises can perform is to clarify the fundamental relationships between time, distance, and vulnerability.

But what about the vulnerability of missiles? If that were cut down, how much would it cut down on the effectiveness of laser satellites and defense? There is no doubt that increasing missile hardness would have such an effect. But how could this be accomplished? Here the numbers are totally divorced from experimental data. Claims have been made that rotating the booster reduces the laser's effect on it. Canavan uses a notional formula for calculating this effect, according to which "a rotation rate of 1 rad/sec would halve the kill rate."[5] But surely this effect varies greatly according to several variables. One is certainly the size of the spot that the beam projects onto the booster. If the beam makes only a relatively small spot on the booster, rotation would relieve the thermal stress. But if the beam bathes the side of the booster, then rotation—at any speed—could provide only little relief, if any. If the flux deposited onto the booster is great enough to destroy it in a short time—say a second or less—and the entire side of the missile is bathed, it is possible that rotation would have no effect at all. Only experiments would offer more than structured guesses on how various rates of rotation would diminish the effects of various levels of laser flux, in various spot sizes, on missiles made of various materials.

How about protecting missiles by hanging shielding from their sides? The April 1987 Report of the American Physical Society is full of numbers purporting to show that hanging or plastering a half-inch of shielding on Soviet SS-18 missiles would substantially protect them against U.S. lasers at the cost of 6 tons of payload—half the weight of the biggest missiles' warheads. But the numbers happen to be wrong because the report assumes incorrectly that the weight of the shielding to be placed on each of the missiles stages is proportionate to the *mass* of that stage rather than to its surface area. Hence, the correct conclusion is that the weight penalty for a half-inch of shielding would virtually wipe out the SS-18's payload. But the matter is more complex than the numbers suggest. Would a missile's skin, which is designed to barely hold together, support tons of materials hanging from it? If one were to combine shielding and missile rotation, what effect would the additional centrifugal force have on missile bodies that barely hold together anyhow? If the vitreous carbon shielding material were supported, is there any reason to believe that it would survive the shaking and rattling of a boosting missile? The numbers that are bandied about in the SDI debate have nothing to say about such things.

Finally, any effort to inject the effects of decoy countermeasures into the numbers game must be rejected as totally unenlightening. The limit case has to be the possibility that some,[6] alas, take seriously, that the Soviet Union might "cover" the boost phase of its ICBMs by exploding multimegaton warheads in space above the launch zones. The heat of "fossilized fireballs" from such explosions would extend for hundreds of kilometers and would mask the heat of the rising ICBM's exhausts. Would more ICBMs be safeguarded by such a stratagem than would be destroyed by it? No one should pretend to know for sure. But having seen rockets destroyed by environmental perturbations such as lightning, and even by temperatures a few degrees off from the optimum, one should be reticent to base war plans on the proposition that many missiles could fly through nuclear fireballs.

Other Phases

The numbers game has not been played extensively with regard to the postboost, midcourse, and terminal phases because any attempt to use numbers to characterize the battle in these phases must obviously be contrived. What, for example, is the hardness of postboost vehicles at any given time? That depends on what they happen to be doing at that time. Are their engines burning? In that case, on balance, they are probably about as hard (or soft) as boosters. On the other hand, when they are coasting, they are probably harder than boosters, and much colder. Because PBVs are much more complex things than missiles, their hardness is not quantifiable. What does it mean to kill a PBV? Because damage to a postboost vehicle may not be catastrophic but might affect warheads and decoys in a variety of partial ways that would ease the job of midcourse and technical defense, that damage cannot be quantified.

As for midcourse, there is no way of disguising assumptions about the effectiveness or ineffectiveness of decoys or discrimination with a costume of numbers. Hence the only quantitative game played in public about midcourse concerns the footprints of (i.e. the areas covered) by very high altitude ground-based interceptors such as ERIS. The differences between rival claims stems from different assumptions about how soon after the DSP satellite first notices that offensive missiles have been launched the ERIS interceptors are sent on their way. The charts that show one ERIS base covering all of North America are correct—but only if the warning is instantly and automatically translated into a launch order. An indecisive man-in-the-loop mode of operation could reduce the "footprint" to next-to nothing—depending on the degree of incompetence.

The quantitative aspect of the problem of terminal defense, for its part, is unmistakably straightforward: For any given target area, will there be more competent terminal interceptors, or will there be more incoming warheads? The answer obviously lies not in the realm of science but in the realm of the military choices that attackers and defenders have made: How many warheads has the attacker directed to which targets? Which of these warheads happened to have been destroyed by earlier defensive layers? How many competent interceptors has the defenders placed where? Since none of these answers can be predetermined—never mind all of them—what conclusions are we to draw? The Soviet Union's official publishing house has a suggestion for American readers:

> In a full scale ICBM strike it is in principle impossible to predict which MIRVS will be intercepted earlier in their trajectories and, hence, how many warheads will reach a target or an area covered by a ground-based or air-launched antimissile system.[7]

On the basis of this fact, the Soviet Union invites Americans to assume that, in principle, every spot of American territory has been targeted by the entire Soviet strategic rocket force for "full scale attack." If we follow the Soviet Union's advice every American must assume that whatever warheads have survived boost and midcourse defense are heading for him and him alone. Since no one could ever ensure that there will be sufficient terminal coverage of any and every place in the U.S. against an "all-out" effort to destroy that very place, then it follows that Americans ought to give up on terminal defense. This line of argument is hardly honest and disinterested. But at least it has the merit of being far clearer than the numbers game played with regard to boost phase.

Conclusion

What, then does the numbers game tell us other than to distrust detailed claims, positive or negative, about how effective "it" would be? The first lesson is that while under some imaginable circumstances a defense would be inconsequential, under many other sets of conceivable circumstances a defense could be very good, if not perfect—certainly good enough to discourage an attack or retaliation. The second lesson is that circumstances are ever so variable. The logical third lesson is that an enormous advantage accrues to whoever goes out of his way to shape those circumstances. In other words a very great range of possibilities puts a huge—but indefinable—premium on initiative.

Hence we also learn how unserious it is to take this wide range of possibilities as a pretext for not building any antimissile weapon until something concrete has been demonstrated in the field. Necessarily, such an attitude ensures that others—the Soviets surely, and if we are very lucky, the French, but certainly not the Americans—will take the concrete steps that will realize some possibilities rather than others.

It should be clear that because its connections with reality are so tenuous, this numbers game is not winnable by anyone. During 1983–1985 an exchange of letters and articles took place between the Union of Concerned Scientists, the Office of Technology Assessment, and certain technicians at Los Alamos National Laboratories about how many satellites would be necessary to kill how many missiles during boost phase. Although the proponents of the SDI claim that the opponents abandoned their positions that thousands of satellites would be needed and that the job of boost-phase defense is unfeasible, in fact, the opponents only conceded the existence of certain mathematical relationships—not the usefulness of boost–phase defenses.

In April 1987, the American Physical Society issued a report chock-full of quantitative assertions based on arbitrary assumptions. Almost immediately, commentators including myself began to point out inconsistencies and gross errors. The authors of the report no doubt will issue a new version of their product purged of the most embarrassing errors and clarifying further how much their conclusions depend on their assumptions. But it would be a mistake to think that this sort of process draws together people animated by different purposes. Not only can different purposes not be reconciled. Neither can opposing assumptions. For example, one can complain about the APS report's requirement for 40-meter-wide telescopes 22,300 miles from the earth for determining the absolute position in space of ballistic missiles with an accuracy of one meter. One can counter that high-altitude surveillance satellites with 3-meter telescopes need only provide rough guidance to low-altitude laser satellites, and that these in turn need only to establish the exact *relative* location of their targets. But so long as there is no program for actually building equipment, one set of assumptions is arguably as good as another. The game is abstract and sterile—the very definition of a pseudotechnical filibuster.

In the end the numbers game shows everyone agreeing that both the U.S. and the Soviet Union possess the technology for taking a large, but uncertain, toll of missiles in space, as well as the technology for defending each individual point on the ground against relatively small numbers of warheads. The only important numbers regarding how well and at what cost the U.S. can turn these technical possibilities into reality could result only from a serious attempt to actually do it.

The quantitative verdict could only come ex post facto. But the character of that verdict would surely be affected not just by who built what devices and how well these devices functioned, but by how quickly they did it. In this as in other forms of conflict, absolute numbers are far less significant than relative ones or, in nonquantitative terms, getting there "firstest with the mostest."

9 / *The Treaty, and the Ties That Really Bind*

Our technical community met my guidance and has designed our SDI research program to conform to a more restrictive view of our ABM treaty obligations [than I believe the treaty itself warrants]. This has entailed some price with respect to the speed of our progress, the overall cost of the program, and the level of technical uncertainty we face at each step of our research. . . . This being the case, the issue of where exactly [the treaty's] boundaries should lie is moot.

—Ronald Reagan, NSDD 192, October 1985

Conventional wisdom has it that the ABM treaty of 1972 bars the way to ballistic missile defense and that the U.S. government is engaged in a serious debate over the meaning of its solemn obligations under that treaty. Conventional wisdom is especially attached to the proposition that one side to the debate, the Reagan Administration, chafes at the limits of the ABM treaty because of its desire to hurry the day of the SDI and is, therefore, looking to find or even to create legal loopholes. The other side, led by Senator Sam Nunn (D-Ga.) and Paul Nitze, one of the American authors of the ABM treaty of 1972 and the chief advocate of arms control in the 1980s, is generally supposed to be scrupulous of legal obligations, perhaps to the point of eschewing obvious loopholes. In fact, neither side in the controversy is particularly concerned with what the letter of the treaty requires. Both are jousting with legal arguments about the treaty to avoid espousing substantive positions about how the U.S. ought to face the possibility of war. Thus the legal debate, like the technical debate and the numbers game, serves to defer onto politically safer "surrogate" fields the substantive policy question with which both sides fear to deal: If the U.S. does not rely on antimissile defense to deal with the Soviet missile force, on what shall it rely?

In fact, the struggle in Washington over how SDI should be affected by past arms control agreements and by the prospect for future arms control agreements is exclusively a struggle over U.S. military policy conducted for domestic political advantage. The struggle is almost solipsistic. At issue are concrete proposals to restrict American forces. But none of the participants has proposed any measure that would actually bring about a restriction of Soviet antimissile forces. The arms control debate—most undeniably in the antimissile field—is a unilateral American exercise— a network of concepts and desires made in America that ties and binds American antimissile programs alone.

The Soviet Union, however, is a full partner in this intramural American exercise. Conventional wisdom has it that the Soviet Union is trying to use the arms control process to "stop the SDI." In fact, the Soviet Union's overriding strategic interest is to prevent or to delay as long as possible the United States' acquisition of antimissile devices that would thwart the Soviet Union's fundamental military tool: the disarming missile strike in the opening phase of war. To achieve this goal the Soviet Union does not have to "stop" the SDI. Rather, the Soviets' "bottom line," to prevent the U.S. from actually producing militarily significant numbers of antimissile devices is entirely consistent with the SDI program as conceived in 1983–84. The Soviets are perfectly ready to trade words for substance. Thus they work to strengthen the hand of those Americans, who, for whatever reason, are working to maintain the SDI in its original Reaganite definition. The practical "compromise" result they seek is a U.S. pledge—tacit if not explicit—not to reap the fruits of any antimissile program during a prescribed number of years. The status quo of the SDI suits the Soviet Union fine. The Soviet Union, however, wants the U.S. to affirm it. This, in practice, would resolve the essential question of policy that underlies the debate over the ABM treaty and SDI. The Soviet Union could then safely count on the logic of that resolution to work through the American policy-making process to ensure that its objectives are met. As we shall see, the Soviet Union has played its cards competently.

"What is not in the treaty specifically," wrote the Abbé de Mably in his classic treatise on international law two centuries ago, "is not in the treaty at all." This need for specificity is the reason why the text of treaties, whether about semiconductors or the extradition of criminals, consists primarily of definitions. This is the reason why treaties are negotiated in the first place. If each side could fully trust the other to perform its part of the bargain, there would be no need for the treaty. But in fact each side wants to make sure that the others' obligations are spelled out so clearly that any failure to accomplish the obligations would be obvious. On the other hand, both sides must trust each other's fundamental intentions; otherwise no definition, no matter how elaborate, could frustrate either party's determination to circumvent it. Balancing these countervailing counsels of prudence is difficult enough with regard to matters tangential to national survival. Doing so with regard to weapons that may save or kill millions is impossible. The U.S. has tended to enter into arms control agreements without a conscious "up front" determination about whether or not the other side's intention is to deprive itself of the capacity to wage war effectively. Rather the U.S. has entered into arms control agreements in the hope that the agreement itself will gradually wean the other side from warlike intentions. Fear spurs democracies toward arms control agreements, and suspension of judgment about the other sides' intentions makes it possible to conclude them. Hence, the sad result of attempts to abstract from conflicts of purpose by arms control agreements is that the agreements have provided the pretext for those governments that wished to disarm to do so. By so doing the agreements made sure that those governments wishing[1] to arm did not have competition.

The Letter of the Treaty

The ABM treaty of 1972 is a typical arms control agreement, indeed an extreme example of its kind. Its "letter" is sufficiently ambiguous to encompass diametrically opposed intentions. This would not seem to be the case from an ingenuous reading of Article I, Section 2: "Each party undertakes not to deploy ABM systems for a defense of the territory of its country and not to provide a base for such a defense." But what is a "base," and what does it mean to "deploy"? The treaty never even tries to define these words. As for the term "ABM system," the rest of the treaty is a halfhearted and foredoomed attempt to define it.

Article II, Section 1 begins: "For the purpose of this treaty an

ABM system is a system *to* counter strategic ballistic missiles or their elements in flight trajectory currently consisting of: . . ." (Emphasis supplied.) Note that the treaty does not say "that can counter," or "that may be able to counter," but rather *"to* counter." In other words, the treaty bans things *intended* as ABMs rather than things that can *serve* as ABMs. This is crucial, because it is impossible to make a case beyond reasonable doubt about what someone intends to do before he does it.

Now, there is no question at all that the Americans who negotiated the ABM treaty intended to banish antimissile defenses forever. Surely they and others who shared their intentions would refrain from acquiring instruments that *could* defend against missiles, because they *would not want* to have them. But what would these Americans do when U.S. intelligence would present them with information about Soviet systems that could defend against ballistic missiles? Would they call them violations, admit that they themselves had been wrong in their view of war in our time, apologize to the American people for having led them astray, and lead a crusade for American ABMs? That would be to expect a lot. To even consider paying such a price they would have to overcome the natural human temptation to find the evidence inapplicable to the case at hand.

The rest of Article II does not help, but rather takes a few more turns around the tautology: (a) "ABM interceptor missiles . . . are interceptor missiles constructed and deployed for an ABM role or of a type tested in an ABM mode . . ." (b) "ABM launchers . . . are launchers constructed and deployed for launching ABM interceptor missiles . . ." and (c) "ABM radars . . . are radars constructed and deployed for an ABM role or a type tested in an ABM mode." Again, note the double element of intention. The item must not only have been constructed for the purpose of antimissile defense but also deployed for that purpose. Needless to say, there can be no objective proof of such intentions.

But what is testing "in an ABM mode"? This "safeguard" is important, because the difference between radars, interceptors, and computers, (or between lasers and optical pointer-trackers) which are quite useful for anti-missile work and similar devices that are not so useful, or not useful at all for this purpose, is not readily apparent. So, the American negotiators thought that they would be hard-nosed. Anything that had been tested as part of a system for countering "strategic ballistic missiles (Article II:1)" would be considered covered by the general prohibition, because according to Article IV, ". . . each party undertakes not to give missiles launchers, or radars other than ABM interceptor missiles, ABM launchers, or ABM radars, capabilities to counter strategic ballistic missiles or their elements in flight trajectory, and not to test them in an ABM mode." The indication that these capabilities had been "given" would presumably be that the devices had been tested "in an ABM mode." But, alas, the treaty never defines the term. The U.S. attempted to insert a none-too-specific definition into the treaty, but the Soviets refused to have it. In 1978, U.S. and Soviet officials meeting in the "Standing Commission" in Geneva reached a secret agreement that began to define "ABM mode." But of course this consultative exercise did not result in a definition that was either comprehensive or legally binding. Also, since it was secret, it could not carry any political weight.

Even if the U.S. had succeeded, however, the very concept of "ABM mode" is inherently too amorphous to be useful. What if a particular device—radar, interceptor, laser—performs in only one mode, and in that mode is useful for many functions, including ABM? Is it then covered by the treaty? The Soviet Union contends that its large phased-array radar at Krasnoyarsk is for space tracking. Without a doubt, the Krasnoyarsk radar can perform that function—but not as well as it can perform ABM work. But nevertheless, it *can* do space tracking. The Soviet Union's SA-12 can and does intercept aircraft as well as reentering warheads. The laser that is to fly aboard the Soviet "Mars probe" of 1988 can probably destroy a ballistic missile in flight, but how can it be called an ABM under the terms of the treaty? By what right can anyone contend that these arguably multipurpose devices have an "ABM mode"? Obviously, the fact that any antimissile device, or part thereof can have more than one function (e.g. antisatellite work) is an open loophole for the development and testing of the very things whose development and testing is specifically prohibited under Article V:1, V:2: interceptor missiles, launchers, and radars that are sea-based, air-based or space-based. By what right can anyone hold that these arguably multipurpose devices have a distinct "ABM mode"?

The treaty, in Article III, allows the deployment of 100 ABM launchers in two (later reduced to one) geographically specified areas. In Article V, however, it stipulates that these launchers should not be made movable. But what is a launcher? If by the term we mean anything that can point an interceptor in the right direction and give it the electrical power it needs to ignite, almost anything can serve as a launcher, so that the restriction is almost meaningless. It is also totally unverifiable. Article V also prohibits the development, testing, or deployment of any mechanism for rapidly reloading interceptors into launchers. The intention of American negotiators was to enforce the principle of one launcher, one interceptor. But who is to say what is "rapid"? "Rapid" compared to what? The treaty never says. Any loading mechanism could always be justified under the treaty on the grounds that it is not as rapid as it could be! Hence the 100 permitted launchers could be legally enabled to fire 1,000, or perhaps 5,000, interceptors. But at least would not the geographic restrictions of Article III render wasteful this multiplication of interceptors in a small area? Not at all *if* one were to provide these interceptors (whose capabilities the treaty does not restrict) with the capacity to make their intercepts at very high altitudes and thus cover continent-size areas. This is precisely what the HOE-ERIS technology has done. Of course the U.S. has decided against deploying this technology for the foreseeable future. But on what basis could anyone argue that the Soviet Union has not incorporated it into its existing ABM or "high altitude air defense" interceptors? If the Soviet Union did not have this technology prior to the early 1980s, it got it when James Harper, a spy, provided it. Hence today, a combination of imprecise legal drafting and technology have drastically reduced the significance of Article III's geographic restrictions.

Consider also that the treaty never once mentions the word "production." Hence the treaty does not in any way restrict the Soviet Union or the United States from producing any and all antimissile devices that anyone's heart might desire. Ah, someone might answer, the treaty does restrict deployment. Alas, however, the treaty does not define, or restrict, or even mention the storage of ABM equipment and consequently does not even attempt to draw a distinction between "storage" and "deployment." At what point does the storage of ABM components become deployment, or even predeployment? Does the difference depend on the distance between the places where the products of factories are stored and the places where they are to be used, or on how long it would take to put the components in working order, or on what? The treaty is silent.

The reason that the treaty never addressed such questions is that U.S. intelligence cannot provide any basis for formulating such answers regarding the Soviet Union. The U.S. simply has no knowledge of how many or what kinds of antimissile components are produced in the Soviet Union, which factories produce which components, or where the components go after they leave the factories. Lest we give the wrong impression, let us now make clear that virtually all the lack of precision in the drafting of the ABM treaty that we have mentioned is due primarily to the scarce nature of the information that U.S. intelligence can provide about Soviet weaponry, combined with the fact that the U.S. political process demands that arms control agreements be verifiable. Given these two strictures, U.S. arms control negotiators had to choose between honestly reporting that it was impossible to write an agreement which was both meaningful and verifiable, or writing agreements which were meaningful but obviously unverifiable, or writing agreements which were arguably verifiable but not terribly meaningful. They chose the latter.

All of the ambiguities in the treaty arise from the difficulties inherent in trying to comprehend, encompass, and limit with language the uses to which men may put the reasonably well-known technologies of radar and rocket interceptors. This inherently problematic task is downright impossible if—as is the case here—it must be performed using the very limited information that U.S. intelligence can supply. But all these difficulties paled in comparison with trying to use treaty language to limit the uses of antimissile technologies that did not yet exist—especially given that U.S. intelligence could not promise that it would provide *any* given level of information about how the Soviets might be employing those technologies, *ever.*

That is why the negotiators dealt with the entire subject of unknown technologies by referring to them as "components capable of substituting for ABM interceptor missiles, ABM launchers, or ABM radars." All that the treaty could promise (in an appendix called agreed interpretation D) was that if such systems or their components were to be "created in the future . . . specific limitations . . . would be subject to discussion in accordance with Article XIII [the standing consultative commission] and agreement in accordance with Article XIV [amendments]."

How else could the negotiators have handled the unknown? Suppose that some negotiators had suggested banning the development, testing, and deployment of laser devices. First they would have had to decide what the definition of such a device should be. If someone in 1972 had the foresight to imagine that on some future day the Soviet Union might announce that it was launching a high-energy laser device into space for the purpose of vaporizing the surface of asteroids (as the Soviet Union in fact announced in 1985), that person might have asked: By what criteria could our treaty allow us to tell the difference between an asteroid-vaporizer and a missile killer? Someone might have proposed a bright-ness of, say, 2.4×10^{20} watts per steradian as an arbitrary definition of an ABM laser. Other negotiators would doubtless have argued about whether this is or is not a sufficient level of brightness to be deemed a true antimissile weapon; indeed, almost two decades later the argument among Americans on such points is preventing the development of any U.S. space laser. Others might have won-dered whether such an agreement might be circumvented by build-ing devices slightly inferior to that level of performance, but in greater quantities. Moreover, the American negotiators of 1972 would not have been able to know that such key performance parameters of lasers as beam quality, jitter in the pointer-tracker, power, performance of the mirrors' actuators, and so on contribute to laser brightness. In 1988 they know, but can't agree, about what levels of performance in these areas are sufficient for a "real" ABM laser. Nevertheless, U.S. negotiators in 1972 would surely have agreed with their successors today that U.S. intelligence could not supply enough information about these performance parame-ters of Soviet lasers to permit the formation of intelligent opinions, never mind definitive judgments about whether a given Soviet laser device did or did not fall into the prohibited category. As a case in point, the U.S. has precisely zero factual basis for judging whether the projected Soviet "asteroid zapper" does or does not violate the ABM treaty. In short, not only can one not define that which one has not yet conceived, but no definition can be a useful basis for action if it refers to unknown terms.

Hence the ABM treaty's treatment of "futuristic" ABM systems is literally the only thing it could be: an agreement to discuss, and to agree about, specific limitations of future weapons as those weapons are created. But, as everyone knows, an agreement to agree is not a deal but an expression of sentiments that each side may regard as it wishes. If it were otherwise, there would be no need for further discussion or agreement.

What, then, can one lawfully do under the ABM treaty? That depends almost entirely on what one *wants* to get away with. Both the U.S. and the Soviet Union can certainly develop and test any and every kind of surface-to-air system for exclusive anti-missile purposes, so long as the interceptors have single warheads and so long as during the test phase the components are "fixed"—whatever that means. There is no limit to the number of large phased-array radars supporting the system, so long as these are on the periphery of the country and oriented outward. There is indeed a limit of 100 operational launchers, but no practical limit on how many interceptors these 100 can launch, or on how "rapidly" they can launch them. There is no limit on the altitude of the interception or on the sophistication of the discrimination. There is no limit on how many interceptors or launchers or missile guidance radars may be produced, or on where they may be stored, or on how quickly they may go from a "stored" state to a "ready to shoot" state—*nothing in the letter of the treaty prevents this time from being measured in microseconds.*

So long as any ABM system or component of it can arguably be said to serve another purpose as well—including the countering of ballistic missiles that are not "strategic," a term not defined in the ABM treaty—there is no restriction whatever in developing, testing or, of course, producing and deploying any of them. The term "ABM mode" has no specific meaning in the text of the treaty. The distinction between air defense equipment and antimissile equipment once had a basis in technology. It no longer does. The distinction between the antitactical and antistrategic missile functions was always a legal fiction. So, either side can build and deploy as many as it wishes of dual-purpose antiair ABM systems, dual-purpose antisatellite ABM systems, and dual-purpose antitactical ballistic missile ABM systems. These can be ground-based, sea-based, or whatever, and of course there is no limit whatever to their capabilities.

As for ABM systems based on physical principles other than radar and chemical-rocket interceptors, either side can build as it talks. In other words, nothing in the letter of the ABM treaty prohibits either signatory from building a good anti-missile defense.

Any of the American negotiators of the treaty would regard the above analysis as nonsense. "Look at the preamble, and at Article I!" Paul Nitze once told this author, pounding his fist into his palm for emphasis. "I'm a lawyer, and I tell you that every provision of the treaty has to be read in the light of the reason why both sides entered into the treaty in the first place: to ban ABMs as a significant factor in the strategic equation."[2] Nitze has a powerful point. Leave aside the fact that eloquence in articulating the purposes of legal instruments does not make up for sloppiness in drafting the instruments themselves. Leave aside also that there is no evidence that the Soviet Union entered into the ABM treaty for the purpose of leaving itself undefended against American missiles. The fact still remains that the meaning of any provision of the ABM treaty does, in fact, depend almost entirely on the extent to which one is animated by the intention to have or not to have antimissile devices for one's own country. However, this point has two very different implications. If one intends not to have an antimissile defense, one does not really need any detailed prompting about what *not* to do. On the other hand, if one intends to have a defense, the letter of the ABM treaty is no barrier. When Henry Kissinger presented the ABM treaty to the Senate in 1972 he warned that if either side sought to use the treaty's terms to gain marginal advantage over the other the treaty would fail. That is why Kissinger emphasized the necessity of both sides being animated by the same spirit of renunciation. But of course that is something that the treaty cannot provide.

Restrictive or Permissive?

Since 1985, a controversy has raged within the U.S. government over how to interpret agreed interpretation "D" of the ABM treaty. But while conventional wisdom has it that the controversy is over the fine print and refers only to what either side may do with regard to "futuristic" weapons, in fact it is over the *spirit* with which the U.S. (and only the U.S., since none of the parties to the controversy have mentioned what may or may not be required of the Soviet Union) shall approach the entire ABM treaty. By sparring about the meaning of commas in the treaty and of negotiators' statements in 1972, both the Reagan Administration and its antagonists sought to avoid joining the issue: Did the American national security establishment do the right thing when it committed the West to vulnerability, or did it commit a terrible mistake? The Reagan Administration could not bring itself to openly break with the past, while its antagonists could not bring themselves to openly defend it. Let us look behind the scenes.

In the spring of 1985, the office of the undersecretary of defense for policy undertook a study of the negotiating record of the ABM treaty to determine whether agreed interpretation "D" should be interpreted as mandating the restrictions on the SDI that the SDIO had already imposed, or whether it should be interpreted as an absence of specific treaty restrictions on "futuristic" ABM weapons. The study concluded that the treaty did not require the SDIO's restrictions. Since the extent of restrictions to be imposed on the SDI is a matter of national rather than departmental policy, the study was sent to an interdepartmental group for review. As expected, the representatives of the Department of State and the Arms Control and Disarmament Agency took a position opposite to that of the study. The dispute was given to the State Department's legal adviser, Judge Abraham Sofaer, to resolve. Sofaer ruled in favor of what came to be known as the "loose," or "broad" interpretation.

At this point, during the summer of 1985, President Reagan was faced with a straightforward choice about policy. The federal government's interagency process had produced a judgment according to which the ABM treaty does not restrict the development of futuristic ABM weapons. The president could have accepted that judgment and could have announced that henceforth the U.S. would develop such weapons as quickly as possible. But to have done so would have been to dispense with the multitrack approach to arms control and the SDI that characterized his presidency. After all, if the U.S. would henceforth acquire futuristic ABM weapons, why should it not be acquiring every other kind as well? In other words, had he so decided, he would have had to argue that the entire ABM treaty had been a bad idea and that its many partisans in his administration, foremost among them Secretary of State George Shultz and Paul Nitze, had counseled the country wrong. He would also have had to drop the dilatory premise at the heart of the SDI program (research yes—weapons no) and depart from the nonpolicy toward strategic warfare so dear to senior military officers.

On the other hand, President Reagan could have rejected Judge Sofaer's judgment, citing his own understanding and his own inalienable responsibility for such matters under the Constitution. He could have announced that, as far as he was concerned, the ABM treaty intended to prohibit futuristic as well as current ABM weapons and that he intended to honor that intention. That would have honored and justified the partisans of arms control in his administration and would not have displeased the military. But, it would have exposed him to uncomfortable questions, among them: "If you accept the purpose of the ABM treaty, why do you arouse false hopes that the nation will be protected against missiles?" and "If you accept the purpose of the ABM treaty, why spend any money on the SDI at all?" Trying to answer these questions would have led to another question, that he was in no position to answer, that is, "What *is* your strategic policy?" In other words, the controversy tended to force Ronald Reagan to do what he likes least: to decide.

Not surprisingly, Ronald Reagan (in a decision announced by George Shultz to a NATO meeting in San Francisco on October 8, 1985) came down squarely on both sides. Yes, Judge Sofaer is correct, the ABM treaty does not really bind us as much as some people say, and yes, the U.S. will continue to restrict its SDI program. There is no rational reconciliation of this self-contradiction. But it is interesting to look at the closely held reasoning that the National Security Council elaborated to explain it and that Ronald Reagan signed.

This document (NSDD 192) begins with the seemingly straightforward promise that "This nation will remain in full conformity with its treaty obligations." But the point of the document is precisely the opposite: the U.S. will follow a particular approach to the SDI even though the treaty does *not* oblige it to. Hence it says, "Our initial and unilateral assertions about what the ABM treaty did restrict concerning advanced defensive technologies is not clearly demonstrable in the terms of the treaty as written, nor in the associated negotiating record. . . . These assertions reflected more our hopes for what could result from the treaty, made in the context of our assumptions about the future at that time, than on objective assessment of what was achieved and mutually agreed by the signed treaty document." In other words, the treaty does not support the policy visions of those Americans who negotiated it. Thus the president declares himself free to do what he wishes.

Yet immediately thereafter in the document, the president freely chooses to conform to the letter of the American arms controllers' spirit while ostentatiously abstaining from espousing or rejecting the purpose that animates that spirit: "Our technical community met my guidance and has designed our SDI research program to conform to a more restrictive view of our ABM treaty obligations. This has entailed some price with respect to the speed of our progress, the overall cost of the program, and the level of technical uncertainty we face at each step of our research." In other words, contrary to what the President had told the American people, he had not really decided, on March 23, 1983, to defend the Western world, subject only to the constraints of technology. Nor, as he made plain in this document, was he constrained by concrete treaty obligations. In fact, he had *chosen* to slow down technology and to impose strictures in the name of the treaty that he recognizes are not required by the treaty. But why?

Ronald Reagan's document continues to dodge the question: "I have carefully evaluated the price that the U.S. must pay for keeping our SDI program within the bounds of our current plans." Well, one might ask, what is that evaluation? How much more quickly, how much more surely, how much more economically could the American people be protected without these restrictions of yours? Is the price trivial or is it not? And what do we get in return for paying for it? But instead of an evaluation there is an assertion of policy protected by a prohibition of questions: "It is not necessary to authorize the restructuring of the U.S. SDI program towards the boundaries of treaty interpretation which the U.S. could observe. This being the case, the issue of where exactly these boundaries should lie is moot . . ." The only explanation for this line of reasoning that cannot possibly be true is the one offered by the document itself: "Under this course, there can be absolutely no doubt of the U.S. intentions to fully meet its treaty commitments."

The most likely explanation is that President Reagan and his chief lieutenants, unwilling to choose clearly for or against antimissile defense or the arms control process, chose both by going slow on both.

President Reagan's political opponents quickly found that they too could profitably play at hiding behind homemade shadows of the ABM treaty. Throughout 1986, as part of their campaign for the congressional elections, leaders of the Democratic Party charged that President Reagan, in his haste for the SDI was distorting and departing from the ABM treaty. But the Democratic Party would demand that Reagan do what he promised, i.e., live by the U.S. treaty obligations. As part of this campaign, Senator Sam Nunn introduced an amendment to the 1986 edition of the Armed Services Authorization Bill requiring the president to turn over the negotiating record of the ABM treaty. With this in hand, Nunn threatened, we would *see* how contrived was Reagan's permissive reading of agreed interpretation "D." The President turned over the record, and on March 11, 1987, Senator Nunn began to deliver to the Senate and to an applauding audience of the major media,[3] a 157-page report advertised as the scholarly refutation of Judge Sofaer's opinion of 1985.

Nunn's report,[4] however, hardly touched the negotiating record for the simple reason that the negotiating record contains no substantial support for his position. Further proof of this came from Senator Joseph Biden (D-Del.), a close associate of Senator Nunn's in this campaign. On the same day that Nunn began his report, Biden introduced Senate Resolution 167, which would bar the use of the negotiating record of the ABM treaty in setting U.S. policy. Nunn's report, however, was a full recitation of the wishes and expectations of the Americans who had negotiated the treaty. This, of course, is something quite different from the negotiating record. Judge Sofaer, and President Reagan, and everyone else in the world were never in any doubt that the intentions of American negotiators had been to ban any and all ABMs now and forever. But Sofaer's contention was that neither the plain language nor the negotiating record would support the thesis that the American negotiators had got their way. Nunn, theatrics aside, did not contest this.

Nunn's move, however, was political. He asserted a point, quoted many distinguished Americans with similar sentiments, and mustered a partisan majority of the Armed Services Committee behind a legislative provision to deny the president funds for any activity deemed to be in violation of his own and his friends' interpretation of agreed interpretation "D." Of course, Nunn did not try to specify in legislative language the differences between the futuristic devices that would be prohibited and the ones that would not—any more than the treaty's original negotiators tried. He did not attempt to, in effect, write a new, unilateral, updated version of the ABM treaty and get it passed into law. Instead, he encouraged the U.S. government to impose such a new version upon itself. His hands would remain clean. Also neither Nunn nor any of his supporters gave the slightest hint that they would somehow try to enforce upon the Soviet Union the same interpretation of the ABM treaty that they tried to foist upon the United States. It was not clear whether or not they omitted consideration of how their action might apply to the Soviet Union because they believed that the Soviet Union is already in compliance with their interpretation. They made no argument to this effect. Indeed there is no evidence that they were any more concerned with the Soviet Union than with the planet Pluto. In fact, both because of lack of specificity and because of its exclusive domestic orientation, Senator Nunn's provision to enforce the "restrictive" interpretation of Agreed Interpretation "D" cannot be understood as international law at all. Rather, it was a maneuver in domestic politics, meant to depict President Reagan as a militarist, whose threat to orderly relations with the Soviet Union was scotched by wise Democrats.

Yet the political clash between a leader of the Democratic Party leading a Democratic Senate in a well-advertised effort to deliver a setback to the flagship of a Republican president's defense policy obscured the fact that, in practice, Senator Nunn's and Ronald Reagan's positions with regard to the ABM treaty were nearly identical. While Reagan claimed we did not have to, and Nunn claimed we did, both concluded that the United States *should and would* act according to a "restrictive" interpretation of the ABM treaty. Without specifying how or why, both went out of their way to honor the American framers of that treaty, especially Paul Nitze. Both were willing to let Nitze and other likeminded people determine how "restrictive" the interpretation should be. Neither wanted antimissile defenses built. Neither let the Soviet Union's activities interfere with this basic decision. These two politicians differed chiefly in their rhetoric. Nunn spoke to a Democratic Party constituency that demands harsh words about armaments. Reagan, whose conservative constituency demands a quite different emphasis, dressed up essentially the same position as Nunn's in words that evoke a future (but surely not a present) in which the U.S. would try to defend itself.

The Effective Treaty

The actual, effective meaning of the ABM treaty for the United States is not a matter for speculation. It is set down in Department of Defense Directive 5100.70, dated January 9, 1973, and in the subsequent Department of Defense Instruction S-5100.71. These documents establish guidelines, committees, and procedures to ensure that "no program which reasonably raises an issue as to compliance can enter into the testing, prototype construction, or deployment phases without prior clearance."[5] In fact as we shall see, this dam in the middle of the creative stream exercises a much more important restraining effect on the creative wellsprings of projects. After all, why waste effort designing something that one will not be allowed to develop into a field-testable prototype? Why not, from the beginning, conceive SDI projects as mere proof-of-principle experiments? The purpose of the Department of Defense compliance program, which has been raised to a higher level since the birth of the SDI program, is explicitly not just to comply with the letter of the treaty but with the spirit that animated American arms controllers. The DOD notes that, where the treaty does not specify definitions, "it is necessary in some cases to set additional standards."

The DOD divides its activities subject to the ABM treaty into three categories. The first is that of "conceptual design or laboratory testing." The DOD—President Reagan's DOD—defines this category by quoting the words of Gerard Smith, the very words that Senator Nunn hurled at President Reagan from the Senate floor in March 1987. Like Smith, the Pentagon starts from the assumption that the ABM treaty really does ban ABM weapons "based on other physical principles." Since these weapons could not be defined in the text of the treaty, it is up to both parties to define them in practice to make sure that whatever they do fulfills the *intention* of the treaty, i.e. that there shall be no defense. This is the heart and soul of the "narrow interpretation."

Hence the DOD makes Smith's words its own: "The prohibition on development contained in the ABM treaty would start at that part of the development process where field testing is initiated on *either a prototype or a breadboard model*" (emphasis mine). Smith said that the reason for so drawing the line is that "early stages of the development process, such as laboratory testing, would pose problems for verification by National Technical Means." But by banning the building of either prototype *or even of breadboard models* (test models in configurations wholly unsuitable for operational use) of new ABM weapons, Smith and the DOD (and Reagan and Nunn) are imposing a control far more stringent than that implied by the criterion of verifiability by national technical means. That control is a self-denying ordinance against the *creation*—indeed the detailed conception—of things that, were they tested, would be evident to national technical means. Hence in what they do these Americans further narrow the "narrow interpretation" that they articulate. Obviously, any distinction between "research," development," and testing" can only be arbitrary. *Intentions*, rather than legal terminology, make the practical difference.

The DOD's second category, "field testing of devices that are not ABM components or prototypes of ABM components" is a logical, but wholly arbitrary, consequence of Smith's intention.

> The Smith statement shows it was clear in 1972 that "development" begins when "field testing" is initiated on either a "breadboard model" or "prototype" of an ABM component. This definition of "development" was used as a basis of ratification by the Senate and has been used as a U.S. government standard for the last thirteen years. The definition of "development," coupled with Article V, leads to the prohibition on testing of "ABM systems" and "components," or their "prototypes" and "breadboard models," which are other than fixed land-based. SDI field tests of space—or other mobile-based devices cannot involve ABM "components" or prototypes or "breadboard models" thereof. All SDI category 2 experiments must meet this criteria [sic].

As we have seen, however, the text of the ABM treaty says nothing that is not tautologic about what is and is not an ABM system or component. Even less does it distinguish between "components" and "sub-components." Nevertheless in practice, according to the DOD, any device conceived and built for eventual testing must not be an ABM component, "prototype," or "breadboard model thereof." Furthermore, although the DOD notes that all discussions of what constitutes testing "in an ABM mode" do not specify what that mode is especially with regard to "other physical principles," it nevertheless makes sure that no SDI "field test" violates its own maximalist definition of that stricture.

Not surprisingly, since the distinction between categories 1 and 2 is so murky, the DOD in practice deals with both categories by designing the projects in them so that in one way or another they come up with something that is obviously not for ABM. The space-laser triad (the ALPHA laser, the TALON GOLD pointer-tracker, and the LODE mirror) have been made "treaty compliant" by redesigning them so that the results will be incapable of achieving ABM performance levels. Moreover, the DOD has separated the three projects and broken down each individual project to make sure that each device will use only part of the set of technologies that would be required for an ABM component. The "compliance" technique here is a combination of scattering and of "designing down."

A decade ago, a megawatt-class laser, integrated with a main mirror and pointer-tracker existed at San Juan Capistrano, California, where it shot down a TOW (anti-tank) missile in flight. Under the SDI this laser was dismantled, and after a four-year effort reassembled at White Sands, New Mexico. But under the new, tighter interpretation of the ABM treaty, this old laser device, whose function is to test the resistance of missiles to lasers, may not shine its light on any missile or its components in flight.

For over a decade, plans have been underway to improve the capacity of the old geosynchronous DSP satellite to identify and track missile boosters. But under the DOD's interpretation of its duties toward the ABM treaty, if and when the U.S. manages to send up a replacement, this device will be deliberately limited in its capacity to serve as an adjunct to the ballistic missile defense mission, because it will not be equipped to immediately process and retransmit the data it gathers. But the DOD's regulators are not sure that this will cripple the device sufficiently and are studying other possible ways of diminishing the potential significance of the device.

Perhaps the DOD will choose to do unto the DSP—follow on what it has done to the Airborne Optical Adjunct. This was made acceptable to our ABM treaty monitors by deliberately limiting the quantity and the quality of the electro-optical detector elements, deliberately limiting the field of view (that is, putting blinders on the system), as well as removing the laser rangefinder for the device. Here, as in other cases where the technology for performing the antimissile mission exists, how much technical ingenuity has been devoted to making each device work as if it were insufficient, but in a way that yields data that, once extrapolated, can be used to argue that the device could perform in an antimissile role. Oh what a tangled web gets woven by self-contradictory policies!

As for the space-based anti-missile rockets, the DOD's regulators had a simple solution: Use them in an antisatellite role. This shows how arbitrary, and ultimately mindless, this system of regulation is. By applying this logic to any given device under consideration— i.e., that it would be used in an antisatellite mode—the DOD's regulators could have dispensed with any and all restrictions. They could have—had they wanted to—but did not.

The DOD's third category involves tests of systems and components intended to be ABMs and specifically allowed by the treaty. The regulators made sure that, as the treaty explicitly requires, each launcher could launch only one interceptor, that each interceptor could carry but one kill vehicle, and that all components not be movable—without regard to the fact that the Soviet Union has clearly violated the first and the last of these rules. But the regulators, working with the designers, went further. The planned terminal imaging radar was not only put in a building, it was designed so that the building would provide the structural support for it. If some day someone decides to shrink this radar and make it mobile, the work will have to start almost from scratch. Why? Certainly the inertia of attachment to old ways played a role, as did the lack of commitment to actually defending against ballistic missiles. But the "spirit" of the ABM treaty contributed to both.

We are lead to the question: What sort of intention animates those in charge of the SDI? Are they committed to defending against ballistic missiles? Or are they committed to the "spirit" of the ABM treaty? They try to postpone the question by repeating the mantra: "SDI is a research program whose purpose is to enable future presidents and future congresses. . . ." Yet the crucial question regarding intention cannot be put off so easily. As the engineers design each device, they must answer the commonsense question, "What's it for?" Each day they go to work they must decide, willy-nilly, whether the intention of the ABM treaty's American authors Gerard Smith, Ramond Garthoff, Paul Nitze, et al. to protect the world against nuclear war by making the West vulnerable to ballistic missiles is a good intention or not. They have to effectively decide whether or not to use their ingenuity to maximize the usefulness of this device for ABM purposes. So, given one kind of will, the ABM treaty is a mole hill. Given another kind of will, it is an impassable mountain.

It is not the engineers' responsibility to resolve such questions. But politicians have refused to answer them, and have thrown to the engineers an impossible challenge: "Do" the SDI, but adhere to the strict interpretation of the ABM treaty. It is impossible, however, to do respectable engineering just as it is impossible to do respectable international law, when the premise for both is a firm resolve to remain stuck in a policy muddle.

What the Soviets Want

The Soviet Union wants the United States to continue to mire its prospects for ballistic missile defense in a web of muddled political and technical decisions and nondecisions. Arms control is the principal means by which the Soviet Union has sought to help Americans weave that web. But Americans, rather than Soviets, are chiefly responsible for the fact that the Soviet Union has a growing monopoly of antimissile defense.

Beginning in 1965, Robert McNamara, Dean Rusk, McGeorge Bundy and a host of lesser officials virtually pestered Soviet representatives in every possible forum with offers of a treaty to ban antimissile defenses. At the Glassboro, New Jersey, summit meeting of 1967, MacNamara actually lectured Soviet Premier Alexei Kosygin on the theme that "offense is good, defense is bad." The Soviets' response was always that it would be immoral not to do everything possible to protect their country. The Soviet Union's own military strategy has always been based on reducing the enemy's ability to do harm by striking at the enemy's armed forces. Thus, when in 1968 the United States successfully tested its Sentinel ABM system, the Soviet Union realized that the U.S. would soon be able to thwart its military strategy. Moreover, Soviet antimissile programs were working with technology much inferior to America's. So the Soviets decided to take the deal that the United States had been offering. But this act was an affirmation rather than an abandonment of the Soviet Union's strategy of damage-limitation. We now know that the signing of the ABM treaty of 1972 did not affect the steady build up of the Pechora class radars and of the rest of the Soviet ABM program, just as the 1972 Interim Agreement on Offensive Forces, which was signed and ratified together with the ABM treaty, did not stop the Soviet Union's acquisition of counterforce missiles. Yet the treaty indisputably stopped comparable American programs and thus helped the Soviet Union to create a very favorable strategic balance for itself. Just as important, the attachment of many American leaders to the hopes they themselves invested in arms control has helped to frustrate any and all initiatives within the U.S. to move that balance back in the other direction.

The Soviet Union's diplomatic strategy has been straightforward: To hold up before the United States the vague promise of a world made peaceful through arms control, to threaten unspecific troubles that would follow a failure by the United States to pursue arms control, and to strongly suggest that—for the arms control process to continue—the United States must prove its "sincerity" by very specific acts of restraint.

The success of that strategy flows from the abundance of influential Americans who are eager to unconditionally press the U.S. government to "take chances for peace." The Soviet diplomatic strategy does not necessarily entail the signing and ratification of arms control agreements. Indeed the scrutiny to which the United States Senate subjected the proposed SALT II treaty had a demystifying effect on the entire arms control process. The aftermath of SALT I, which shamed so many American officials by directly contradicting the sales pitches they had made on behalf of the treaties, also had lowered the willingness of the United States body politic to sacrifice military programs for the sake of arms control. So, the Soviet Union prefers to protract the arms control process, thus keeping before Americans as many hopes as possible to embrace, as few specifics as possible to criticize, and as many opportunities as possible for Americans to shape United States military programs in terms of arms control, for as long as possible.

The Soviet Union's diplomatic effort to enmesh American strategic defense in arms control was ready to go public only 40 days after the Senate had passed the first Wallop amendment. On August 11, 1981, Soviet Foreign Minister Andrei Gromyko conveyed to the United Nations a draft treaty "Banning the Development of Any Weapons in Outer Space." The Soviet Union, said Gromyko, had always wanted space to be demilitarized. It was acting now because the risk that outer space would be militarized "recently has been increased." Lest anyone doubt the purpose of the exercise, Gromyko made clear that the danger consists of the possible deployment in space of "such types of weapons which cannot be defined as weapons of mass annihilation." Interestingly enough, given Senator Nunn's claims that the ABM treaty forbids futuristic antimissile weapons in space, Gromyko argued that the treaty was needed because existing treaties do not do the job.[5] Similarly, the official "Political Observer" of TASS, the Soviet news agency, also said that "the existing treaties and agreements still do not preclude" such weapons. These could be "of the existing type" on "spaceships of multiple use," or of types that might appear in the future.[6]

In the months that followed, this effort was overshadowed by the intense campaign to prevent the deployment of United States' missiles in Europe. The Soviet Union's antispace arms campaign began again in the summer of 1983. It is significant that the Soviet Union's reemphasis of this campaign followed a plea for help that a group of prominent American scientists, led by Richard Garwin, Hans Bethe and Wolfgang Panowski, addressed to Yuri Andropov, the former chief of the KGB who at the time held the office of General Secretary of the Communist Party of the Soviet Union. This happened immediately after Ronald Reagan's speech of March 23, 1983.[7] However, since in late 1983, the Soviet Union was making the Euromissile question the touchstone of U.S.–Soviet relations, it was poorly positioned to draw the United States into a dialogue on space. Between November 1983 and January 1985, the Soviets boycotted arms control talks in protest against the deployment of the Euromissiles. This meant that while they could denounce the SDI, and work up common arguments with their American friends, they had nothing to offer the United States in return for concessions on the SDI, no way of formulating palatable concessions, and no forum.

In the fall of 1984, after it was clear that their intransigent attitude was not going to help elect a U.S. President more to their taste, the Soviets asked for new arms control talks, which began with high-level conversations in December of that year and moved to Geneva in March 1985. The Soviets made no secret of their chief intention in these talks: to stop any U.S. anti-missile programs. The United States refused to negotiate about space alone. The Soviets were quite willing to satisfy the United States by talking about President Reagan's proposal for reducing offensive arms so long as the United States would talk about the SDI. But, at that time, according to United States Ambassador Henry Cooper, the Soviet's antiSDI proposal still consisted of the treaty it had first proposed in 1981, the premise of which is that *no treaty currently in force* does the job.

Not until May 1985 is there any evidence that the Soviet Union framed its demands on Geneva in terms of enforcing a particular interpretation of the ABM treaty of 1972.[8] It is surprising, and surely no credit to their perspicacity, that the Soviets waited so long to lay hands on the principal lever that American arms controllers, themselves, were already using to stymie the progress of American defenses. Whether or not the Soviets shifted their effort to the struggle for the reaffirmation and specification of the ABM treaty at the suggestion of anti-SDI Americans, by the late spring of 1985 it was common knowledge in arms control circles that a major battle was going on in Washington over whether or not the ABM treaty should be construed as prohibiting the development of futuristic ABM weapons. Common sense and past practice argued strongly to the Soviets that their arms control proposals be tailored to influence this struggle. Many influential Americans are committed to enforcing the "spirit" of the ABM treaty upon their country. Why not strengthen their hand?

Hence, the Soviet Union began to sound the theme: "In the Treaty it is stated with utmost clarity that the creation of any ABM systems of space basing is strictly prohibited . . . Observance of the ABM treaty is incompatible with efforts to prepare for the creation of arms banned by the Treaty."[9] The United States' loud protestations that the SDI program was carefully crafted to stay within the ABM treaty, that the United States had no intention of abrogating it, ever, and that Reagan was interested in "restoring the integrity" of the treaty, made the Soviet position plausible in American public discourse. Equally plausible was the initial Soviet proposal that this position logically implied: Let's talk about the ABM treaty, and about how to make sure that SDI remains in compliance with it. Already by late 1985 the discussions between the United States and Soviet "space arms' " delegations in Geneva were on this topic.

The Soviet bargaining position was to offer—as yet—unspecified cuts in offensive weapons in exchange for the United States' adherence to the proposition that would have an unmistakable impact on Americans, namely: Observance of the ABM treaty is incompatible with efforts to prepare for the creation of arms that would violate the purpose for which the treaty had been made. Much of the American press, following the lead of the State Department, hailed this Soviet position as the budding "grand compromise." What is supposedly grand about this compromise is that it follows the lines of SALT I—the ABM treaty and the Interim Agreement on Offensive Forces. Both sides agreed at that time to do without antimissile defenses in exchange for limits on offensive missiles.

The very fact that the United States government accepted it as a basis for discussion represented victory for the Soviet Union on the essential point: The United States would continue to refrain from committing itself to actually having any antimissile devices.

Only the details of that suspension of commitment remained to be decided. However, so long as the suspension remained in effect, there was no need to rush a decision. From the Soviet point of view, the negotiations were nevertheless essential because, although in his October 1985 decision Ronald Reagan had chosen to adhere to the "narrow" interpretation, he had only made a promise to himself. The object of the negotiations would be to have him nail down that promise as solemnly as possible. A treaty would not be essential for this purpose. The discussions would give the American bureaucracy the incentive to draw up more guidelines, and to police itself.

On January 15, 1986, the Soviet Union went public. Mikhail Gorbachev presented the most startling arms control proposal to date. Essentially, he accepted the proposals that Ronald Reagan had made in 1981 and 1982 about reducing intermediate-range ballistic missiles in Europe to zero, and reducing the stocks of American and Soviet readily deliverable long-range missile warheads by 50 percent. The price? An American commitment to abandon plans for antimissile defense.[10]

This put the Reagan administration in a bind. Its arms control proposals had been made in the earnest expectation that they would not be accepted, or that if they were they would contain serious reductions in the Soviet Union's huge stock of counterforce missiles. Yet here was Gorbachev urging an immediate unspecified 50 percent reduction, holding out the prospect of ultimately eliminating all missiles, and putting Reagan in the position of a quibbler if he insisted on picking over which missiles and warheads would and would not be cut. On the other hand, Reagan could not easily reject the proposals because, at least on the surface, they were his own! To reject them, the administration would have had to reject arms control.

Over the months that followed, the Reagan administration chose to praise the proposals, but to demur that it would never "negotiate the SDI." After the administration had thus made it unmistakable to the American public that its attachment to the SDI was the only thing that stood between the world and a massive reduction of nuclear weapons, Gorbachev dropped the other shoe. On June 4, the Soviet delegation in Geneva formally proposed that both sides would recommit themselves to the ABM treaty for 15 years. During that time research on antimissile systems would be permitted. But both sides would agree not to test or deploy antimissile weapons in space.

The Soviet offer was perceptively crafted so that the Reagan administration could have its politically cherished SDI program, *and* its politically cherished arms control deal. To reap these fruits would require changing nothing in the SDI program. All the Reagan administration would have to do would be to agree that for a certain number of years, the program would bear no fruits. The advice to President Reagan from within his administration was predominantly along the following lines: Since we do not plan to even decide whether to build any antimissile weapons for a number of years, the Soviet Union is offering us something for nothing.

This was essentially the deal that Gorbachev almost squeezed out of Ronald Reagan at Reykjavik in October 1986. Gorbachev invited Reagan, right then and there, to work with him to define the limits of activities permitted under the ABM treaty. Reagan balked. Later, in a nationally televised address to the nation he explained that he was perfectly ready to agree to observe the ABM treaty for 10 years, but that the definitions of prohibited activities that Gorbachev proposed amounted to "a new version of a 14-year-old ABM treaty that the Soviet Union has already violated. I told him we don't make those kinds of deals in the United States."

Why did he do this? Since, soon afterward, Reagan voluntarily renounced for the remainder of his administration the option of deciding whether to build antimissile weapons, it is unlikely that he balked at Reykjavik in order to actually protect that option. More likely, he did not take Gorbachev's deal because to have done so would have been to destroy the political image of the SDI. So powerful is that image that, regardless of the content of the SDI program, so long as it is not visibly "bargained away," it remains the administration's certificate of achievement.

But the pressure of the logical bind into which the Soviet Union had placed the Reagan administration only increased after Reykjavik. As the *New York Times* editorial writer put it:

> Mr. Reagan had the chance to eliminate Soviet and United States medium-range nuclear weapons in Europe, to work toward a test ban on his terms, to halve nuclear arsenals in five years and to agree on huge reductions later. He said no.

> SDI as a shield remains utopian, inconceivable without one miraculous technical breakthrough after another. Perhaps an argument can be made that this visionary bird in the bush is worth the sacrifice of the Soviet bird in the hand. But so far, the President has not made the case, only asserted it.[11]

So under this pressure, Reagan proceeded to make precisely the "kind of deal" with the Soviet Union that he told the American people he would not make. But instead of doing it openly and in one swoop, he let it happen piecemeal through the interplay of people and priorities well established in the U.S. government. Hence Reagan's signature, rather than veto, of a congressional mandate to adhere to the narrow interpretation. The effect is that of a treaty. But it is subject neither to Senate ratification nor to public scrutiny.

Beginning in February 1987, a series of conversations began in Geneva between Paul Nitze for the United States and Y. P. Velikhov for the USSR on how to apply the spirit of the ABM treaty to current circumstances. Similar conversations got under way in the Standing Consultative Commission, a body established by the treaty of 1972 to "resolve" American questions about Soviet compliance. Of course, the substance of these conversations is secret. During the fall of 1987 one Ashton Carter, who headed the OTA's attack on SDI and who was employed by Paul Nitze, conducted discussions with the various parts of the SDIO regarding the acceptability of a list of restrictions proposed by the Soviet Union. He issued no orders. But the effect was the same as if he had. Of course, no meeting-of-the-minds that occurs in such conversations is legally or politically binding on the United States. So, in a formal sense, Reagan kept his promise. But those conversations are an effective guide for much of the Reagan Administration and the American national security bureaucracy. Just imagine a technical bureaucrat deciding whether to submit or not submit a proposal to his superiors for a piece of the SDI. If the item or experiment seems to be agreeable to both Nitze and Velikhov, it stands a greater chance of being approved than if it fell into the category of "treaty controversial." The bureaucrat does not want to waste his time! Another bureaucrat might pick up his daily stack of press clippings and read a journal article by Paul Nitze entitled "ABM Treaty Permitted Activities."[12] Why should he not consider it binding?

As for much of the press and the Senator Nunns of this world, they are bound by the Nitze–Velikhov talks for the entirely sufficient reason that they wish to be bound by them. Indeed—and this is the overriding point—they wish the SDI to be bound by self-denying ordinances regardless of any conversations or agreements with the Soviet Union. The talks with the Soviet Union provide an excuse.

This is why Senator Nunn's campaign to restrict the United

States to the "narrow" interpretation of the ABM treaty is based so overwhelmingly on the statement of intentions by American officials. Those intentions, not any text, are the ties that really bind, stunt, delay, and deform the SDI program. The Reagan Administration's unwillingness to alienate the prominent individuals who embody those intentions makes nonsense of its toying with the idea of a "broad" interpretation of the ABM treaty. How "broad" or "permissive" can it be if the administration honors the purpose for which the treaty was signed—no defense—and is talking with the Soviet Union about how to fine-tune the breadth and narrowness of the United States' obligations under the treaty? Ronald Reagan can protest *ad nauseam* that the talks are not legally binding. He is legally correct. But the Anatoly Dobrinyns of the Soviet Union know that both the Reagans and the Nunns of America much prefer to toy with legal shadows than to confront hard choices. The Dobrinyns want to help their American interlocutors spend their terms of office in comfort—and to offer up years for the locusts to eat.

The Crux

The fundamental choice is no more a legal one than it is a technological one. The Americans who made the ABM treaty made it to give weight to their own particular view of the world and of nuclear weaponry. This is a view that proceeds from the belief that the invention of the atomic bomb was and will forever be the paramount event in history, that this event established perpetual military equality between the U.S. and the Soviet Union, and that nothing can ever happen to change that. Indeed, nothing that has happened—not counterforce missilery, nor any ABM program anywhere, has changed the views of the American authors of the ABM treaty. Their view is internally consistent. So long as one gives any credit at all to this view, any attempt to make a "broader" or "more permissive" interpretation of the ABM treaty cannot be for real.[13]

On the other hand as we have seen, if one rejects the American arms controller point of view, and to the extent that one looks at the treaty as an unwelcome obstacle in the way of a desirable goal, it is no obstacle at all. Indeed the ABM Treaty has not prevented the Soviet Union from building the nine huge radars that are the backbone of its ABM battle-management, from running production lines for every other component of a nationwide ABM system, from producing the SA-12 mobile ABM, from producing high-energy lasers that are soon to go into space, and from doing a host of other things that some U.S. officials prohibit other U.S. officials from doing. If the American goose looked at the ABM Treaty as does the Soviet gander, a "broader" or "more permissive" interpretation could only be a whistle-stop on the track to rejection of the entire treaty. In any case, the legal debate is a cop-out.

10 / *What Is to Be Done?*

Wherefore make up your minds once for all.

—Pericles, first oration

And I will restore unto you the years that the locust hath eaten.

—Joel 2:25

Both the Reagan Administration and its opponents have tried to avoid making responsible, public choices about ballistic missile defense. Thus it is incorrect to suppose, as does conventional wisdom, that the struggle between Ronald Reagan and his opponents over the SDI is important. Both Ronald Reagan and Sam Nunn have opposed putting any money into the nation's military budget to buy even one antimissile interceptor of any kind, regardless of whether it is made with old, young, or middle-aged technology. The Reaganites' vociferous support of the SDI clothes this bare fact in a way that appeals to the Republican rank and file. Democratic politicians, for their part, must pick their cover more carefully. Their hard-core leftist supporters demand a forthright rejection of ballistic missile defense. Also, the logic of partisanship demands denigration of Reagan's most famous creature, the SDI. Yet the public opinion polls continue to indicate that the SDI is a popular symbol. So, Democratic politicians invariably support "SDI research" while cutting funds for what they describe as "technically dubious" or "premature" aspects of it. The hard-core left knows that this means "no defense." Yet, since the SDI program does not involve building any antimissile device, no one, least of all the Reagan administration, can charge Democratic critics of the SDI with trying to sabotage the people's protection.

In short, by 1986 the interplay between the Reagan Administration and its Democratic critics had turned the SDI into something of a political nonissue. Yet the deepening of the United States' strategic predicament had raised once again the issue that Ronald Reagan buried on March 23, 1983, that is, why not build and deploy such antimissile protection as we can?

Two Choices, Or Three?

Perhaps the starkest of many illustrations of how the SDI has declined as a political issue occurred during the 1986 Senatorial campaign in Colorado. The Republican candidate, Congressman Ken Kramer, had been a leader in the drive for antimissile defense since the late 1970s. As a member of the House Armed Services Committee he had initiated the idea of an Air Force Space Command, played a large role in its establishment in 1982, and was generally credited with the fact that both the Space Command and the Consolidated Space Operations Center (the nation's principal command center for military satellites) were being built in Colorado. By 1986 tiny Colorado vied with California for having reaped the most concrete benefits from the nation's interest in space defense. In addition, the state's electorate was more friendly to national defense than the national average. Kramer's opponent, Congressman Tim Wirth, was a textbook liberal, a lifelong opponent of missile defense who had voted to cut SDI funds. Kramer, then, should have had no trouble putting Wirth on the wrong side of the majority of Colorado's voters, and keeping him there.

Yet quite the opposite happened. Wirth rejected the charge that he was anti-SDI and proved his point by showing that he had in fact voted to spend billions of dollars for the SDI budget year after year. Sure, he had also voted to make a number of cuts to correct some of the president's technically unsound proposals, to save the people's money, and to stay within the ABM treaty. But how could anyone depict this as antidefense action? Even President Reagan had said the U.S. should honor the ABM treaty. Moreover Wirth's campaign stressed that the changes in the SDI that Wirth had voted for were approved by Congress as a whole, were well supported by eminent scientists, and were certainly not anti-SDI. After all, President Reagan himself had agreed to compromise about those changes and had signed the bill. If anybody was anti-SDI and out of tune with the president, said Wirth's campaign, it was Kramer, who had been pushing for immediate deployment schemes that the Department of Defense itself had found technically unsound and, at the very least, premature, *and* that President Ronald Reagan himself had fought against. Thus, the antidefense Wirth successfully—and indeed rightfully—depicted himself as being closer to the Washington consensus on the SDI, a consensus effectively shared by the Reagan administration, than was his pro-defense opponent.

Thus also, the stated objective of the amendments proposed by Senators Proxmire (D-Wis.), Johnston (D-La.), Bumpers (D-Ark.), and Chaffee (R-R.I.) in 1986 and by Senator Nunn in 1987 was not to eliminate SDI, but rather to lay down legislative guidelines to keep it within bounds that the amendments' authors deemed proper. Although the amendments differ in many ways they have one thing in common: All would allow money to be spent to develop a variety of technologies, so long as no plans whatever were made to embody any of those technologies in any device that might be in any way usable to kill a missile. Since the Reagan Administration had no intention of crafting any anti-missile device, it had a hard time making much of a stand against these amendments. It could not argue that if Congress had agreed to the administration's proposal to spend $5.2 billion in fiscal year 1988 rather than the roughly $3 billion proposed by the opposition, or if Congress rejected the left's restrictive language, the people would be protected any more than if Congress had done otherwise.

In other words, given the "research only" character of the SDI, the left's restrictive amendments were political freebies for their authors. Everyone knows that voters won't get terribly angry at congressmen and senators simply for tampering with the president's options. Why should anyone care whether a future president will be constrained from exercising an abstract option thirteen years hence, or eighteen years hence, rather than ten years hence as he had planned? The leftist opposition diffused even that slight threat by offering an incentive to the Reagan administration to compromise with, and thus approve of, its restrictions. If you compromise, and accept our strictures, the left proposed to President Reagan, we will allow you to spend a few more hundred million dollars, and you can claim something of a victory.

The Reagan administration began winning this sort of "compromise victory" on the SDI in 1984 and never tried for any other kind. Hence, the SDI battle has been over nothing more than marginal political advantage. The results have given marginal political benefits to both the Reagan administration and to its Democratic opponents. Neither side risked the voters' ire by publicly championing a clear position about ballistic missile defense. Accordingly, the battle over SDI has been profoundly irrelevant to the strategic predicament of the United States.

The only political battle relevant to the United States' strategic predicament was not over the SDI at all but over something else— something that, whether called "early deployment" or "partial deployment" amounted to one version or another of the common-sense approach rejected by the Fletcher Panel and the Reagan Administration: Do what you can with what you've got. Not surprisingly, those who wage this battle are precisely the ones who had waged it before the Reagan administration became involved. Their leaders, in the late '80s as in the late '70s, are Senators Wallop (R-Wyo.), Garn (R-Utah), Hollings (D-S.C.), and Heflin (D-Ala.), and Congressmen Kemp (R-N.Y.) and Courter (R-N.J.).

Inevitably, these people found themselves in conflict with both the Reagan administration's SDI and with the anti-SDI movement. Between 1983 and 1986, they suffered from the logical contradiction of being SDI's most fervent supporters while, in fact, working from premises entirely different from those that underlie SDI. These "supporters" found it attractive to associate themselves with President Reagan's popular rhetoric about SDI. But again and again they were embarrassed—as Congressman Kramer was embarrassed—when opponents of ballistic missile defense effectively claimed to be closer to President Reagan's position than they. After all, throughout their time in office, President Ronald Reagan, his secretary of defense, and officials of the SDIO did not go to the Wallops, Kemps, and Courters to work out the scope and details of the program. Rather, the Reagan administration's stock-in trade was to negotiate with the Sam Nunns and Les Aspins of the Congress.

These "supporters" cut a sad figure with their letters-to-the-president, written more in sorrow than in anger, asking Ronald Reagan to propose antimissile weapons or at least to back their own proposals. These letters typically began and ended with flattery of the President for having made a "historic decision" for which generations of Americans would praise him. Of course, the signatories knew that no "historic" decision had been made and were trying to butter up and nudge the president into making one. Alas, precisely such sweet reasonableness assured the president and his appointees that they had nothing to fear from the signatories and that they could afford to treat them with contempt. So, the "supporters'" laboriously crafted arguments served only as the butt of jokes in White House staff meetings.

Between 1983 and 1986, the press did not report that there existed an "early deployment" side to the SDI debate. The reporters for the *New York Times* and the *Washington Post* with whom this author has spoken have argued that this side did not deserve coverage because it was not having an impact on the program. They have a point, but by failing to mention this movement—complete with its lack of influence at the time—the national press gave its readers the mistaken impression that the controversy between Ronald Reagan and Sam Nunn (and their compromises as well) were about the essential question "Shall we build antimissile weapons, and if not, on what shall we base our strategic policy?" But this was an incorrect impression, and hence bad reporting. In fact, the pro- versus anti-SDI controversy was empty posturing. The real choice before the nation was between two forms (Reagan's and Nunn's) of elaborate procrastination, on the one hand, and the antimissile weapons advocated by the "early deployment" movement on the other.

This began to be clear around the middle of 1986.

The Death of the SDI and the Birth of "Early Deployment"

In March of 1986, in order to bolster their drive to cut the SDI's funding, and to embarrass President Reagan, the leftist opposition discovered the SDI's undeniable Achilles' heel: The technology being developed by the program could not demonstrably (maybe not even possibly) defeat the "responsive threat" that is the program's movable benchmark with the level of assurance that the program demands. This incongruity had always been at the center of Senator Wallop's critique of the SDI. But whereas Wallop had denounced this incongruity as artificial and had rejected both the very notion of the "responsive threat" and the SDI's standards of performance, the left uncritically accepted all of the SDI program's own standards, and eagerly embraced the incongruity.

Wallop et al. had expressed dismay at the incongruity to demand that it be resolved in favor of action. The left had expressed glee in order to demand that the program rid itself of "premature" technology demonstrations, and limit itself to basic research aimed at a deeper understanding of the very difficult problems of ballistic missile defense. Hence, also, the program's funds should grow little, if at all.

The opening shot in this campaign was a staff "study" delivered to Senator William Proxmire on March 17, 1986. The study was a review of the SDIO's plans and an account of interviews with its officials. It clearly speaks with the voice of many people in the program who support "long term research"; who term every-thing else, in the words of a senior scientist at the Livermore National Laboratory, "a series of sleazy stunts," and who object to talk of building ABM devices because it "is driving good people out of the program." The "Proxmire Report," as it has come to be known, is not an assault on SDI from the outside, but an expres-sion of what SDI had become.

As regards boost-phase defense, which everyone agrees is very important, the "study" reported that the SDIO, under the cover of budget cuts, had dropped any pretense that it was interested in chemical lasers because of "operational limitations"—though no one argued they are not feasible. At the same time the study praised the major shift of funds to Livermore's free-electron laser, although it faces "significant difficulties" and doubts about its basic feasibility. This shift, says the report, was among many in favor of which "critics"—i.e., people such as Proxmire, Nunn, the Union of Concerned Scientists, etc.—had long argued.

But the problems of boost-phase defense, says the report, go far beyond weapons and sensors. "During the past two years every new SDIO assessment of Soviet capability . . . invariably deems the Soviets substantially more capable than the previous assess-ment." For example, the report notes, "Sandia scientists reported that fast-burn boosters would not necessarily degrade the weight that could be lifted into space. . . . Livermore's scientists have concluded that fast-burn boosters would not necessarily degrade Soviet capability to put warheads and decoys in space; as a matter of fact, Soviet fast-burn boosters might even be able to dispense several mini-buses of warheads [instead of a single bus, as is now done] which would further complicate the post-boost-phase de-fense." Naturally the report does not say that these wondrous "discoveries" by Sandia and Livermore, never mind the SDIO's discovery of operational limitations in chemical lasers, were not the result of trials of weapons against weapons, or even of labora-tory experiments, but of people punching their favorite assump-tions into computers and getting their favorite answers. Yet it was sufficient to accomplish the report's purpose that these conclu-sions were undeniably bought and paid for by the SDIO and that the SDIO did not disavow them.

The most important of the SDIO's charges against itself noted by the Proxmire report was that boost-phase defense would most probably not work because it would be impossible to ensure the survival of any defensive devices in space. The Proxmire report published the names of a long list of conceivable countermeasures,[1] nearly all of which exist only in the realm of the imagination, and reported in detail on only one, to the effect that no one in the SDIO could figure out how to enforce "keep-out zones" against antisatellite weapons, including "space mines." The reason it was infeasible to enforce "keep-out zones" was that doing so would involve a commitment to destroy even objects declared to be civilian satellites if their owners insisted on putting them too close! It speaks volumes about the U.S. government that it would consider this a technical point rather than a challenge to policy. In the same way and for similar reasons, when a U.S. frigate in the Persian Gulf was hit by a missile launched from an airplane that had been allowed to get too close, some U.S. officials spoke of the failure of the ship's electronic instruments to provide unambiguous proof of the airplane's intentions. But electronic instruments report things, not intentions. In space, just as at sea, the enforcement of keep-out zones becomes technically challenging to the extent that inept policymakers impose unrealistic "rules of engagement."

The Proxmire report's most interesting suggestion about survivability was that the Soviet Union could be expected to successfully disguise and decoy its means of attack on U.S. defensive satellites, while the U.S. could not expect to disguise and decoy its defensive satellites to confuse attackers. Of course, it did not report any reasons for this attitude on the part of anyone at the SDIO—there could be none. But the attitude itself is remarkable. To support this attitude the report quotes a paper on infrared research in the Soviet Union that says "They believe that there are no absolutes in weapons technologies, that any weapon cannot only be countered but also warped so that it appears to be something it is not. . . ."[2] Indeed the Soviets do believe that, because they are intensely interested in making their own space assets survive, while others' perish. But does the SDIO believe that *the U.S.* can successfully use those very techniques to beat the Soviets in the field of "signature modification" and decoying?

From this passage in the report, one must conclude that the SDIO does not so believe: "If the Soviet defense develops a capability to discriminate between a warhead and a decoy, it will likely be capable of discriminating during an attack between *defensive* weapons and decoys." (Emphasis added.) But the major premise of the rest of the report is that to discriminate between decoys and warheads is a hopeless task—*at least for the U.S.!* That premise is constructed out of "anticipated problems" such as the detonation of warheads in space. Such explosives would supposedly downgrade the performance of discrimination sensors while at the same time, inexplicably, not affecting the flimsy decoys or the warheads. This is similar to the assumption, also alive in the SDIO, that boosters could shield themselves by flying through "fossilized fire-balls" of nuclear detonations. Accordingly, says the Proxmire re-port, "S.D.I. scientists and General Abrahamson himself have con-cluded that passive discrimination alone will not be effective in the midcourse phase. Hence the report says proudly: ". . . some projects such as the Space Surveillance and Tracking System have been downgraded because they depend on passive discrimination."

The Proxmire report's whole point was, why not be honest and go all the way? Why not acknowledge openly what the SDIO is already saying through its "best" people and by its operations? Why not acknowledge what the president's science adviser George Keyworth has been saying since March 23, 1983: "Whoever is presi-dent in the early 1990s will have—sufficient information to think seriously about deployment." That means that *today* we do not have it and hence we should not be trying to think seriously about antimissile devices. All the talk about "breakthroughs" is nonsense. There have been none. Why not acknowledge that antimissile de-fense is a pipe dream that deserves only long-range research?

The SDIO's feeble response consisted of quibbling with minor details. For the SDIO's response to have contradicted the study's thrust, the SDIO would have had to renounce its own reliance on the "responsive threat" and explain why it did not value the conclusions that these teams at Sandia and Livermore—composed of people whom it had paid and honored—had drawn from the "responsive threat." To effectively counter the Proxmire report, the SDIO would also have had to reverse its decisions to slow down near-term defensive weapons. Above all, it would have had to renounce its founding tenet: That its job was only to investigate a theoretical possibility about which no intelligent judgment could be made until at least the 1990s.

For similar reasons, the SDIO issued an equally lame response to a similar "study" pushed by antidefense activist Sidney Drell during his tenure as president of the American Physical Society in 1986.[3] The SDIO stated "We would not have made several of the assumptions they made in defining the technical require-ments." But which ones? The "study" had charged that Livermore's free electron laser, on which the SDIO had placed so many hopes was getting nowhere near the wavelength, power levels, and consis-tency of operation that the SDIO had programmed for it. The SDIO's one-page response did not claim otherwise, but meekly pointed out that nevertheless some progress was being made.

All of this is to say that by 1986 the logic of the choices that Keyworth, Cooper, MacFarlane, and Fletcher had made in 1983 about the direction, personnel, and intellectual framework of the SDI had finally caught up with the program. So, between 1984 and 1986 acting according to that logic, mindful of the president's two-track policy with regard to the SDI and arms control, and mindful of the Air Force's opposition to ballistic missile defense, the SDIO's director, Air Force Lieutenant General James Abrahamson, had chosen to throttle the programs leading to near-term weapons. He had bet the future of the SDI on the ability of far-term technologies to make enough "breakthroughs" to sustain interest for many years to come. But by mid-1986 it was clear that the two showiest parts of that bet, Livermore's linear accelerator free electron laser and the companion effort to transfer high-power laser beams through the atmosphere were not paying off. Abrahamson was left with all of the liabilities that one might have feared from the course he had pursued and with none of the advantages.

When, by mid-1986 it became clear that Congress would not approve more than about $3 billion for SDI for fiscal '87—roughly the amount that had been projected for this field prior to the president's speech, it became clear to Abrahamson and to everyone else who was paying attention that the SDI, as conceived in 1983, had just died. Ronald Reagan and Sam Nunn would fight over its flag. But the originally planned progression of a comprehensive SDI system through research, then development, and finally to a deployment decision was just not going to happen.

At this point, the real struggle came to be over whether the United States would have some form or another of "early deployment" (i.e. it would build forthwith such devices as it could), or whether the U.S. body politic would put off any serious talk of antimissile defenses for a long time.

In the last half of 1986 the SDIO, for its part, began to reemphasize some of the directed energy and electro-optics programs it had just finished deemphasizing. Also, by default, the rocket interceptors (both ground-based and space-based) that were occupying a small part of the SDI budget (and had been playing an even smaller role in the SDIO's plans) began to loom large in the SDIO's rhetoric. Because, beginning in 1986 an increasing number of the SDIO's programs were being placed under "black" security classification, it is difficult to lawfully discuss the extent to which the SDIO has reemphasized such programs as chemical lasers and the AOA. That is, not only has detailed information about these programs been restricted to very few people, but those who come to know that information come under the most serious obligation that U.S. law can impose to maintain secrecy.

The general fact of this reemphasis, however, is general knowledge among those close to the program. Two things must be said of it. First, almost the sole reason for the security is to avert embarrassing questions. Why did the SDIO once decide that chemical lasers just would not do, and why it has since decided that they might just do after all? Every journalist who covered the birth of the SDI program is sure to have copious notes from authoritative-sounding official briefings that denigrated chemical lasers. Surely, either the SDIO was wrong then or it is wrong now. Regardless of that, what does it mean for the U.S. to be "looking favorably" on this weapon the basic technology for which has been lying about for most of a decade? A "favorable attitude" that did not involve the immediate building of a missile-killing weapon would be laughable. In the best of circumstances, the administration would have to explain why so many people wasted so much time. Most uncomfortably, however, high officials would be asked: So, you've decided to build a space-based laser. Who in the U.S. military will have the "Role and mission" to use it? How have you decided to handle the problems of survivability in space? Having definitely decided that ballistic missile defense is a good thing, what other devices will you build? What are your concrete plans for protecting the U.S.? Have you now decided that the ABM treaty is not in the interests of the U.S.? What *have* you decided? Why?

The second thing to be said about the fact that more of the SDIO's programs have become "black" is this: While "blackness" can indeed cover such small programs as may proceed from indecision, it cannot protect the existence, the scope, and the objectives of any large programs that might follow from decisions that might be taken to be serious about any weapon. Hence the new "blackness" in the SDI world is a cover for indecision.

The SDIO's newfound enthusiasm—by default—about rocket interceptors, however, was shouted from the housetops, although it, too, was a reversal of position. Ever since late 1981, retired General Daniel Graham, former director of the Defense Intelligence Agency, had been promoting a plan for antimissile defense featuring large numbers of rocket interceptors in orbit and labeled "High Frontier." Although the framers of SDI had never taken the High Frontier plan seriously enough to proselytize against it as they had against chemical lasers, they had nothing but contempt for High Frontier. But now, in the fall of '86, the humble, inexpensive, experiment carried aboard the Delta 180 rocket that (although it did not intercept anything) showed that existing instruments had the ability to home in on the junction between a missile and its plume, represented something terribly important to the SDIO: success, and something to divert attention from the impasse into which the program had worked itself.

Yet this enthusiasm too was of the indecisive variety. Did the SDIO actually propose to the secretary of defense that the U.S. *deploy* space-based rockets with all of the preparations and consequences (construction of transportation facilities, assignment of roles, missions and forces, and either renunciation or re-interpretation of the ABM treaty) that this would entail? No. Rather, it proposed, and the secretary proposed to the President, the engineering development of the space-based rocket weapon and the scheduling of a decision about possible production and deployment for two years later. This proposed step forward, which would have carried the U.S. decision-making process to where it had been *circa* 1981, proved too much for the Reagan Administration.

As regards the ground-based interceptor rocket ERIS, the embarrassment was of another kind. Here was the scion of the HOE intercept of June 1984, the only dramatic success that had occurred under the SDI (although it had been started long before the SDI). Here was proof, if anybody wanted it, that *something*, could be done. And yet the SDIO was much more reticent about ERIS than about the space-based rockets. This was because it was really very hard to convince anyone that there was any more than *one* decision left to make about ERIS, namely, do we want it or not? But that was precisely the decision that the Reagan administration was trying to put off. Also, in order to fit ERIS into the SDIO, the SDIO's leadership would have to disown the assumption by now well ingrained in the SDIO that no midcourse kill system is worthwhile since we do not have the "interactive discrimination" needed to defeat hypothetical "balloon decoys."

Of course a decision to deploy ERIS would make sense only if the U.S. also decided to build large-phased-array radars and the Airborne Optical Adjunct to provide discrimination. But to make such decisions one would have had to renounce both the Reagan administration's basic ambiguity about policy, and the rest of the SDI establishment's procrustean intellectual edifice. This the SDIO's leadership could not bring itself to do.

In sum, the change of heart and mind at the top of the SDIO that occurred in mid-1986 produced something less than a coherent appeal to the president and to Congress.

For the politics of SDI, the second half of 1986 was more significant, because it went a long way toward dispelling the Reagan administration's obfuscation of the fundamental question. The process got under way in July, when the "usual suspects"—Wallop, Kemp, and Courter—joined by five other colleagues, wrote a letter to the president, much like others they had written, urging his support for reorienting the SDI to production and deployment. They also asked for a meeting with the President in August to make their case. But the White House chief of legislative liaison, William Ball, did not notice that these men were no longer coming for an audience at the foot of the throne. This time they were coming to get a straight answer to the question "Are you with us or against us, or are you in the fight at all?"

To dilute the prodeployment people's effect on the president, Ball arranged for the presence of eight other Republican legislators, all of whom were cool to antimissile defense. With sixteen guests, plus the president's staff, and only thirty minutes allowed for the meeting, the chance of serious talk was nil. This mockery on top of yet one more act of evasiveness proved to be the last straw for the prodeployment people. They did not attempt to argue, but instead warned the President about the parting of the ways that was occurring.

Congressman Jim Courter set the taunting tone by asking President Reagan what would have happened if John Kennedy had treated the moon program a⌐ Ronald Reagan has treated ballistic missile defense: "Do you think we would ever have gotten to the moon, Mr. President?" Reagan sputtered in anger at that and similar barbs. A month later, as Reagan was preparing for his summit meeting with Mikhail Gorbachev in Iceland, the essence of the message that the prodefense people had delivered that day appeared as an op-ed by Congressman Jack Kemp et al. in the *Wall Street Journal:* Unless the SDI program actually provides for protective weapons, "no one will support it, including ourselves."[4] The "early deployment movement" had formally detached itself from the dead body of the SDI.

The "usual suspects" however were only the legislative tip of a much larger movement of diverse people making diverse proposals for early deployment. Some, like Henry Kissinger,[5] simply stated that in their view the U.S.—Soviet strategic balance had worsened to the point that only the building of American defensive weapons could rescue the situation. Of the specific proposals, the simplest was that of Martin Anderson of the Hoover Institution who, the reader will remember, had first raised the idea of missile defense within the Reagan campaign staff. Anderson proposed that the

U.S. purchase 100 ERIS interceptors, and deploy them at Grand Forks, North Dakota, according to Article III of the ABM treaty. These 100 interceptors, argued Anderson, would give the entire U.S. absolute insurance against an accidental launch of Soviet missiles, as well as against the possibility that one of the world's Qaddafis might acquire some ICBMs. Incidentally, these 100 interceptors would somewhat complicate a serious Soviet attack on the U.S. and might be the core of a larger American defense force later. After all, argued Anderson, every great journey must begin with a small step.

The Reagan Administration publicly ignored and privately rejected Anderson's proposal precisely because to take a small step into this field would raise questions it did not want to deal with about where it wanted to go and why it was not going faster. To begin with, if we deploy these 100 interceptors, do we take care to maximize their effectiveness or not? If it were our purpose to make that little defense the best it could be, would we pursue it in ways that, while respecting the letter of the treaty, would contradict its antidefense spirit? For example, would we begin to make the reloading as fast as we could make it without infringing some convenient definition of "rapid"? How many ERISes would we produce beyond the 100 on the launch pads? Where and in what state of readiness might they be stored? If our purpose was to make our defense the best it could be, why stop at 100 ERISes? Why limit ourselves to ERIS at all? But if the administration's purpose were *not* to make that little defensive deployment the best it could be, it would have to explain why not. The 100 ERISes would suffer the fate that the United States' only ABM site suffered via the Kennedy amendment of 1975. The administration would be discredited. Rather than deal with such uncomfortable matters, the Reagan Administration chose to remain in the limbo provided by the perpetually unresolved pseudotechnical and pseudolegal questions about the grand "SDI system."

Then there was Zbigniew Brzezinski's proposal for a layer of space-based interceptor rockets plus a layer of ground-based interceptor rockets deployed near U.S. ICBM fields. The idea was intended to diminish the Soviet Union's confidence in its ability to carry out a counterforce strike. Although Brzezinski's proposal offered little to the population, it did address the United States' most pressing strategic problem in a down to earth manner. Just a few defensive weapons, he argued, would create some uncertainty on the attacker's part. More would create greater uncertainty and boost deterrence further.

Finally, near the end of the year, as some in the SDIO were arguing within the administration for permission to do engineering development on space-based rockets, Robert Jastrow, a Dartmouth professor collected and published their views, proposing 11,000 interceptors in orbit for boost-phase protection, 10,000 ERIS interceptors for midcourse, and an undetermined number of HEDI interceptors for terminal protection. The ensemble, according to Jastrow's government sources would be 93 to 99 percent effective (against precisely 1200 ICBMs, 11,200 warheads and 10,000 decoys) all for a cost of $121 billion (neither more nor less), and could begin deployment seven years after the decision. While the numbers regarding performance and cost that Jastrow reported had little meaning, his was one more voice repeating what more and more people were coming to realize: that the SDI program, whatever it was, would not deliver "the system" in the foreseeable future but that, nevertheless, lots of technology is available to more or less (depending on whose views one heeds) fill our needs for antimissile defense. If the U.S. was not using any antimissile weapons to remedy its strategic weaknesses, this was not due to a shortage of technology.

In 1986 the early deployment movement received an unexpected boost from abroad. One of the staples of the struggle over the SDI has been the U.S. State Department's warning that "the Europeans" dislike the SDI so much, and are so attached to arms control, that should the U.S. forsake the ABM treaty for the sake of antimissile defense, it would "lose" Europe (whatever that means). This warning has had its intended effect. For example, in September 1985 as President Reagan was considering whether to endorse a more "permissive" view of agreed interpretation "D" of the ABM treaty, this line of argument was an important factor in his decision. Not surprisingly, some of the most somber warnings have come from Richard Burt, a longtime advocate of arms control serving as Reagan's ambassador to Bonn. Washington was truly surprised, then, when Germany's minister of defense, Manfred Woerner, published an article in the Winter 1986 *Strategic Review* advocating immediate defense against ballistic missiles.

Woerner's article is all the more interesting because he evidently felt compelled to treat the SDI as a distraction to the case he was making. The SDI is a fine thing and full of hope for mankind, Woerner begins. Germany is proud to participate and looks forward to the SDI program's decision milestones in the 1990s. Meanwhile, says Woerner, Europe in general and Germany in particular have a problem: all those Soviet ballistic missiles of various ranges, ready and able to decapitate NATO's armed forces as a prelude to an invasion. These missiles are becoming so accurate that they can perform their decapitating mission without nuclear warheads. Hence, he concludes, we should consider the missile problem as a practical part of the conventional threat.

By this rhetorical maneuver, Woerner sought to remove the subject of antimissile defense from the a priori, abstract disputes that have enmeshed SDI and nuclear matters in general. Woerner then asks what we can do about this great conventional threat? Quite a lot, he answers. As the Soviet Union has shown, the technology of modern air defense can be extended to cover much of this conventional missile threat. Germany will provide such a defense for itself forthwith. Then he drops the other shoe: Naturally, because it is impossible to tell whether a missile or warhead is carrying a nuclear or conventional explosive, our antimissile devices will protect us against nuclear as well as conventional warheads. Woerner ends the article with another ritual bow to the SDI and with good wishes for the next century. Meanwhile Germany is using its participation in the SDI program to inject high technology into its "tactical air defense system."

This gentle lesson was not lost on anyone who follows military affairs. Nor was France's quieter development of its own ground-based antimissile weapons, the SA-90. The essence of that lesson is that while the U.S. government was using some of America's best minds to find pretexts for procrastination, others were building defenses to the best of technical capacities that do not approach those of the U.S.

As 1986 ended and 1987 began, the "early deployment" movement in the United States had grown to include just about every defense expert associated with the Republican party, as well as some, like Brzezinski, normally associated with the Democratic party.[6] Moreover, virtually the entire corps of Republican party activists in the U.S. had become aware of the existence of a split between the Reagan administration's "pro-SDI" position and the "pro-early deployment" position—and they vigorously supported the latter. The final proof of this is that by the end of 1986—with the notable exception of Vice President Bush—every Republican candidate for the presidential election of 1988 had declared himself in favor of "early deployment." These candidates for the most part had no grasp of the details. But they did grasp the essence of the matter: There exists a program called the SDI that is working on some antimissile system, which, if it ever works, will be tremendous. But a long time must pass before it is ready. Meanwhile, we should do what we can with what we've got. One of these candidates, Congressman Jack Kemp, made that point into a central pillar of his campaign.

That is why when Secretary of Defense Weinberger gave the impression on January 12, 1987 that the Reagan administration was on the brink of approving the Defense Department's proposal for engineering development of the space-based rocket weapon, the press mistakenly concluded that the Reagan administration had made the decision to give in to this constituency. But this was never close to being so. The Defense Department never even *took up*—never mind resolved internally, never mind submitted to the president—the question of who would be responsible for using the weapons thus developed, and how room would be carved out for these weapons and their associated services within the defense budget. By never coming to grips with the question of "early deployment" in January 1987, the Reagan administration chose to heed the reticence of another constituency: the senior officers of the U.S. armed forces.

The Main Opposition

Conventional wisdom wrongly assumes that far-left groups such as the Union of Concerned Scientists or the Stanford arms control program are the principal brakes on the Reagan Administration's zeal for the SDI. In fact, the Reagan Administration regards leftist opposition to the SDI a public relations asset. The real brake is Reagan's and Weinberger's total deference to senior military officers, and the unwillingness of senior military officers to confront the organizational and budgetary questions that a commitment to strategic defense necessarily implies.

Until 1987, the military's hostility to strategic defense, although well known to "insiders" was unknown to the public, largely because the press was comfortable with painting the picture of the SDI as the Pentagon's bid to militarize space, but also because the military confined its hostility to restricted channels. In 1987, however, senior military men felt the need to oppose the early deployment movement was urgent enough to speak more openly and to voice their antidefense views to reporters "on the record." The press, perhaps feeling the need to do more against antimissile defense, began to cover the antidefense activities of various Pentagon boards.

In May 1987, for example, General John T. Chain, commander of the Strategic Air Command and surely the most important operational commander in the U.S. Air Force, speaking at an Air Force Association symposium criticized the very idea of an antimissile defense as destabilizing: "If the Soviets build an SDI then that means I'm going to have to have a larger bomber force. . . . The day that we end up with an SDI system on both sides . . . this country may have 1,000 [or] 2,000 bombers." His conclusion: "With S.D.I. we will have nailed the door shut and left the windows open. . . . Once we build a shield against incoming missiles, then we have to worry about bombers delivering gravity bombs, delivering standoff missiles, delivering cruise missiles, and submarines and ships delivering air-breathing cruise missiles." The general spoke this way to make two points. To build antimissile defenses is to give up the comfort that our acceptance of vulnerability has brought us. If we take seriously one kind of vulnerability we will have to take seriously other kinds. That will mean doing an awful lot of things that we are not doing. Worse yet, it will mean not doing many of the things that we are doing. The figure of 1,000 to 2,000 bombers was surely picked out of thin air, but the intention was specific: Whatever money the country spends on antimissile defense cannot possibly, for any reason, be taken out of current commands.[7] However, the thrust of General Chain's presentation was that these terrible problems should be faced later rather than sooner.

At the same symposium another highly placed Air Force General, Harley A. Hughes, who also serves on the Joint Chiefs of Staff, not only made the point that the SDI's funds should come from outside the military budget. He also explained why the military is moving so unenthusiastically to make antimissile defense happen. You see, the idea of defending the country did not come from the military system. Because of that, the military never had got around to drawing up a statement of operational requirement. And certainly no major program could get started without one. But General Hughes assured the audience that they were working on it. He did not need to add the words "with all deliberate speed."[8]

In June of 1987 officials of the Joint Chiefs of Staff openly criticized a move by the SDIO to get the Defense Acquisitions Board to give preliminary clearance to putting the question of deployment of rocket satellites into the Pentagon's regular budget process, i.e., to formally posing the question about actually building antimissile devices. The main charge was simply that the plan would absorb money that should go elsewhere. This naked bureaucratic ploy was thinly veiled with the assertion that since certain technical and bureaucratic problems have not yet been solved, consideration of entry into the regular budget process is premature. Note that this fight was not over proposed expenditures. Rather it was over one of about four steps preliminary to that fight!

One of the bureaucratic weapons wielded in June '87 was a report by the Defense Science Board, whose full text the military leaked to the *Washington Post* on July.[9] This self-perpetuating group has often thrown against ballistic missile defense the weight of the fact that it is the bureaucratic representative of "science." But seldom have its arguments been scientific. This occasion was no different. Its report refers exclusively to managerial–bureaucratic criteria that must be met "over the next couple of years" as prerequisites for any decision to try to defend the country. Its key "scientific" point is that ". . . there is presently no way of confidently assessing: (1) system performance against requirements [of the Joint Chiefs of Staff], (2) system cost, or (3) schedule." Moreover, "The technology [to ensure] . . . the survivability of the [space based weapons] is still uncertain. . . . Funding requirements for the plans we have seen, however, exceed the [Pentagon's five-year budget plan] and greatly exceed the amounts presently under discussion in the Congress." Of course the DSB "strongly support continued work on S.D.I."

College courses in physics or electronics will not help one to decipher this scientific report any more than battlefield service will help one to understand the senior military's position. But anyone who has experienced bureaucracy will find their meaning crystal clear: The Pentagon's eminent gentlemen don't want to see American antimissile weapons approved, deployed, and most of all paid for. If the United States follows the tortuous course that they have laid out, dots their i's and crosses their t's, history will continue to go into the books without an American antimissile defense. Any student of history would be hard put to find an example of a major human enterprise that reached fruition by following such an approach. Rather, the successful ones have followed Theodore Roosevelt's answer to bureaucratic–scientific reservations about the Panama Canal, namely: "Make the dirt fly!"

But why don't the senior military and their establishment want defense? Without speculating, we must note that they simply value other things more. When Congressman James Courter met with members of the Joint Chiefs of Staff in the spring of 1987 to discuss the reasons for their reticence, they reportedly "rolled their eyes" and indicated it would be totally unrealistic for them to come to grips with the obviously divisive problems that would attend introducing missile defense into the U.S. armed forces.

There is nothing surprising in this. Military officers are no exception to the "iron law of bureaucracy," according to which regardless of the purpose for which the organization was established, it tends to end up serving the personal interest of its senior members. Perhaps the most shocking example of any military's organizational self-absorption was the French Army before and during most of World War II. Not only did its senior officers refuse to make proper preparations, because they would have disrupted well-established patterns of behavior. But in 1940, even as German panzer divisions were killing French draftees by the thousands and were occupying Paris, they continued to put concern for the cohesion and budgetary welfare of the senior officer corps ahead of anything else. For this reason they were the principal lobby for surrender to the Nazis. It is entirely normal that senior officers should stubbornly and self-interestedly continue to walk in the ruts of habit.

It is normally up to nonbureaucrats—civilian leaders or extraordinary military men—to wrench a bureaucracy out of its ruts and onto new paths by breaking old careers and making new ones. Leaders can only reason with bureaucracies by manipulating the things they hold dearest, i.e. by working on the reason by which they run. The real question, then, is why the president and his secretary of defense allowed the military bureaucracy to pursue its priorities instead of theirs.

Anyone who experienced the Reagan administration knows that this abdication was the result both of conscious choice and of the mental limitations of President Reagan and of the bulk of his appointees. Senator Wallop once closed a long phone conversation with President Reagan—during which the President had agreed with Wallop's arguments for early deployment—by pressing the president on what held him back. "The chiefs," replied Ronald Reagan. "I just can't substitute my judgment for theirs." Thus the only people with the lawful authority to force the hand of the military chiefs declined to question the intellectual and moral basis of the chiefs' position. In sum, the bureaucrats acted like bureaucrats, but the president did not act like a president.

That is why when in February 1987 Secretary of Defense Weinberger explicitly disavowed any intention to deploy defenses based on "off-the-shelf technology" by claiming, "There is nothing on the shelf," he insulted the intelligence of everyone who had been pushing specific antimissile weapons for almost a decade. Weinberger undoubtedly represented the president's firm position. But that position was literally incredible to anyone but bureaucrats. Even the Proxmire report had stated, "There is no doubt that the United States could build some type of antiballistic missile system today that would be of limited effectiveness against a Soviet nuclear attack." The "early deployment" movement was arguing that the U.S. should stretch the limits of the possible. Weinberger and Reagan might have countered by trying to argue in some detail that, for whatever reason, the weapons the U.S. could order immediately would not be worthwhile. But that is not where they were coming from. They had given the matter over to the bureaucracy, had made their appointments, and were comfortable with the endless limbo that the bureaucracy produced.

The U.S. Defense Force

When the Reagan Administration thus closed the door on any decision to build antimissile devices, it freed the early deployment movement of any residual obligation to take its views into account. This made for a certain economy of thought. Instead of asking themselves How do we get the president to do something? those who looked beyond Reagan (as 1987 advanced so did the number of such people increase) began to ask instead: What is to be done?

Common sense says that the first part of any large-scale enterprise must be to gather a nucleus of people who *want* to do the job, to charge them with the solemn duty to do it, to set dates by which the product should be delivered, to give them a general idea of how to proceed, and then to feed in the resources as required. Conventional wisdom notwithstanding, the Reagan Administration had not established the SDIO to be such an instrument.

First, the SDIO was not filled with people who were either organizationally or, for the most part, personally committed to antimissile defense. Although it is nominally a separate organization directly under the secretary of defense, the SDIO is actually peopled by members of the Army and Air Force, and a few from the Navy. These servicemen's careers continue to be determined by their parent services, which view ballistic missile defense as a threat to their corporate interests. Were the military officers assigned to the SDIO to pursue vigorously the mission of ballistic missile defense (assuming that this were encouraged by the SDIO, which it is not), they would thereby sacrifice their own careers rather than further them. As it is, the SDIO is like any other joint service organization in the Pentagon—a place where the services' representatives accommodate each other's interest. Nor can the director— Air Force General James Abrahamson—or anyone else inspire the organization with his own purpose so long as he is, by charter, the executor of an executive committee of Pentagon officials of which he is the lowest-ranking member. Perhaps the fact that the SDIO's organization does not link the interests of the personnel with performance of the job would have been less significant had the organization been staffed with people selected specially because they possessed an inner drive to do the job. But, in fact, those who set up the organization in the first place went out of their way to make sure that there was not a "true believer" in missile defense among the organization's early leaders. In time, a few did develop "fire in the belly." But they never formed a "critical mass" for the sufficient reason that the career-motivated majority recruited its own kind for staff positions, consultancies, and contracts.

Second, in affairs of government, nothing substitutes for a mission. A mission is a license to act. But the Reagan administration was careful not to give the SDIO the mission to defend the United States or the right to ask for the funds to carry out such a mission. Third, given Parkinson's law, and the Reagan administration's decision not to follow the example of John Kennedy's moon program in setting a date for delivery of the product, it is anything but surprising that the SDIO's research program generated endless demands for more research. This is so especially because it should have been (and probably was) obvious to anyone who knows the Pentagon that, unless required to do otherwise, the services' R&D establishments would continue to follow the pattern into which they had grown, namely constant redefinition of tasks, deferral of decisions, gold-plating, exorbitant costs, and stretch-outs. In short, establishing the SDIO was not the first decisive step toward a defense but living proof that nothing is more futile than to give charge over new things to people without the will, the authority, or the means to achieve them.

The logical starting point for anyone interested in antimissile defense, then, was to create an organization that would be everything that the SDIO was not. Regardless of their preferences for individual defensive weapons, or how much they expected from those weapons, thoughtful members of the "early deployment movement" agreed on this.

The first to act on this logic was Senator Wallop. On April 2, 1987 he introduced a bill (S-900) to establish a new military force— a fourth military service alongside the Navy, Army, and Air Force— and to endow it with the mission "to defend the United States from all types of aerial threats, including aircraft, ballistic missiles, cruise missiles and other types of missiles, and in the event of war, to provide intelligence from, and secure and retain control of space for the military forces of the United States."[10] Bright and well-intentioned people, said Wallop, might well argue against any of his bill's particulars. But anyone who did should be obliged to propose other ways of accomplishing the mission and explain why these other ways would do as well.

The military service proposed by the Wallop bill would be dedicated from the top down to the accomplishment of its mission—it would have no conflicts of interest. Like the other armed forces, the Defense Force would be headed by its own civilian secretary, and military chief of staff. These officials would review the applications of any officer or enlisted man in the armed forces who wished to transfer into the Defense Force. This is akin to the procedure through which Admiral Hyman Rickover filled the United States nuclear submarine force with people literally hand-picked for both unusual ability and for dedication to the mission. The Defense Force would absorb the physical facilities, equipment, contracts, and select personnel of the Army Strategic Defense Command, the North American Aerospace Defense Command (NORAD), the Air Force Space Division, the Unified Space Command, all space activities of the Navy, and the space support elements of the office of the secretary of the air force (i.e. the "black" intelligence programs); plus such other elements and assets of the Department of Defense as the secretary of defense would deem necessary and proper to accomplish the Defense Force's mission. A few of the SDIO's assets and contracts would be in this later category. At its very inception, then, the Defense Force would be taking over approximately 80,000 existing civilian and military employees and a yearly budget of perhaps $50 billion. This set of people, facilities, equipment, and contracts makes up much of the nation's existing technical base for military space activities. If it were pulled together under leadership clearly oriented to the strategic defense mission, it would translate the United States' abundant technical capabilities into defensive assets.

The Defense Force would develop defensive devices, procure them, and prepare to use them in combat. The bill would direct it to prepare forces as quickly as possible to defend against threats "as defined by the best intelligence available to the United States." This is to counter the cult of the "responsive threat" so prevalent in American military R&D. To counter other aspects of the culture of "gold-plate, delay, and waste," the bill would exempt the Defense Force from any and all Pentagon regulations governing R&D, and procurement for a period of ten years. During that period, the secretary would make such rules as seemed reasonable.

The bill would also direct the Defense Force to take

> such actions as may be necessary to develop and produce proto-
> types of the following systems within the times frames specified:
>
> (1) A space-based rocket system for intercepting and destroying bal-
> listic missiles soon after their launch and for defending United States
> space-based satellites. Such system shall be space tested within 18
> months after the date of the enactment of this Act.
>
> (2) A space-based laser weapon system for intercepting and destroy-
> ing ballistic missiles soon after their launch. Such system shall be
> space tested within four years after the date of the enactment of
> this Act.
>
> (3) A ground-based anti-missile system for intercepting ballistic
> reentry vehicles just outside the earth's atmosphere. Such system
> shall be tested, including all elements of such system, within three
> years after the date of the enactment of this Act.
>
> (4) A mobile, ground-based anti-missile system for intercepting bal-
> listic reentry vehicles in the upper atmosphere. Such system shall
> be tested within two years after the date of the enactment of this
> Act.
>
> (5) All necessary support systems for the systems specified in para-
> graphs (1) through (4), including—
>
> > (A) radar systems;
> >
> > (B) command, control, and communication systems;
> >
> > (C) battle management systems; and,
> >
> > (D) space transportation and logistics systems.

The systems cited are those that the Department of Defense knows
are feasible and that it has taken steps to restrict. The purpose
of this provision is to make sure that Congress and the president
have the chance to accept or reject the protection that actual devices can give, rather than waste both years and billions of dollars
in pseudotechnical, abstract arguments over the feasibility of some
mythical overall system.

The bill challenges those who would dispute the necessity of a
wholly new service to propose an executive order giving the defense
mission either to a new or expanded command within the Army
or within the Air Force. Such an order would transfer to that
command all of the resources that the Wallop bill would transfer
to the proposed USDF. But no order could convince the Army or
the Air Force's senior officers to give their best to this new and
different force growing within their house. Besides, if all went
well, this new or expanded command would eventually develop
into something controlling hundreds of satellites and thousands
of ground-based missiles. It would become as big as one of the

existing services—or bigger. The logic for this "branch" to separate from the service within which it grew would be more compelling than that which had led to the separation of the U.S. Army Air Corps from the U.S. Army in 1947. Why then not simply do the job correctly from the beginning as the Soviets did when they established the PVO (their aerospace defense force) as a separate service?

Those who would dispute the Wallop bill's measures to focus defensive weapons on the "threat" defined by intelligence rather than by unconstrained imagination properly have the burden of showing the marginal utility of the time and money that the U.S. spends chasing after the "responsive threat." Suppose for a moment that the U.S. had built the entire safeguard system it gave up in 1972. How would the defensive technology of 1972 perform against the offensive missiles and decoys that the Soviets actually possessed at the close of the 1980s? Alas, it would perform very well! It would also be instructive to review any argument in favor of the marginal utility of the regulations that, over the past generation, have made the military's R&D and procurement process what it is today. Why not just wipe them away and start fresh? That is surely what the nation would do in wartime.

Finally anyone who would argue against the Wallop bill's mandate to actually build prototypes of all of the systems the United States can build should be prepared to propose other means of preventing ballistic missiles, once launched, from landing on the U.S. He should also be prepared to argue that there is a reasonable chance that his proposal would produce defensive devices in roughly the same period as the Wallop proposal, and that his proposal is not merely dilatory. Usually the arguments against legislatively mandating the production of weapons are couched as arguments in favor of executive flexibility. But in this case, such arguments would have to defend self-denial in the name of flexibility. At any rate, the Wallop bill contains a challenge to quibblers: If after passage of the bill, the executive branch could propose a different list of weapons—perhaps with different timetables—and argue that it is a better list, let it do so!

The Wallop bill's point is to force an open, politically responsible choice between doing or not doing all that can be done in the field of antimissile defense. Opposition to the bill stems not so much from any of its details, but rather from the fact that its very existence is a challenge to put up or shut up. But that very challenge is what makes the bill valuable.

The Pentagon's response to S-900 helps to show that the real struggle is between the Pentagon's status quo, and proposals such as Wallop's that would force the Pentagon's hand.

The office of the secretary of the Air Force, in a memorandum for the general counsel of the Department of Defense, dated April 29, 1987, stated: "In summation, the proposed legislation will not solve problems, it will create problems such as competing demands in a fiscally constrained environment with no attendant increase in combat capability. Defense of the homeland is provided by existing organizations. A new military department is not required."

The memo claims that the North American Aerospace Defense Command (NORAD) is "responsible for the air defense (bombers, cruise missiles) of North America." But the Air Force knows perfectly well that NORAD's mission is only the *peacetime* observation of North American airspace, and that NORAD does not have enough equipment even to stop the fleet of low-tech, drug-running planes that enters the U.S. every day—much less to stop state-of-the-art Soviet Blackjack and Backfire bombers and cruise missiles. But the unmistakable point is that the Air Force is entirely satisfied with this state of affairs. The memo also states that the Unified Space Command is "tasked with the missions of space defense and space control." This is true. But the memo does not mention that Space Command does not have any operational weapon with which to carry out that mission. Furthermore, the first Commander of Space Command, General James Hartinger, USAF, told this author that if Space Command were to press for such weapons, "the big boys in the Air Force" would be terribly upset at the "new boy on the block staking claims to their money." So the corporate Air Force, and perforce Space Command, are satisfied with hanging out the sign advertising "space defense." But they are equally satisfied in their total inability to provide any.

The memo concedes that "no command is tasked today with the mission of ballistic missile defense." But it argues that such an assignment would be "premature" because "existing efforts in this arena are confined to the strategic Defense Initiative Organization's work of developing and exploiting enabling technologies." What would happen if and when "operational capability" were achieved? The Air Force's position is that the mission ought to go to that eager tiger, the Space Command. The Air Force gives every sign that it would treat the ballistic missile defense mission as vigorously as it treats the space defense mission.

The official position of the Joint Chiefs of Staff makes the Air Force look eager by comparison. Its memorandum to the general counsel of the Department of Defense, dated 28 April, 1987, states boldly: "The current joint command structure and the four Armed Services provide for adequate defense of the United States." In other words, the nation's senior military leaders are fully satisfied with the current strategic situation of the United States. The Soviet force of counterforce missiles, the growing Soviet antimissile defenses, the lack of any American nuclear targeting plan that would do the U.S. any good, all the events and thought processes of the past twenty years that have made nonsense of MAD—these might as well not have occurred for all the JCS care. What we have is good, by definition.

Then the JCS's memo delivers its detailed critique. The proposed Defense Force "is inconsistent with D.O.D. structure. . . . The United States Space Command is currently assigned the space support, space control, and ballistic missile defense planning missions and is fully capable of executing those missions." It would be difficult to imagine smugness based on lesser capabilities.

The memo takes S-900 to task for wanting to "divert scarce resources," for proposing to develop, procure, and operate a strategic defense system "based in large part on technology not yet proven," and for proposing to bypass DOD rules "in order to deploy strategic defenses in the quickest possible manner." No, says the JCS! "Strategic defense systems need to undergo the scrutiny of the full acquisition process, not only to ensure viable system concept but also to support the systems against their critics." With such support from the JCS, anti-missile defense needs no critics! The JCS are fully satisfied with the "process" that produced MX ten years after the SS-18, in time to be obsolescent, and in numbers that are strategically irrelevant. The JCS are also fully satisfied with what funds in the field of ballistic missile defense have purchased in recent years: uncounted research papers intended in substantial part to satisfy the "requirements" of critics. The JCS want more of the same. The memo removes any doubt about the convergence of personal, material interest between the nation's senior military leaders and the thousands of people, from Sandia to Stanford, who make a living opposing antimissile defense.

The JCS memo culminates by asserting that the "Findings of the Congress" contained in S-900 are "an oversimplification of the facts." These "findings" are that the American people established the Constitution, among other purposes, to provide for the common defense; that the principal threat to the American people's physical safety is the Soviet Union's force of missiles and bombers, that the U.S. currently has no means of stopping these engines of destruction if they are ever launched, and has no plans of acquiring such means. The JCS do not attempt to contradict any of these propositions but, rather, state that "our current offensive nuclear deterrent strategy has deterred the Soviet from ballistic missile and aerial attack for several decades." The JCS neglects the fact that deterrence succeeded because of a U.S. nuclear superiority that has now disappeared and concludes that "should we identify deployable systems in our SDI research program" we would study changes to current strategy.

No one reading the Pentagon's reactions to S-900 can doubt that its opposition to the defense mission is deep-rooted, and that if the mission is ever to be performed a special organization will have to be created and staffed with people differently motivated. But who will create it? Conventional wisdom has it that unless strategic defense becomes an ineradicable part of the American scenery in Ronald Reagan's presidency, it will be swept away. Nothing could be farther from the truth.

After Reagan

The impulse for using the most modern means available to defend against Soviet missiles did not come from Ronald Reagan and will not disappear with him. That impulse stems from the confluence between the successes of modern technology and the failure of the American establishment's military policy of the 1960s and 1970s to tame the Soviet strategic war-fighting buildup through arms control. Since no American has yet proposed, or is likely to propose, any means of forcing the Soviet Union to adhere to the spirit of any future agreement any better than it has adhered to the spirit of agreements that are technically "in force," one may confidently bet that the Soviet Union will not voluntarily reduce its hard-won ability to fight, survive, and win a war against the United States. Indeed, all indications are that given programs under way in both countries, the gap between Soviet and United States strategic offensive forces will continue to widen. The choice for the Western world is no other than to accept the Soviet Union's usable military superiority indefinitely with all of the consequences that entails, or to try to undermine that superiority by actually building enough antimissile devices to do so. Ronald Reagan neither discovered this condition nor began the military programs needed to remedy it. Ronald Reagan's presence in office is not necessary to highlight this predicament. On the contrary, his reassuring presence has served to blurr it.

Ronald Reagan must leave office on January 21, 1989. That is nearly six years after he first told the nation that he would try to provide the United States with antimissile protection. Only two years after the end of the Reagan presidency, more time will have passed since March 23, 1983, than elapsed between John Kennedy's announcement in 1961 that the U.S. would put a man on the moon and the Eagle's landing on the Sea of Tranquility in 1969. This period, of course, is much longer than the fewer than four years between Pearl Harbor Day and V-J day, during which the U.S. produced 296,429 aircraft, almost 100 aircraft carriers, 71,062 naval ships in all, 86,333 tanks, two and a half million military trucks, plus jet planes and the atomic bomb from scratch. Yet by January 21, 1989, while a variety of antimissile devices will be rolling off Soviet production lines, the U.S. will still be unable to protect itself against even one missile. Indeed, the U.S. government will remain officially "agnostic" about *whether* to ever propose to the Congress that we try a defense, while the senior military's opposition will remain undisturbed.

This is not to suggest that Ronald Reagan is antidefense. Rather, Ronald Reagan used talk of the SDI as one of many countervailing rhetorical axes on which to rest his presidency. He thus engaged in, and fostered, almost a decade's worth of pseudotechnical and pseudolegal debate that relieved the pressure on his administration to resolve its internal contradictions over policy. This provided him and his chief appointees with a certain comfort. As a result, however, he will have left the United States somewhat farther away from any solution to its strategic predicament than it was in Jimmy Carter's time. Also, his handling of the antimissile option has certainly rendered it a shopworn thing for anyone who follows him. Nevertheless, nothing has dulled the American people's appetite for self-protection.

Whether that just appetite is satisfied will depend on the political process. That means electing a president who wants antimissile defense and who is both willing and able to override and restructure the U.S. military to get it. It also means forcing Congress to vote on proposals clear enough in their intention and effects so that the sovereign American voter will be able to pass judgment on how his congressmen and senators are affecting the prospects for his physical safety.

Mr. Morton Kondracke, usually one of America's more perceptive analysts of government, got it precisely wrong when he wrote in the April 16, 1987, *New Republic* that the issue of antimissile defense should not become entangled in politics. He argued that the complex legal and technical issues involved should be left to Senator

Sam Nunn and others similarly inclined, who would produce a compromise that everyone would find sensible. In fact, however, as we have seen, the technical and legal issues are not the real barriers to antimissile defense. The real barriers are bureaucratic inertia and, above all, the tendency of many public officials not to want to play their proper roles. In a democracy, politicians are supposed to frame choices so that the voters can exercise their sovereignty. But politicians know that if they do this, some will see their proposals—and themselves—rejected. So the *déformation professionelle*, the occupational hazard, of politicians in a democracy is to avoid issues like the plague—to let the important matters of the day be decided by bureaucracies, "bipartisan commissions," or the courts. Failing that, they tend to create shadows of issues with which they can more safely joust. This is what Ronald Reagan and Sam Nunn have done with the SDI. Of course, this has prevented a coherent choice being made about military policy, and it has kept the American people from exercising responsibility for their own fate.

It is easy to imagine the compromise by which the politicians and officials to whom Mr. Kondracke referred might try to depoliticize strategic defense. The U.S. would order full-scale engineering development of ERIS interceptors and formally make room in the five-year defense plan for 100 of them, to be deployed in a strict treaty-compliant manner. This would be presented to the American people as the realistic first fruits of the SDI together with an American pledge to abide by the ABM treaty for another ten years, during which the U.S. and the Soviet Union would negotiate about the possibility of introducing more antimissile devices on both sides while reducing offensive weapons.

It is easy to see how such a compromise would serve the interests of presidential candidates who are principally beholden to antidefense constituencies but who want to persuade the average American voter that they are not. Anyone sponsoring this "compromise" could legitimately claim to be offering the American people more protection than Ronald Reagan ever did. At the same time, such candidates could claim to have deflated and brought down to earth the claims of those who, since the late 70s, had been talking about serious protection from the Soviet missile force. They could present themselves as serious managers of a complex, dangerous, but basically static situation. The sponsors of such a compromise could count on praise from the Joint Chiefs of Staff and from the professional antidefense groups as well.

Of course such a compromise would hide rather than resolve

the important choices that face the American people. Should the U.S. have been building antimissile defenses for the past thirty years or not? Were the American authors of ABM treaty wise statesmen or fools? By what means do we plan to hold the Soviets to the terms of the next arms control agreement? Why do we not use these means to hold them to the terms of agreements that are currently in force? Is the Soviet Union's counterforce missile force important, or not so important? How shall we target our nuclear weapons? What is the maximum benefit that the U.S. could achieve through retaliatory strikes? How, then, shall we deal with the Soviet Union's immense, growing, and increasingly mobile counterforce missile force? How shall we take into account the Soviet Union's anti-air and antimissile defense? How can we put ourselves, our sons, and fellow citizens into military forces that are wholly vulnerable to Soviet ballistic missiles when Soviet military forces are increasingly protected by SA-12 antimissile systems—among others? Do we really want the Soviet Union to be the only country with high-energy lasers in space? Yes or no, and why? Is the Pentagon bureaucracy a fit judge of efficiency, and is it to be trusted regarding fundamental matters? Do we accept as normal and desirable or do we wish to change a military–technical system that took twenty years to deliver the MX? Shall we build the best defense we can with the tools at hand, or shall we continue to mark time while others build? These and other questions deserve clear answers.

No doubt, just as some candidates and other public figures will try to forestall answers, others will find it in their own interest as well as in the public's interest to provide them. It is impossible to foretell who will prevail.

But it is easy to see why anyone, Republican or Democrat, liberal or conservative, whether in the executive or legislative branch, who honestly seeks to deal with the threat posed by an increasingly capable Soviet ICBM force will inevitably turn to ballistic missile defense. In our time, there is simply no alternative, just as in Aristotle's time there was no good alternative to walls.

What then is the future of the SDI? Given its history of self-contradiction and its association with the politics of Ronald Reagan, and since the structure of the SDIO does not lend itself to the development of weapons much less to their operational use, anyone who wants to be serious about ballistic missile defense will likely stay as far away as he can from these creatures of the Reagan Administration. The SDIO may well be preserved as a kind of nursery, bank, or clearing-house for useful technology. But anyone who wants antimissile protection will choose, or create, an operational command within the armed forces and give that command the authority to create the weapons. This is how such things have happened in the past, and this is how they must happen in the future, because it is in the nature of things.

Notes

I/*The Myth of an SDI Program: An Overview* (*pp. 1–19*)

1. K. T. Keller, former chairman of the board of Chrysler, was charged with responsibility for all missiles. His committee's work later resulted in practical missiles such as the surface-to-air Nike and Terrier and the air-to-air Sparrow. But in the field of ICBMs the Keller commission's gold-plated definitions helped to delay the U.S. for about five years.
2. Joint Chiefs of Staff, *Military Posture Statement: Fiscal Year 1987*, p. 27.

2/*The Millennium* (*pp. 20–36*)

1. Bernard Brodie, ed. *The Absolute Weapon* (New York: Harcourt, Brace, and Co., 1946).
2. Ibid., p. 40.
3. Ibid.
4. Ibid., pp. 46–47.
5. Ibid., p. 80.
6. Maxwell Taylor, *The Uncertain Trumpet* (New York: Harper and Row, 1960), p. 184.
7. U.S. Department of Defense, News Release No. 980–62, pp. 4–5.
8. U.S. Department of Defense, *Posture Statement: Fiscal Year 1966*, p. 47.
9. Ibid., pp. 49–50.
10. T. K. Jones & Scott Thompson, "Central War and Civil Defense," *Orbis* (Fall 1978). T. K. Jones summarized this study's findings before Congress as follows:
    a. Soviet civil defense (including crisis evacuation of cities) could reduce fatalities, in a U.S. retaliatory attack, to no more than 10 million people.
    b. Survival of the work force is by far the more important factor influencing industrial recovery of a nation following nuclear attack.
    c. Next in importance is survival of capital assets, with the survival of machinery being more important to prompt recovery than the survival of the buildings that housed the machinery.
    d. During World War II, the Soviets evacuated over 1500 industrial

    enterprises, including 85 percent of their aviation industry, east of the Urals.

    e. Techniques shown in Soviet civilian defense manuals for "hasty hardening" of industrial equipment provide for covering machinery with earth or sandbags.

    f. Boeing tested these techniques in Defense Nuclear Agency tests, one involving detonation of 500 tons of TNT.

    g. These tests confirmed that hardening to a level of 20 to 40 pounds per square inch (psi) is easily provided by a light covering of earth. Hardening to levels of 60 to 150 psi can be obtained by packing machinery in crushable material (such as metal "chips" produced by machining operations).

    h. Given execution of Soviet civil defense plans, including those for protecting industrial equipment and the work force, it was believed that the USSR could recover from a nuclear war in two to four years, whereas the U.S. could not recover in less than twelve years.

    i. Nationwide planning and preparedness for crisis actions to protect U.S. industries was estimated to cost a total of $200 to $300 million for 40 to 80 psi protection. (The cost of preparedness to develop 200 to 300 psi protection was much higher, an estimated $2.5 to $3 billion). Studies would need to be made of the protection problems unique to each industry (e.g., steel) before planning would be started.

11. U.S. Department of Defense, *Posture Statement: Fiscal Year 1969*, p. 46.

12. For example, Albert Wohlstetter, "Bishops, Statesmen, and Other Strategists on the Bombing of Innocents," *Commentary* June 1983; Leon Sloss et al., "Evolution of U.S. Nuclear Targeting Policy," *Strategic Review*, Spring 1985. But note that the chairman of the Joint Chiefs of Staff officially reported to the Congress that "we used to" target population "per se.": Senate Committee on the Budget, *Hearings, First Concurrent Resolution on the Budget, Fiscal Year 1977*, Vol. III, 94th Congress, 2nd. Session, p. 141.

13. That combination depends first of all on the pressure (over and above atmospheric pressure) that a silo can withstand before ceasing to function. U.S. Minuteman silos reportedly can withstand 1000 pounds per square inch, whereas Soviet SS-18 silos can withstand 7200 psi. Next, the combination depends on the *accuracy* of the warhead, since the force of the blast is inversely proportional to the cube of the distance from the center of the blast. Thus, accuracy is many times more important than the nuclear weapon's yield. For example, whereas in 1967 the Soviet Union had to load a 25-megaton bomb on its SS-9 missile (accuracy, worse than one half mile) in order to have a 90 percent chance of destroying a Minuteman silo, since 1980 each of the ⅔-megaton warheads atop the SS-18 (accuracy about .1 mile) would have the same effect. By contrast, the U.S. Minuteman III's Mark 12A warhead, also with an accuracy of .1 mile but with a yield of only .33 megatons, has about a one-in-three chance of destroying a 7200 psi Soviet

silo. The warhead for the MX also yields .33 megatons. But since its still classified accuracy is considerably better than .1 mile, it stands a good chance of destroying Soviet silos. MX is thus a true counterforce weapon, like the SS-18. But of course the Soviet Union has made a commitment to have a vast store of true counterforce warheads. The United States has not.

14. Albert Wohlstetter, *Commentary*, June 1983, p. 26.

15. The most significant exceptions are represented by editorials in the *New York Times* and speeches by Senator Malcolm Wallop of Wyoming, the state where the MX is deployed.

16. Secretary of Defense, Posture Statement for Fiscal Year 1978, p. 78.

17. For example, John Newhouse, *Cold Dawn* (New York, Holt Rinehart & Winston, 1973); Raymond Garthoff, "Mutual Deterrence and Strategic Arms Limitation" *International Security*, Summer 1978; *Paul Nitze*, "Assuring Strategic Stability in an Era of Detente," *Foreign Affairs*, January 1976; Henry Kissinger, Report to the Congress, June 15, 1972.

18. U.S. Central Intelligence Agency, *Soviet Civil Defense*, No. 178–10003, July 1978. General Altunin's speech was excerpted in *Strategic Review*. Winter, 1983 p. 98. Altunin's statement was co-signed by Dimitri Ustinov, then Defense Minister of the Soviet Union.

19. Ibid.

20. Ibid.

21. Senate Committee on Armed Services Hearings, Department of Defense Authorization for Fiscal Year 1979, Part 10, 95th Congress, 2nd. Session, April 1978, p. 7197.

22. T. K. Jones and Scott Thompson, *Orbis*, Fall 1978. Also see Senate Committee on Armed Services, 95th Congress, 2nd Session, 1978, *Hearings: Civil Defense*, p. 49.

23. Senate Committee on Armed Services, 95th Congress, 2nd Session, 1978, *Hearings: Civil Defense*, p. 49.

24. House Armed Services Committee, *Hearings on Military Posture for Fiscal Year 1979*, Part 6, 95th Congress, 2nd. Session (1978).

25. Ibid., p. 22.

3/*The More Things Change . . . (pp. 37–57)*

1. In a nutshell, the technology of rockets involves propulsion, and guidance. Propulsion requires the manufacturing of fuels—the burning of which delivers as much energy as possible per unit weight—of means to adjust their rate of burn precisely, as well as of light and durable casings. By the 1970s, these technologies, which date back to ancient China, seemed to have reached the natural limits of chemical energy. Guidance systems depend on sensors—inertial, radar, and optical. These in turn depend both on the art of miniaturization and on data processing, which allows them to divide space and time into ever smaller pieces in order

to calculate ever more precisely. The functions of missile guidance and battle management have improved along with the speed, accuracy, and reliability of data-processing systems. There seems to be no natural limit to such improvement.

2. The Air Force has fought attempts by Congress to procure more than 100 B1-B bombers because it has been developing an advanced technology bomber, dubbed "Stealth," which may better penetrate Soviet air defenses by reducing the aircraft's exposure to Soviet radars. In this author's opinion, it is a venture whose significance is overblown. It is indeed possible to reduce the radar cross section of even huge objects to next to nothing by arranging the object's shape so that any radar waves that strike it return in the direction whence they originated. *But this feat is clearly impossible from all angles simultaneously.* Moreover, even from the most favorable angle, the "stealthiest" of objects may be seen—albeit indistinctly—by old-fashioned radars whose long waves flood the object. The Soviet Union's SA-10 radar is mounted on towers because so much of the populated USSR is flat. Almost any radar will have reasonable capacity against cruise missiles if it is located on high ground. The Nike Hercules, by the way, had excellent low-altitude capacity.

3. Walter McDougall, *The Heavens and the Earth: A Political History of the Space Age* (New York: Basic Books, 1975). I am indebted to Prof. McDougall for many insights into the U.S. space program.

4. Vannevar Bush, in McDougall, Ibid., pp. 101–102.

5. Benson Adams, *Ballistic Missile Defense* (New York: American Elsevier, 1971), p. 35.

6. Ibid., p. 32.

7. Ibid., p. 36.

8. The best discussion of the concept of cost-effectiveness is by Michael Altfeld, "Strategic Defense and the Cost Exchange Ratio," *Strategic Review*, Fall 1986.

9. U.S. Congress, Hearings before the House Subcommittee of the Appropriations Committee on the Safeguard Antiballistic Missile System, 91st Congress, 1st Session (Washington, D.C.: U.S. Government Printing Office, 1969), pp. 18–19.

10. For a full statement of McNamara's position that the Soviets would not build as many missiles as the U.S., much less a large fleet of counterforce missiles, see: Interview with Robert S. McNamara, "Is Russia Slowing Down in the Arms Race?", *U.S. News & World Report*, April 12, 1965, pp. 8, 52. See also, Robert S. McNamara, Address to the Editors of United Press International, September 18, 1962. Cf. U.S. Department of Defense, Posture Statement for FY-1980 and for FY 1983. Cf. U.S. Department of Defense, *Soviet Military Power*, 1985.

11. Henry Kissinger, Remarks on June 15, 1972, *Documents on Disarmament, U.S. Arms Control and Disarmament Agency, 1972*, p. 305.

12. McGeorge Bundy, speech to the Annual Meeting of the International Institute of Strategic Studies, London, September 6, 1979.

4/A Leap in the Dark? (pp. 58–92)

1. The KH-11 is the United States' principal means of taking pictures of the Soviet Union. This satellite began operating in 1977. In 1979, William Kampiles, a junior CIA employee, was convicted of selling to the Soviet Union the KH-11's operating manual. He was sentenced in federal court to forty years in prison.

2. See, for example, Calvin Sims's "Electronic Imaging Gains," *New York Times*, June 5, 1986: "Earlier this week, Kodak introduced a monochrome electronic imaging camera for industry called Megaplus, that employs its new sensor. . . . George Gayle of Arthur D. Little said this advance in sensor technology had come a little sooner than expected. 'If you look at the evolution of the industry, it was only a few years ago that we had 150,000 pixels,' he said. 'It's quite exciting to realize we now have over a million.' "

3. The accuracy, and therefore the counterforce capacity of the SS-19, has been a subject of controversy since 1974. The CIA's position in 1974–1979 was that the SS-19 did not have sufficient accuracy to be a counterforce warhead. The technical rationale for its judgment was based on a calibration of data from technical indicators, which assumed that the differences between various figures were not significant. The political reason for the CIA analysts' judgment was that they preferred to conclude the Soviet Union either was not trying to create, or had not succeeded in creating, a war-fighting missile force, and that therefore the U.S. should not deviate from the policy of mutual assured destruction.

   In 1976, however, President Ford appointed a group of distinguished outsiders to determine whether the U.S. intelligence community's data would support different conclusions. The section of this group (known as the "B-Team") concerned with missile accuracy, headed by Dr. Roland Herbst, concluded that in fact the statistical chances of the errors in the accelerometer data being random were only .05, that the SS-19's accuracy was about .12 nautical miles, that the SS-19 was a counterforce weapon, and that the Soviet Union's ICBM force had been built to "fight, survive, and win a war against the U.S." In 1979 the CIA changed its National Intelligence Estimate 11–3–8 to agree with the B-Team's. Senators Daniel P. Moynihan and Malcolm Wallop conducted a colloquy on the floor of the U.S. Senate to remark on these events.

   In 1982, however, the CIA reopened the question of the SS-19's accuracy and reached its pre-1979 conclusion. The intelligence community, led by CIA, successfully ignored repeated demands by Congress that it allow its new conclusions to be challenged by a body of outsiders constituted as was the B-Team. The latest of these demands was in the form of a successful amendment to the Intelligence Authorization Act for Fiscal 1987. This author's conclusion about the data on which the intelligence community rests its current conclusion is that it is even less substantial, even more open to various interpretations, than the pre-1979 data, and that in 1987 the CIA's position on this point is even further on the extreme edge of optimism than it had been ten years earlier.

4. It is necessary to point out here that simply serving on a committee does not necessarily teach a senator anything. Even more than horses, senators cannot be forced to drink the water to which their assignment leads them. A few, however, take an interest in their field and use the Senate's enviable authority for compelling information. Thus they sometimes become genuinely expert in a field. By general agreement of the members of the Senate Select Committee on Intelligence, Malcolm Wallop knew more about the business than all of them put together.

5. Malcolm Wallop, "Opportunities and Imperatives of Ballistic Missile Defense," *Strategic Review*, Fall 1979. For the context of Senator Wallop's article, see James Canaan, *War in Space* (Harper and Row, 1982), especially chap. 8. Also see David Hoffman, *Washington Post*, March 3, 1985, p. 1, for a concise retrospective on the background of strategic defense and Senator Wallop's role in it.

6. Drew Middleton, "U.S. Science Seeking Sure Missile Killer," *New York Times*, November 25, 1979.

7. See the *Wall Street Journal*, February 11, 1981, p. 6; and April 23, 1982, p. 5.

8. On October 25, 1979, Zeiberg had said: "I am not losing any sleep over the prominence of laser or particle beam [weapons] in space. This is not something we need to worry about for a long time. The proponents of this technology are far more optimistic than available scientific and engineering data justify. . . ."

9. Letter from Robert Fossum, director of DARPA, to Senator John Culver, Senate Committee on Armed Services, June 15, 1980.

10. *Wall Street Journal*, June 23, 1980, p. 22; *Los Angeles Times*, April 2, 1980, p. 9; *New York Times*, February 10 and March 3, 1980; *Washington Post*, January 11 and April 1, 1980.

11. *Aviation Week and Space Technology*, February 18, May 22, and October 30, 1978; September 1 and October 15, 1979; February 4 and June 16, 1980; *Business Week*, June 4, 1979; and *Commentary*, May 31, 1980.

12. Congressional Record, July 1, 1980.

13. Ibid.

14. The group's other members were Bruno Augenstein of the Rand Corporation, Joel Bengston and Arthur Biehl of R & D Associates, Robert S. Cooper of Satellite Business Systems, Peter Franken of the University of Arizona, Edward Gerry of W. J. Shaefer Associates, Harold Lewis of the University of California, Santa Barbara, Victor Reis of Lincoln Laboratory, Jack Ruina of MIT, Marvin Stearn, a consultant, and Herbert York of the University of California, San Diego.

15. See *Aviation Week and Space Technology*, July 28, 1980. The battle over the prodefense plank at the 1980 Convention was between Senator Wallop and Representative Jack Kemp (aided by William Schneider, later undersecretary of state) on one side and Senator

Tower, aided by Rhett Dawson (later a principal White House staffer), on the other. Tower and Dawson were faithfully reflecting the views of the Pentagon. The man in charge of the defense side of the platform, Richard V. Allen, sided with Wallop and Kemp, and gave Tower the thin satisfaction of toning down Schneider's draft a bit. Thereafter Dawson brushed off the controversy, saying that "the platform doesn't mean anything anyhow." It certainly did not to him and to Tower. The press, however, took it seriously, and the number of articles on the subject increased.

16. Nevertheless, such talk increased, but thenceforth it was addressed primarily to the uninformed. See Kosta Tsipis, *Arsenal* (New York, Simon & Schuster, 1983). Also see articles by the same author and Richard Garwin in *Scientific American*, from 1982 to 1984. Another source of nonsense in this field is the Union of Concerned Scientists, whose technical strawman is a hypothetical (and infeasible) 100-megawatt laser based in a thoroughly irrational geosynchronous orbit. This canard found its way into the normally fastidious *Time* magazine (April 4, 1983, p. 22) presumably over the objections of its technically competent aerospace reporter, Jerry Hannafin. The same *Time* article also contains a blooper that should be obvious to anyone even slightly acquainted with technology: "But to date, lasers have been consistently effective only on relatively slow-moving targets. For example, a laser was turned successfully on a wire-guided anti-tank missile traveling at a relatively pokey 500 m.p.h. . . ." A moment of reflection is enough to realize of course that the actual speed of the target does not affect the difficulty of interception by a speed-of-light weapon, one way or the other. Only the *angular* velocity, i.e., the speed at which the weapon is required to swivel in order to track the target, affects the difficulty. That, of course, is greater if the target is close, and less if the target is far away. In the test *Time* mentioned, the *angular* speed of the laser weapon was about 100 times as great as it would be shooting boosters 1,000 kilometers away! The biggest canard, however, has been the 424-page *Report to the American Physical Society of the Study Group On Directed Energy Weapons*, April 25, 1987; see Angelo M. Codevilla, *Commentary*, September 1987.

17. Although much of the press commentary was favorable, it was uninformed. The outstanding exception was the almost weekly coverage of developments in the space weapons field by Clarence Robinson, then senior military editor of *Aviation Week and Space Technology*, between 1980 and 1984.

18. Congressional Record, U.S. Senate, May 13, 1981, p. 54977.

19. Ibid.

20. For the best unclassified summary of this report, see *Aviation Week and Space Technology*, April 12, 1982, p. 16.

21. The best account of the relationship between wavelength and power in defensive situations is in Maxwell W. Hunter, "The Space Laser Battle Station," *Journal of Defense Research*, Winter 1982, p. 287, Fig. 31. Parts of this article are classified.

22. Congressional Record, Senate, May 13, 1982, p. S-5093.

23. Letter from Senator John Tower to Senator Malcolm Wallop, March 9, 1982.

24. *Aviation Week and Space Technology*, July 18, 1983.

5/*The Best and the Brightest* (*pp. 93–114*)

1. Malcolm Wallop and Angelo Codevilla, *Washington Post*, February 6, 1983, "Outlook," p. 1.

2. *Aviation Week and Space Technology*, July 18, 1983, pp. 18–21.

3. Harold Agnew, General Atomic Technologies; Major John Toomay, U.S. Air Force (Ret.); and John Gardner, of the Office of the Secretary of Defense.

4. Eastport Study Group, *Summer Study, 1985.* A report to the Director of the Strategic Defense Initiative Organization, December 1985.

5. Unidentified defense department official, quoted in *Aviation Week and Space Technology*, October 31, 1983, p. 77.

6. *Washington Post*, November 10, 1983.

6/*The Empty Core* (*pp. 115–132*)

1. On June 16, 1961 the *New York Times'* lead editorial commenting on Weinberger's proposed $1.3 billion, five-year defense plan asked how much safer the U.S. would be after having spent that enormous sum than before. Weinberger's Pentagon never attempted to show a plan that, if worse came to worst, would spare the American people the worst that the Soviet Union might do—simply because Weinberger's Pentagon does not think in such terms.

2. The following is an unclassified summary of Gershwin's testimony, the essence of which is the same as the U.S. Department of Defense's presentation of Soviet strategic defense purposes in its annual publication *Soviet Military Power*, and as the Arms Control and Disarmament Agency's 1986 report on Soviet violations of the ABM treaty.

3. In October 1984 the Soviet Union announced that it would place a high energy laser device on a probe to the planet Mars in early 1988. In March 1985, a group of Soviet technicians visited the manned Space Flight Center in Houston to explain to their startled American counterparts that this device is meant to vaporize the surface of asteroids on the way to Mars, for the purpose of spectrographic analysis. This explanation makes no sense. The fact remains that the Soviet Union will have a high energy laser in orbit. It is more than likely that it will never get out of orbit and on the way to Mars. It is certain that the U.S. will not know that laser's capabilities. But it is quite likely given the state of the art in laser weaponry that any ballistic missile flying within a few thousand kilometers of that device could be shot down.

4. U.S. Department of Defense, Annual Posture Statement for Fiscal Year 1987, Washington D.C., January 1986.

5. Ibid., pp. 73–75.

6. U.S. Department of Defense, Annual Posture Statement for Fiscal Year 1988, Washington D.C., January 1987.

7/*The Menu* (*pp. 133–161*)

1. *Time*, February 21, 1987.

2. The George C. Marshall Institute (1987), *Missile Defense in the 1990s.*

3. Ibid. The report cites the need for ten surveillance satellites in orbits 1000 miles high. This is incomprehensible. Given that the horizon of a satellite at that altitude is only 3000 miles, ten satellites could manage to cover little more than a 6000-mile-wide swath of the earth—but surely not all of it!

4. See Joseph Miller, "Chemical Lasers," *Quest*, Spring 1980, for the best unclassified account of this technology.

5. *Report of the Study Group on Directed Energy Weapons to the American Physical Society*, April 24, 1987 (p. 424).

6. The George C. Marshall Institute, *Missile Defense in the 1990s*, p. 38.

7. Norman Polmar, "The U.S. Navy, Phased Array Radars," *U.S. Naval Institute Proceedings*, April 1979.

8/*The Numbers Game* (*pp. 162–175*)

1. C. Cunningham, "Critique of Systems Analysis in the OTA Study of Directed-Energy Missile Defense in Space," Lawrence Livermore National Laboratories, DDV 840007, August 30, 1984.

2. For much of the subsequent discussion we are indebted to Gregory Canavan et al., *Comparison of Analyses of Strategic Defense*, Los Alamos National Laboratories, February 1985.

3. Ibid.

4. Ibid.

5. Ibid.

6. George C. Marshall Institute, *Missile Defense in the 1900s*, p. 19.

7. Soviet Scientists Committee for Peace Against Nuclear Threat (Moscow: Mir Publishers, 1986), p. 68.

9/*The Treaty, and the Ties That Really Bind* (*pp. 176–202*)

1. See Malcolm Wallop and Angelo Codevilla, *Arms Control Delusion* (San Francisco: Institute for Contemporary Studies Press, 1987).

2. Paul Nitze, Conversation with Angelo Codevilla and Senator Malcolm Wallop, Senate Russell Office Building #206, June 1985.

3. For example see the editorial praise of Senator Nunn in the *New York Times*, March 18, 1987.

4. Congressional Record, Senate, March 11, 1987.

5. Foreign Broadcast Information Service, USSR International Affairs, August 12, 1981, p. AA16.

6. Ibid., p. AA19.

7. *Aerospace Daily*, May 2, 1983, p. 7.

8. TASS, "Geneva: What has the first round of talks shown?" May 27, 1985.

9. Ibid.

10. *New York Times*, January 16, 1986. See Malcolm Wallop and Angelo Codevilla, op. cit. chapter 7, for a full analysis of this proposal.

11. *New York Times*, October 15, 1986.

12. Paul Nitze, "ABM Treaty Permitted Activities," *National Defense*, April 1987.

13. There is a precedent for the Reagan administration's announcement that it would not be bound by the terms of the treaty while not departing from the strategic thought and the force posture that underlie that treaty. In May 1986 Ronald Reagan announced that, after adhering for over five years to the terms of the SALT II treaty that, he said, had never been ratified, had been violated by the Soviet Union, and would have expired if it had ever been in force, he would cease doing so. However, on August 5, 1986, he issued a statement that said: "we will exercise utmost restraint as we modernize. . . . We do not anticipate any appreciable growth in the size of U.S. strategic forces. . . . We will not deploy more strategic nuclear delivery vehicles or more strategic ballistic warheads than does the Soviet Union."

10/*What Is to Be Done?* (*pp. 203–233*)

1. Soviet threats and countermeasures SDI might face include:

antisatellite weapons	ground-based lasers
electronic countermeasures	x-ray lasers
space mines	pellets in orbit
paramilitary forces	proliferation
depressed trajectories	clustering ICBM launches
booster hardening, spinning	fast-burn boosters
quick PBV release	maneuvering
salvage fusing	penetration aids
decoys	antisimulation
masked warheads	saturation attack

2. Richard E. Thomas, "Long Wave Infra Red Research in the Soviet Union," Texas A&M University, March 1984.

3. See Angelo M. Codevilla. "How Eminent Physicists . . ." *Commentary* September, 1987. The American Physical Society's working group delivered its report to the SDIO for review in late 1986.

4. Congressman Jack Kemp et al., the *Wall Street Journal*, September 1986.

5. *Washington Post*, June 4, 1986

6. The following names are included in a list of signatories to "pro-early deployment" letters to President Reagan: Malcolm Wallop, Jack Kemp, Jim Courter, Duncan Hunter, Dan Quayle, Pete Wilson, Jeanne Kirkpatrick, and Edward Teller.

7. "SDI plan draws military critics," *Washington Post*, June 28, 1987.

8. Ibid.

9. "Document File," *Washington Post*, July 10, 1987.

10. Congressional Record, Senate, April 2, 1987.

Index